With Her in Ourland

Volume 1. No. 1. NOVEMBER 1909

THE FORERUNNER

BY

Charlotte Perkins Gilman.

CONTENTS

1.00 A YEAR THE CHARLTON COMPANY
67 WALL ST. NEW YORK **.10 A COPY**

This drawing, depicting a woman and man mutually supporting a child who stands atop a globe, appeared as cover art on every issue of *The Forerunner*. The drawing symbolizes Gilman's cooperative approach to social problems and foreshadows the narrative conclusion of the Herland/Ourland saga realized in the final issue of *The Forerunner*.

With Her in Ourland

Sequel to *Herland*

Charlotte Perkins Gilman

EDITED BY

Mary Jo Deegan and Michael R. Hill

WITH AN INTRODUCTION BY

Mary Jo Deegan

PRAEGER

Westport, Connecticut
London

The Library of Congress has cataloged the hardcover edition as follows:

Gilman, Charlotte Perkins, 1860–1935.
     With her in Ourland : sequel to Herland / Charlotte Perkins Gilman
; edited by Mary Jo Deegan and Michael R. Hill ; with an
introduction by Mary Jo Deegan.
       p.   cm.—(Contributions in women's studies, ISSN 0147–104X ;
no. 159)
    Includes bibliographical references and index.
    ISBN 0–313–27614–5 (alk. paper)
    1. Gilman, Charlotte Perkins, 1860–1935. With her in Ourland.
2. Feminism and literature—United States—History—20th century.
3. Women and literature—United States—History—20th century.
4. Social problems in literature. 5. Social problems—Fiction.
6. Sex role in literature. 7. Feminism—Fiction. 8. Sex role—
Fiction. 9. Women—Fiction. I. Deegan, Mary Jo, 1946. II. Hill,
Michael R. III. Title. IV. Series.
PS1744.G57W5 1997
813′.4—dc21   96–51135

British Library Cataloguing in Publication Data is available.

A hardcover edition of *With Her in Ourland* is available from
Greenwood Press, an imprint of Greenwood Publishing Group, Inc.
(Contributions in Women's Studies, Number 159; ISBN 0–313–27614–5).

Library of Congress Catalog Card Number: 96–51135
ISBN: 0–275–96077–3

First published in 1997

Praeger Publishers, 88 Post Road West, Westport, CT 06881
An imprint of Greenwood Publishing Group, Inc.

Printed in the United States of America

The paper used in this book complies with the
Permanent Paper Standard issued by the National
Information Standards Organization (Z39.48–1984).

10 9 8 7 6 5 4 3 2

This edition
is dedicated to
Erin, Kelly,
Lydia, and Jack Johnson-Hill,
peripatetic travelers in Ourland,
and to the memory of
George Elliott Howard
(1849–1928),
Nebraska sociologist and president of the
American Sociological Society,
in whose personal copies of *The Forerunner*
we first encountered the complete
Herland/Ourland saga.

Contents

Introduction:
Gilman's Sociological Journey
from *Herland* to *Ourland*

Mary Jo Deegan

When Charlotte Perkins Gilman's *Herland* was republished in book format in 1979 and touted as "a lost feminist utopian novel," *The New York Times Book Review* concluded, "May the goddess smile on those who have rescued the book from its long oblivion." *Herland* portrays a cooperative society composed only of women where mothering is the central political and personal activity. The women live a pastoral existence and peaceably develop intelligence, wit, grace, and independence. They give birth parthenogenetically, and sexuality is primarily experienced through giving birth rather than interpersonal activity. *Herland* ostensibly presented a utopian separatist fantasy, and Gilman was easily championed as a witty, feminist visionary.

With Her in Ourland: Sequel to Herland is the equally "lost," largely unknown continuation of *Herland*. It resumes the adventures of *Herland*'s central protagonists, Ellador and Van, but turns from utopian fantasy to challenging analyses of social fissures that plague us yet today. Gilman (1916) published *With Her in Ourland* during 1916 in *The Forerunner* as a continuation of *Herland* (Gilman 1915). No less witty, no less sage, Gilman's long-ignored, sociologically informed critique in *With Her in Ourland* suggests neither feminist separatism nor quixotic escapism, but calls for reason, social action, and cooperation between the sexes. Thus, I conclude, a perspective on *With Her in Ourland* is required that explicates the intellectual unity of the Herland/Ourland saga and details Gilman's distinctive sociological networks, influences, and vision. And finally, I observe, it is also helpful to have at hand a brief accounting of the transformational rules through which Gilman converted her nonfiction sociological work into the fictional mode exemplified by *Herland* and *With Her in Ourland*.

GILMAN AND VAN AS SOCIOLOGISTS

My interpretation of *With Her in Ourland* adopts a sociological viewpoint informed by sociobiography, feminist theory, and the disciplinary history of sociology. The sociological viewpoint may be foreign to students of modern literary criticism, but it is important here precisely because Charlotte Perkins Gilman was, among other things, an accomplished sociologist. Students of literature may be surprised to learn that Gilman is one of several writers (including Simone de Beauvoir, W.E.B. Du Bois, Harriet Martineau, Mari Sandoz, and others) who produced nonfiction social science as well as fiction, including sociologically informed novels.

Given my professional training and identity in sociology, it struck me when I first read *Herland* to discover that Van, a central character in Gilman's story, was a sociologist. And, when I later encountered *With Her in Ourland* serialized in *The Forerunner*, I was doubly struck that Van, the male sociologist, continued as a major figure. Gilman employed Van as a foil on which to skewer the assumptions and practices of patriarchal sociology. What a treat! My professional immersion in sociology guided my reading and subsequent understanding of the Herland/Ourland saga. In offering this sociological introduction to *With Her in Ourland*, I pursue a disciplinary avenue in which I am most conversant and at home. The equally important task of literary criticism per se is hereby entrusted to hands other than mine.

The republication of *Herland* was a signal event in American letters, but what *The New York Times* reviewer, Louise Bernikow (1979), did not appreciate, and what Ann J. Lane's (1979) introduction to *Herland* did not sufficiently stress, is that *Herland* and *With Her in Ourland: Sequel to Herland* comprise a unitary intellectual and literary framework. The republication of *Herland* as a separate novel, presumably complete in itself, revived critical interest in Gilman's work and, at the same time, truncated Gilman's larger aim and condemned Gilman's Herland/Ourland saga as a whole to misinterpretation and even greater oblivion.[1] *Herland*, taken by itself, stops mid-story, leaving readers with an erroneous understanding of Gilman's social vision and feminist worldview.

With Her in Ourland shares many strengths of *Herland*. Both works are clever and shrewd, clearly present an idealized female culture, and emphasize human potential for love and harmony. The sequel, moreover, proposes to reform Ourland. It outlines major progress in human evolution, exhibiting mythic dimensions far beyond amusing fantasy. Gilman is less pessimistic about human relations in the second volume than in the first. The chaos and hatred of Ourland did not defeat her belief in human nature and social improvement. Gilman is more courageous and daring in this second volume because she confronts a world at war. Her ridiculing of racism, particularly American racism, was remarkable for its opposition to Jim Crow society.

With Her in Ourland challenges most interpretations of *Herland*, especially those criticisms that discuss only the first half of the Herland/Ourland story. Few literary appraisals point to the thematic tie between the two parts. Marsha Smith's (1989: 131) comparative analysis is an insightful exception:

> The aerial approaches to Herland and Ourland are paralleled in the two narrative constructions, juxtaposing the male gaze and the female gaze. When the men first fly over Herland, they see large expanses of well-tended and fruitful terrain. When Ellador flies over Ourland for her initial view, the First World War is in full progress and she sees a war-damaged terrain. The comparison is deliberate. The male sees the world in terms of availability; the female sees the world as a battlefield, a place where conflicting desires rip apart and destroy the fruitful body.

By understanding such linkages between the two parts of the Herland/Ourland saga, we more fully understand Gilman's complex feminist perspective.

With Her in Ourland continued Gilman's expository device of strangers in a strange land. In *Herland*, three men found a feminist utopia. Gilman summarized the plot thus far in a brief synoptic preamble to *With Her in Ourland*:

> Three American young men discover a country [Herland], inhabited solely by women who were Parthenogenetic, and had borne only girl children for two thousand years; they marry three

of the women. Two of the men and one woman leave the country of Herland to return to America; Jeff Margrave remaining with his wife, Celis, a willing citizen; Terry O. Nicholson being expelled for bad conduct; and Ellador electing to go with her husband Vandyck Jennings.

Ellador was Van's instructor and guide to Herland. In the sequel, Gilman reversed these roles. In *With Her in Ourland*, Van and Ellador travel to the "Real World," Van's world—Europe, the Orient, the United States—in which Ellador is a stranger and an eager student and Van is her guide. The conversations and adventures of Ellador and Van continue to entertain, inform, and challenge Gilman's readers, just as they did in *Herland*.

Gilman, through Ellador, evaluates Ourland according to the principles of Herland and the precepts espoused by Ourlanders in the U.S. Constitution and the Bill of Rights. Ellador's investigations and comparative studies make her increasingly suspicious of Ourland, and she questions the meaning of marriage to a man who would defend the brutality and inequity of Ourland. Indeed, the layered complexity of "The Return" to "the Big New World—the Real World" (as Ellador calls it) takes *With Her in Ourland* well beyond the status of a mere sequel.

Gilman moves the scene of action, in *With Her in Ourland*, to the real world where women can make meaningful differences. This is no small matter, especially for understanding Gilman's feminist philosophy. Ellador asserts at the start of *With Her in Ourland*:

> I understand that men are different from women—must be, but I am convinced that it is better for the world to have both men and women than to have only one sex, like us. We have done the best we could, we women, all alone. We have made a nice little safe clean garden place and lived happily in it, but we have done nothing whatever for the rest of the world. We might as well not be there for all the good it does anyone else.

In fact, Ellador praises the global possibilities of a heterosexual world:

> "It must be nobler to have Two," she would say, her eyes shining. "We are only half a people. Of course we love each other [in Herland], and have advanced our own little country, but it is such a little one—and you have The World!"

Gilman's Ellador bravely leaves the all-woman utopia of Herland to learn everything she can about Ourland, to confront the challenges of everyday life in Ourland, to seek opportunities for advancement and change in a world shared not only by men and women generally, but also with her new husband. Despite this ponderous assignment, Ellador's inquiries and disputations often make for hilarious satire. On the whole, *With Her in Ourland* is intellectually more difficult than *Herland*. It does not begin with easy utopian escapism but with the extraordinary problem of surveying Ourland and the complex, real world task of integrating and applying the positive lessons of Herland to the lived realities of Ourland.

Readers familiar with *Herland* will find that *With Her in Ourland* presents an unexpected resolution to Ellador's task. Readers who want to experience this surprise unspoiled are advised to put this introductory essay aside and turn directly to the text of *With Her in Ourland*. In the final pages of this essay, I disclose Gilman's unexpected plot twist. Suffice it to say here that *With Her in Ourland* radically extends the meaning of *Herland* and completes our understanding of Gilman's overall purpose.

It is understandable that *Herland* has enjoyed well over a decade of renewed popular and critical reception since its recent republication (Gilman 1979). *Herland* is a delightful romp and it is rewarding that Gilman's humorous and playful side—well-known in her era—is recognized more widely today. Nonetheless, appreciating Gilman's wit, humor, and political punch remains a matter of taste, and—for some—debate. For example, Lane (1979: xvi) revels in *Herland*, but notes "where *Herland* skips and sprints, *Ourland* trudges." Conversely, Phoebe-Lou Adams (1979: 99), who reviewed *Herland* for the *Atlantic Monthly*, observed that the dialogues between the male visitors and "the isolated Amazons prickle with amusing jabs at the male-dominated society of 1915," but lamented that Herland itself, the utopia, "is as dull as such inventions usually are." Perhaps literary dullness, like love or laughter, is where you find it: in the eyes of the beholders.

A more serious controversy contends that *With Her in Ourland*, unlike *Herland*,[2] is rife with bigoted, myopic views. Gilman, Lane (1980: 200–201) wrote:

> shares many odious attitudes upheld by the intellectual community of a hundred years ago. In some of her writing, in *Ourland* in particular, and in her private correspondence, she expresses beliefs that are anti-Semitic, chauvinist, and racist. Although such sentiments dominated the intellectual circles of the country, and although Gilman represents the least outlandish wing

in these circles, still her ideas are dreadful and they seriously mar
her contribution as a social analyst and theorist.

This view, championed by Lane, strategically distances *Herland* from *With
Her in Ourland*, unnaturally obscuring the unity of the Herland/Ourland
saga. But *With Her in Ourland* is Gilman's commentary on *Herland*; it
transposes Herland's abstract principles into Ourland, a real, seriously
flawed world anchored historically in generations of cultural practices to
which Gilman and all writers of any given era are necessarily party. It is
Gilman's strength that—much more often than not—she saw perceptively
beyond many social biases of her time.

Shall we vilify *With Her in Ourland* because it contains a few (and it
really is only a few) ethnocentric lapses? I think not. Maureen Egan (1989:
118) put the case more generally:

> It is clear that there is much in her work to disagree with a
> century or so later, but it is also clear that Gilman's application
> of the major intellectual discoveries of her day to the problem
> of woman's condition made a contribution that was original and
> powerful.

Gilman's social critiques in *With Her in Ourland* are original and powerful.
They remain cogent and surprisingly contemporary. The complete Her-
land/Ourland saga, despite occasional imperfections (now more wisely seen
with hindsight), clearly merits our attention and analysis.

Both halves of the Herland/Ourland saga are barbed, entertaining, and
sometimes extremely funny; neither bogs down in plodding didacticism.
Beyond genuine entertainment value, however, the Herland/Ourland saga
is grounded in Gilman's persona as a sociologist—and it is to this aspect of
Gilman's work that I draw the reader's attention.

The paths to sociological understanding are myriad and reach a variety
of destinations—but the more meaningful routes are traveled by analysts
cognizant of the lived experiences and pressing social realities of historical
actors, such as Gilman. Against the backdrop of Gilman's biography and
the publication of *With Her in Ourland* in Gilman's magazine *The Forerunner*, I outline the interpersonal and organizational networks that linked
Gilman to the movers and shakers of American sociology (especially Jane
Addams, Edward A. Ross, and Lester F. Ward). I also detail the epistemological threads (including feminist reform Darwinism, cultural feminism,
Fabian socialism, and critical pragmatism) in Gilman's complex, distinc-

tive, and sophisticated sociological worldview.[3] Hopefully, this provides the historical and intellectual background needed to appreciate Gilman's sociological framework and the social critiques she delivered in *Herland* and *With Her in Ourland*.

LOCATING THE HERLAND/OURLAND SAGA IN *THE FORERUNNER* AND IN GILMAN'S BIOGRAPHY

Gilman's life and ideas reflected her oppression and repression as a woman in a manmade world. She rebelled against these injustices and bore the personal costs of living and leading a failed revolution (Gilman 1892, 1898, 1911, 1935, 1995). A rich lodestone of Gilman's writings on feminist issues is found in her remarkable journal, *The Forerunner*. It was here that *Herland* and *With Her in Ourland*, as well as several other of Gilman's so-called "lost" books, were published. *The Forerunner* was an intellectual and political platform from which Gilman addressed the world through essays, poetry, and fiction. *The Forerunner* reflects Gilman's life experiences, insights, and abilities as a writer—and, through such works as the Herland/Ourland saga, gave life and form to a coherent and vigorous social philosophy.

The life of Charlotte Perkins Gilman fascinates readers today much as it did during her lifetime—when Gilman's views and activities were frequently grist for comment in daily newspapers. Her charisma and courage; her stunning wit and penetrating intelligence; her visible, public confrontations with the male establishment; and her preemptive suicide in 1935 (when confronted with the specter of the end stages of terminal cancer) account in large measure for this fascination. The personal and problematic dimensions of Gilman's life make compelling biography[4] and autobiography (Gilman 1935).

Charlotte Perkins Gilman was born in 1860 into middle-class surroundings and enjoyed the advantages of life in an extended family of thinkers that included Harriet Beecher Stowe and Catharine Beecher. When Gilman was two years old, her father, an intellectual man, abandoned her mother—resulting in financial strain for her mother and a lasting sense of rejection in Charlotte. A strong love-hate relationship marked Charlotte's interactions with both parents. Gilman's childhood and adolescence included unhappy episodes, but simultaneously she flourished on the intellectual riches provided by her playmates, cousins, aunts, and uncles.

Gilman's education was a combination of institutionally structured and self-directed schooling. By age fifteen, Gilman had completed only four years of formal instruction, but this was typical during the 1870s (M. A. Hill 1980: 41). She was, however, a voracious reader. Charlotte entered the Rhode Island School of Design in 1878 but did not graduate. This mixture of intellectual challenge from within her family circle, self-directed study, and excursions into formal schooling resulted in what Mary A. Hill (1980: 57) calls a teenage education that "was quite a fascinating venture."

As an adult, Gilman swept through her era in a blaze of notoriety. She was an intellectual and charismatic whirlwind who drew attention and controversy wherever she went, whenever she spoke or wrote. Charlotte's highly publicized divorce from Walter Stetson and her subsequent decision to give her daughter, Katherine, to the safekeeping of one of Charlotte's closest friends (a woman who married Gilman's former husband) generated derision and public scorn.

Gilman suffered alternating periods of depression and anxiety, possibly a bipolar mood disorder. The pain of female dementia is memorialized in Gilman's (1892) chilling, semiautobiographical account of "The Yellow Wallpaper." Gilman's "manic" phases were characterized by brilliant, productive outbursts of activity and movement—she wrote *Women and Economics* (Gilman 1898), for example, at an incredible pace during a brief period of time. Nevertheless, many projects, especially *The Forerunner*, required—and received—steady, sustained effort over a period of years.

Gilman was a prolific author (Scharnhorst 1985). In addition to *Herland*, she is admired today for *Women and Economics*, a brilliant analysis of women's status that remains a powerful statement on the gendered intersection of the home and marketplace. Less well known is Gilman's independent journal, *The Forerunner*.

Gilman published *Herland* and *With Her in Ourland: Sequel to* Herland serially in monthly installments in *The Forerunner* during 1915 and 1916. In *The Forerunner*, one finds editorial commentaries, social and economic essays, stories, and poems by Gilman that accompanied each episode of *Herland* and *With Her in Ourland*.[5] Gilman was the publisher and sole contributor to each monthly issue during the journal's seven-year run from 1909 through 1916. *The Forerunner* was an ambitious, massive, multifaceted enterprise over which Gilman exercised total editorial and intellectual control.

The context of publication makes it clear that Gilman conceived *Herland* and *With Her in Ourland* as interconnected parts. Readers of *The Forerunner* knew that when the *Herland* narrative concluded in the December 1915 issue it was resumed without interruption in the January 1916 issue under the title *With Her in Ourland: Sequel to* Herland, a subtitle devised by Gilman. The division of the Herland/Ourland saga into "two parts" was a nod to the symmetry of the twelve-issues-per-year format of *The Forerunner*. The sometimes redundant quality that some critics note today in *Herland* is attributable to Gilman's monthly need to remind her readers "where matters stood" as her story unfolded (M. R. Hill 1996). And, by prefacing the initial installment of *With Her in Ourland* with a brief synopsis of *Herland*, Gilman underscored the continuity between the component parts of the Herland/Ourland saga.

Gilman unequivocally and cheerfully ended *The Forerunner* in 1916 and the last installment/chapter of *With Her in Ourland* appeared in the final, December issue. *The Forerunner* and the Herland/Ourland saga, especially, marked the culmination of Gilman's lifework as a sociologist. The reduction in Gilman's productivity after this time was congruent with the experiences of many female sociologists whose roles and participation in American sociology began a sharp decline. This gendered occupational sea change was tied directly to the unhappy fortunes of cultural feminism in the U.S.A. after 1916 in what became an increasingly patriarchal discipline (Deegan 1988a).

The Forerunner and its cornucopia of essays, poems, and stories, such as *Herland* and *With Her in Ourland*, reflect not only Gilman's private trials and experiences, but also her immersion in a variety of lively intellectual currents and personal relationships with a host of nationally prominent scholars, writers, and social activists. Among these influences, Gilman's sociological sensitivities and her links to the men's and women's sociological networks were central to the development of her ideas. Gilman defined herself professionally as a "sociologist." Thus, to locate the intellectual and collegial context of the Herland/Ourland saga as it unfolded in *The Forerunner*, it is vital to establish Gilman's sociological credentials and survey her sociological relationships and resources.

GILMAN'S SOCIOLOGICAL AFFILIATIONS AND NETWORKS

The vigor of Charlotte Perkins Gilman's renaissance within several cognate disciplines (history, English, women's studies, American studies, and philosophy) is not matched in sociology.[6] This is unfortunate because *Herland* and *With Her in Ourland* are replete with ideas mirrored in Gilman's sociological experiences, contacts, and nonfiction treatises. The consequences of Gilman's disciplinary oblivion in sociology cut two ways. First, readers untrained in sociology lack close familiarity with the sociological framework in which *Herland* and *With Her in Ourland* are anchored, thus missing part of the fun as well as the intent of Gilman's sociological critiques. Second, sociologists who wrongly dismiss Gilman as "not a sociologist" blind themselves to the sociological import of Gilman's fiction, especially *Herland* and *With Her in Ourland* (Deegan 1987). Failure to recognize women such as Gilman as sociologists is a loss for everyone.

Gilman was an independent, radical scholar who worked outside the formal confines of the ivory tower. Nonetheless, her sociological authority was recognized by leading male founders of the discipline, notably Edward A. Ross and Lester Ward. Gilman labored within a network of female sociologists, of whom Jane Addams is today the best known. Gilman's incisive sociological work—as well as the accomplishments of the males who acknowledged her, and the achievements of most other early women sociologists such as Addams—was ignored after 1920 by an ambitious generation of male academics who rewrote sociological history to their own liking and for their own self-serving purposes (Deegan 1988a, 1991, 1995). Fortunately, Gilman is gradually being re-recognized as a major sociologist.

GILMAN THE SOCIOLOGIST

During Gilman's lifetime, she was a well-known member of the men's and women's sociological networks. Her powerful role was similar in many ways to that of Jane Addams, one of Gilman's close friends and colleagues (Deegan 1988a; M. A. Hill 1980: 272–282). Gilman's work, however, as well as that of Addams and many other women sociologists and like-minded men, is largely ignored by today's patriarchal historians of sociology. Determining today who is a founder of sociology is a gendered political process that shapes contemporary sociological theory, research, and practice.

Before Gilman's ideas can be recognized as sociologically relevant, however, doubters must be convinced that Gilman was actually a sociologist. Skeptical patriarchs who repeatedly deny Gilman an honored place in sociological history—let alone confirm her continuing relevance—appear congenitally unable to comprehend that Gilman was in fact a sociologist, that she knew and worked professionally with other powerful sociologists, or that she devoted much of her life to the development and advancement of sociological ideas. The record documenting Gilman's sociological persona is clear, however.

American academicians tend to rate appointment to a sociology professorship as the single, qualifying hallmark of a genuine sociologist—and in so doing define the practice of sociology in their own image. But sociology is a large enterprise spreading well beyond ivory tower academics. A useful approach to the classificatory problem is Dirk Käsler's (1981) five criteria for defining a sociologist.[7] Käsler defined a person as a sociologist if they met one of his criteria. Charlotte Perkins Gilman met all of them:

1. Gilman taught sociology, not as a formally appointed professor in the academy but as a freelance lecturer who spoke frequently on college campuses. (Gilman was, in fact, offered an academic position but she declined the appointment.)
2. Gilman was a charter member of the American Sociological Society and remained a member for twenty-five years.
3. Gilman wrote sociological articles and books, including articles and comments published in the influential *American Journal of Sociology.*
4. Gilman identified herself as a sociologist.
5. Gilman was defined by many others as a sociologist.

Further, academic sociologists do not always recognize that a person need not be solely a sociologist to make major contributions to the discipline. Jane Addams, for example, was a sociologist and a social worker (Deegan 1988a). As Gilman was indeed a sociologist, she was also a writer, editor, lecturer, feminist, and an independent spirit. Whatever else one concludes about Gilman, she was unequivocally a sociologist.

A few sociologists now admit Gilman to the canon. For example, techniques and rationales for introducing Gilman's writings into sociology classrooms are explored by James L. Terry (1983), Deegan (1988b), and Susan Gotsch-Thomson (1990). Bruce Keith (1991) summarizes Gilman's intellectual biography from a sociological perspective. Charles Lemert (1993) includes a selection from *Women and Economics* in his reader on *Social Theory.* Patricia Lengermann and Jill Niebrugge-Brantley (1996) are rewriting the history of classical sociological theory—wherein Gilman plays an important part. And Michael R. Hill (1996) outlines *Herland* with a sociological eye. The door is opening, but students trained in mainstream patriarchal sociology are still largely oblivious to Gilman's sociological contributions and work. Such ignorance is all the more costly because Gilman traveled in illustrious sociological circles, and we have as much to learn from her forgotten contacts and associates as we do from Gilman herself.

GILMAN'S SOCIOLOGICAL WORLD

Collegial patterns in early American sociology were divided by gender into men's and women's networks. There were, however, overlapping points between the gendered groups, and Gilman traveled in both networks. In California, she forged strong links to Edward A. Ross and Lester F. Ward. Gilman's contacts with the women's network were anchored in Chicago and her friendship with Jane Addams at Hull-House. In Chicago, Gilman experimented with social settlement work and briefly interacted with sociologists from the University of Chicago. These sociological contacts provided Gilman with experiences and insights that reverberate in the pages of *Herland* and *With Her in Ourland*.

Sociology in Gilman's era was a young, ambitious discipline; it was a new intellectual invention. Ellador, for example, suggests in *With Her in Ourland* that Van's ancestors could be forgiven some of their mistakes because they did not have sociology to guide them. Gilman's ties to academic sociology can be placed in temporal perspective by noting that the first issue of the *American Journal of Sociology* appeared in 1895; the first American graduate program in sociology, the Department of Sociology at the University of Chicago, was established in 1892; and the American Sociological Society (now the American Sociological Association) took form only in 1905.

The Men's Sociological Network

Gilman's friends in the male academic network were intellectual pioneers who wove ideas from history, politics, biology, economics, religion, and other sources into the newly emerging discipline of sociology. They were not trained in sociology. As Ellador might have put it, "how should they? there were no schools that offered majors in sociology." These early men became sociologists through self-directed study, imagination, and the will to make a better world through rational thought, careful research, and intelligent social action. Gilman's ties to Lester F. Ward and Edward A. Ross, two of the most important male sociologists during the discipline's formative era, linked Gilman to an emerging network of male sociologists.

The penultimate chapter of *With Her in Ourland* opens with a discussion between Ellador and Van in which the latter concedes, "Of course, there is no getting around Lester Ward." Unlike many authors mentioned in *With Her in Ourland* (such as Helen Hunt Jackson, Mark Twain, Charles Dickens, or John Muir), Lester Ward is probably unknown to many readers today. In the formative era of American sociology, however, Ward was a major sociologist whose work influenced Gilman. Likewise, the work and person of Edward A. Ross, also an admirer of Ward, further impressed Gilman.

Gilman's introduction to the male academic network took place not in Chicago—the emerging center of academic sociology—but in California. On the west coast, she read Ward's ideas and met several progressive social scientists at Leland Stanford Jr. University. Her host for these face to face introductions was David Starr Jordan (appointed president of Leland Stanford Jr. University in 1891). He assembled an energetic, reform-minded group of social scientists and supported the emerging work in sociology by hiring a man who became a major figure in the field: Edward A. Ross.

Edward Alsworth Ross: Ross arrived at Stanford in 1893 where he taught Richard Ely's brand of critical economics before being fired, in 1900, in what became a celebrated academic freedom case. Ross had earned a doctorate under Richard Ely's tutelage at Johns Hopkins University, and M. A. Hill (1980: 245) suggests that the Ely connection eventually brought Gilman, Ross, and Helen Campbell together. President Jordan's decision to hire men such as Ross created a climate for sociological sparks, and it was into this milieu that Jordan invited Gilman to visit the Stanford campus in 1894.

During March 1894, Jordan asked Gilman to lecture at Stanford University, and she accepted. Following her lecture, a tea was given in her honor and she met several members of the faculty. A month later, she was again invited to lecture and again feted at an evening reception. Although the exact circumstances of Gilman's first meeting with Ross are unknown, M. A. Hill (1980: 245) suggests the two met near the time of Gilman's Stanford lectures.

Ross was a tall, stunning and charismatic figure. Outspoken on controversial issues, he was bound for both fame and trouble. Ross wrote several works that helped put American sociology on a sound footing, and he was elected president of the American Sociological Society for 1914–1915 (Weinberg 1972; M. R. Hill forthcoming).

Ross and Gilman both displayed high-profile personalities and became lifelong friends. The bond went deep: just days before Gilman took her life in 1935, she revealed her fatal intentions in a letter to Ross and his wife (Ross 1936: 244). We know that Ross (1936: 60) admired Gilman albeit in a chauvinistic way: "Charlotte Perkins Gilman, niece of Henry Ward Beecher, was a dear and intimate friend of ours. She was the most brilliant woman I have known and had the most beautiful head I have ever laid eyes on." More directly, in a letter to Gilman on 25 December 1923, Ross acknowledged the role her work played in framing a book Ross (1922) had just published: "I hope you have seen my little book 'The Social Trend' which contains a chapter 'Women in a Man Made World' which will interest you. I got my start out of your 'This Man Made World,' but gathered evidence of my own."[8] Gilman rarely gave Ross his due in print, although she praised Ross's 1911 book on changing Chinese society in a brief review in *The Forerunner* (Gilman 1912c).

Ross and Gilman marched to the beat of similar progressive drummers. Ross advocated free silver, a populist proposal that called for both a gold and silver monetary standard; and he opposed hiring Japanese laborers in favor of American-born workers (Ross 1936: 64–86). Ross's pro-labor yet nativist views reflected the curious blend of occasional bigotry and genuine political courage that sometimes flawed Gilman's work at places in *With Her in Ourland*.

Lester F. Ward: Ward was born in 1841 and later became E. A. Ross's uncle by marriage. Ward's early writings influenced Ross, the latter asserting "that his association with Ward was the equivalent of a postdoctoral degree" (quoted in Borgatta and Meyer 1959: x). The two corresponded frequently from 1891 to 1912 (Stern 1938–1949).

Ward gave American sociology its first comprehensive and systematic theoretical exposition. From his training in biology, he derived a reform-oriented theory of social systems that countered the evolutionary fatalism of British sociologist Herbert Spencer. Ward, a lifelong civil servant, sold his home to finance the publication of his foundational work, *Dynamic Sociology* (Ward 1883). Following other major publications and election to the first presidency of the American Sociological Society in 1905, Ward entered the academy late in life. He was professor of sociology at Brown University from 1906 until his death in 1913 (Ross 1913).

Ward and Gilman first contacted each other by mail. Ward wrote an admiring letter to Gilman after the publication of her social Darwinist poem, "Similar Cases" (Gilman 1890)—wherein she compared and contrasted the evolution of animals and humans. Thus began a lifelong correspondence. Gilman, in turn, was strongly influenced by Ward's (1888: 266) article in *The Forum* in which he asserted "that in the economy of organic nature the female sex is the primary, and the male a secondary element." Ward drew together a synthesis of cultural feminism and a reform Darwinism that employed "organic" and "scientific" metaphors.

Gilman eventually met Ward face to face on 26 January 1896 in Washington, D.C., at the twenty-eighth annual Woman's Suffrage Convention. They had already corresponded several times, making this an exciting meeting for her. Gilman's diary records her pleasurable first encounter, her dining with Ward, and, on 28 January, going "to a reception given me by Prof. and Mrs. Ward" (M. A. Hill 1980: 264–265).

Gilman considered Ward "quite the greatest man I have ever known" (M. A. Hill 1980: 265). Ward's (1888) article on "Our Better Halves" inspired her in *Women and Economics* and was, in Gilman's (1935: 187) opinion, "the greatest single contribution to the world's thought since Evolution." When Ross subsequently asked Gilman why she did not append a bibliography to *Women and Economics*, Gilman (1935: 259) responded: "I had meant to, but when it came to making a list of the books I had read bearing on the subject, there were only two! One was Geddes' and Thompson's *Evolution of Sex*, the only other article, Lester F. Ward's, in that 1888 *Forum*."

Gilman particularly admired Ward's concept of "gynaecocracy," elaborated in *Pure Sociology* (Ward 1903; Gilman 1910). Gilman (1911) took up the concept, and, in the preface to *The Man-Made World*, she wrote:

> Assuming the Gynaecocentric Theory to be the true one—that the female is the race type, and the male, originally but a sex type, reaching a later equality with the female, and, in the human race, becoming her master for a considerable historic period—this book gives a series of studies of the effect upon our human development of this unprecedented dominance of the male, showing it to be by no means an unmixed good.

Ward denounced whole cultures for their treatment of women, especially India and Germany, as does Gilman in *With Her in Ourland*. He strongly criticized the Adam and Eve myth in "the Hebrew Bible," and again Gilman followed suit with a slam at the patriarchal bias of the Hebrew tradition in *With Her In Ourland*. Gilman acknowledged Ward's influence publicly and privately with great admiration and generosity (Gilman 1913). Gilman's (1911) dedication of *The Man-Made World* to Ward reveals the extraordinary esteem in which she held the man and his ideas:

> *This book is dedicated with reverent*
> *love and gratitude*
> *to*
> *Lester F. Ward*

Sociologist and Humanitarian, one of the world's great men; a creative thinker to whose wide knowledge and power of vision

we are indebted for a new grasp of the nature and processes of
Society, and to whom all women are especially bound in honor
and gratitude for his Gynaecocentric Theory of Life, than which
nothing so important to humanity has been advanced since the
Theory of Evolution, and nothing so important to women has
ever been given to the world.

Given such admiration, it is no surprise that Lester Ward received direct,
sympathetic mention in *With Her in Ourland*.

Ward, on the other hand, rarely acknowledged Gilman's influence
publicly, although he did do so on occasion. For example, he cited her as
"a woman" who "has clearly brought out this cosmological perspective in
her poem 'Similar Cases' " (Ward 1906a: 541), and Ward's enthusiasm for
her 1890 poem endured for years. Lane (1990: 7) wrote that: "Lester Ward
described himself as having roughly blocked out from the slab the statue
which Gilman then refined with a fine-point chisel." Ward generally failed
to acknowledge Gilman's brilliant nonfiction works in his writings, nonetheless. In fact, he drew her spirited (and understandable) ire by suggesting,
long after her public embrace of his gynaecocentric theory, that his idea
had been ignored by American intellectuals (M. A. Hill 1980: 266).

The Ward-Gilman correspondence and their mutually compatible organizational activities reveal the intellectual ties between these pioneering
sociologists. In response to Gilman's continued pressure for recognition
from Ward, and having sent him a copy of her *Human Work* (Gilman 1904),
Ward replied:

> I have read your book. I could hear my own voice all the time.
> But, of course, it was not an echo. It is pitched much higher than
> I can strike and differs also entirely in timbre. I have always told
> Dr. Ross that all I could do was to block out the statue from the
> slab in rough strokes, and he must finish it up. Now you come
> along and touch it up with a fine-pointed chisel.[9]

On other occasions, through letters, Ward influenced Gilman's thinking
by recommending books for her to read.[10] Organizationally, Gilman
(1907a, b) participated—quite likely at Ward's invitation—as a formal
respondent to two papers given during the first meeting of the American
Sociological Society in 1906 when Ward presided as the organization's first
president.

In sum, Ross and Ward were Gilman's links to the intellectual ferment in the early days of academic sociology. Allen (1988: 43) notes that Ross and Ward "gave her a sense of belonging to an elite vanguard of intellectuals, leading the way to a socialist, nonsexist world." Gilman talked with Ross and Ward in depth about ideas, books, principles, theory, and practice. Allen (1988: 43–44) compares Ross and Ward to Gilman's learned father but, unlike her father, they listened to her and validated her work: "They encouraged her to believe that creating a comprehensive moral system, established on the foundation of scientific sociology and expressed in plain language, was the most important work she could undertake." In pursuing that charge, Gilman distinguished herself as a theorist, and she became a liaison between the ideas and goals of the men's and women's sociological networks.

The Women's Sociological Network

A notable and energetic cohort of women sociologists flourished from 1892 to 1920 in what I call the golden era for women in sociology (Deegan 1991, 1995). Jane Addams of Hull-House in Chicago was a leader in this remarkable group. Through Addams, Gilman was linked to the heart of the women's Chicago-based network in sociology. Chicago was also the emergent hub of academic sociology. From its founding in 1892, the Department of Sociology at the University of Chicago dominated the formation of the discipline from 1892 until at least the mid-1930s (Faris 1967; Kurtz 1984). When Gilman moved from California to Chicago in 1895, she arrived in the midst of newly opening sociological horizons.

From California to Chicago: Gilman and Addams met in 1894, during the California Woman's Congress that Gilman helped organize. On 13 February 1894, Gilman (1994, II: 573) noted in her diary that she went to a "very enjoyable and interesting" reception for "Miss Addams." The following day, Addams addressed the group and Gilman (1994, II: 573) enthused that it was "a splendid meeting."

Addams, in turn, wrote that seeing Gilman was the "one bright spot in San Francisco."[11] Gilman (1935: 170–171) recalled Addams's appreciation of her work, and noted Addams's discovery that Gilman was ostracized in California. Gilman felt misunderstood and despised in California where she was the target of rumor and yellow journalism. "What the creeping slanders were I never knew," wrote Gilman (1935: 171), "There never were any distinct 'charges,' never the least hint of anything against my 'character,' in the usual line." In this milieu of innuendo and suspicion, *The*

Impress, a journal Gilman co-edited with Helen Campbell, failed financially after only twenty weekly issues. "This fiasco," Gilman (1935: 173) concluded, "was what showed me my standing in that city."

Gilman, virtually penniless, left San Francisco via train for Chicago in 1895. The California newspapers took their parting shots. On 25 July 1895, the San Francisco *Chronicle* announced Gilman's departure with the following headlines:

GONE TO LIVE AT HULL HOUSE
The Work of a California Woman.
Charlotte Perkins Stetson Departs.
Will Labor With Jane Addams in the
Social Settlement of Chicago.[12]

The *Chronicle* article correctly noted that Gilman would be a "guest" of Jane Addams, but the newspaper erroneously promoted her to the position of Addams's "first assistant" and chauvinistically focused on Gilman's physical attributes while reducing the intrepid, peripatetic Addams to mere "prettiness": "[Gilman's] slender figure and dark face, with its deep clear eyes, will be seen much in Chicago's crowded ways, and will be a decided foil for Miss Addams' delicate blonde prettiness."[13] The Los Angeles *Times* of 25 July 1895 drew pointed attention to Gilman's personal life, concluding: "Mrs. Stetson will be remembered in Southern California for her literary work done in Pasadena and for the sensational divorce suit brought by [her] husband, a Rhode Island artist."[14]

Her departure from California was a new beginning. "The sense of hope and power rose up afresh as the train rolled eastward" (Gilman 1935: 180). Shaking the California dust off her feet and its hostility from her spirit, Gilman spent the next month visiting Helen Campbell at the University of Wisconsin in Madison where Campbell was briefly a professor and a student of the noted economist Richard Ely. Much rested, Gilman arrived in Chicago.

Jane Addams: When Addams invited Gilman to come to Hull-House, Gilman quickly accepted (M. A. Hill 1980: 255). Addams was a role model, a charismatic public figure, an intellectual, and the head resident of the pioneering social settlement, Hull-House. Gilman was drawn to the sociological enterprise and particularly to "women's work" within the discipline as exemplified by Addams. They responded well to each other. They shared an era and a generation; both were born in 1860, both died in 1935.

Addams and Gilman remained lifelong friends and joined forces on several projects after Gilman left Hull-House and Chicago. Both women worked on *The Woman's Journal*, a feminist magazine that advocated women's emancipation (M. A. Hill 1980) and one of the few women's publications that addressed working women's issues, which both Gilman and Addams actively supported (Gilman 1911, 1912a, b). In 1915, Gilman and Addams also participated in the beginning of the women's peace movement (Hobbs 1987; Addams, Balch, and Hamilton 1915). In addition to specifically feminist activities, they shared intellectual ties in sociology. Both Addams and Gilman joined the American Sociological Society (ASS) during its founding year, 1905, and were active in the ASS for more than a quarter of a century.

Addams genuinely impressed Gilman. M. A. Hill (1980: 275) recounts that Gilman responded in amazed disbelief when Houghton Gilman (her second husband) did not know of Addams or her work:

> Not know Jane Addams! . . . Jane Addams of Hull House! Not know Hull House & Jane Addams. Behold the deficiencies of a college education. Why Jane Addams is one of the noblest, wisest, strongest, sweetest women in the world, and Hull House is the greatest "Social Settlement" in America. Get "Hull House Maps and Papers" right off, and improve your mind.

The deep ties between Gilman and Addams extended to their core ideas about the world and its reconstruction.

A Three Month Visit at Hull-House: Hull-House was the most famous U.S. social settlement and a vibrant center of women's intellectual activity. Its numerous "residents" lived communally and worked toward increased power for the poor in the surrounding neighborhood—especially for immigrants and the disenfranchised (Deegan 1988a; Woods and Kennedy 1911: 53–64). Gilman stayed at Hull-House from approximately September 1895 to early December 1895.[15] Her work at Hull-House was precisely what she needed: "The wise kindness with which she [Addams] took me in for a three months' visit had an immediate effect in counteracting my California newspaper-made reputation" (Gilman 1935: 184). This was an exciting time to be at Hull-House, just as the Residents of Hull-House (1895) published their groundbreaking sociological study of the Hull-House neighborhood, *Hull-House Maps and Papers* (Deegan 1988a: 33–54).

In addition to Addams, a remarkable group of women sociologists lived and worked at Hull-House and many were students or faculty at the

University of Chicago. Gilman respected these women, and they thought highly of Gilman and admired her subsequent work. Florence Kelley later wrote to Gilman that "the residents are waiting in rows" to read *Women and Economics*.[16] Kelley, a resident, ardent socialist, and interpreter of Friedrich Engel's works, was engaged at that time in a battle against sweatshops that exploited women and children's labor in the garment industry (Deegan 1991).

Gilman felt at home. The pragmatic and intellectual work at Hull-House was directly tied to that of Wisconsin's Richard Ely—the mentor of her friend and colleague, Helen Campbell, and Jane Addams's "sociological grandfather" (Davis 1973: 102). Gilman (1935: 184) remembered these months as vibrant and personally fulfilling:

> The change was sudden and great. To Hull House came distinguished people, humanitarian thinkers from all over the country, and from other countries, too. Here was companionship, fellow feeling, friendly society. My verse was known and liked, new friends were made, [and] there were lecture engagements.

Gilman's audience included her sister residents and likely such Chicago intellectuals as John Dewey, George H. Mead, and William I. Thomas. The latter frequented Hull-House during these years and often wrote on similar topics. Gilman worked through topics in her Hull-House lectures that appeared later in major publications, especially *Women and Economics* (Gilman 1898) and *Human Work* (Gilman 1904). Gilman (1935: 186) noted that during her year in Chicago:

> The social philosophy I was teaching included my organic theory of social economics, later developed in *Human Work*; the theory of the economic independence and specialization of women as essential to the improvement of marriage, motherhood, domestic industry, and racial improvement; with much on advance in child culture.

She understood and admired the social settlement and its communal lifestyle—although she did not ultimately choose the latter for herself.

Unity Settlement and Helen Campbell: Five Months of Struggle: December, 1895–April, 1896: In December 1895, Gilman left Hull-House to become a resident of Unity Settlement on Chicago's north side. Unity Settlement was an outgrowth of "an industrial school for girls begun in 1876" and was organized under the auspices of Unity Church (Woods and Kennedy 1911:

47). When Gilman took up quarters at Unity, the neighborhood was a mixture of factories and tenements boasting a population of Irish and Swedish immigrants. Gilman's experience at Hull-House was clearly positive, but she was soon disappointed with life at Unity.

If Gilman imagined herself at the center of a vibrant social settlement at Unity similar to that at Hull-House, the dream did not materialize. She was cheek by jowl with the urban industrial wastelands that later greeted Ellador in *With Her in Ourland*. In dramatic contrast to the liveliness of Hull-House with its many residents, Gilman felt isolated and increasingly despondent. She became depressed by her life in "Little Hell" and described her neighborhood in somber, grim images:

> The loathly river flowed sluggishly near by, thick and ill-smelling; Goose Island lay black in the slow stream. Everywhere a heavy dinginess; low, dark brick factories and gloomy wooden dwellings often below the level of the street; foul plank sidewalks, rotten and full of holes; black mud underfoot, damp soot drifting steadily down over everything. (Gilman 1935: 184–185)

Not wanting to endure this situation alone—and citing "the unreliability" of her health (Gilman 1935: 185)—she encouraged her friend Helen Campbell, to assume the Head Resident post at Unity. Campbell immediately pulled up stakes in Wisconsin and joined Gilman in Chicago.

Gilman was temporarily much happier with this arrangement. Working among the poor, Gilman forgot her own problems: "It was a pleasant family life, though planted in the midst of misery. Among so many poor why should I worry over my own poverty" (Gilman 1935: 185).

Gilman's grim picture of the Unity Settlement was echoed in Campbell's (1898) writings from this period. Campbell wrote a bleak account of the district in a thinly disguised description of an unnamed, unsuccessful settlement on the north side of a western city. Here, Campbell (1898: 598) noted the stench from a nearby gas company that dumped its industrial refuse into a sluggish river filled with "a creeping pestilence, known to all men to carry death in every drop of its festering current, its existence a menace, a warning, and a disgrace." The debased environmental quality of the district was all the more oppressive because the settlement residents could not improve it. Despite complaints, letters, interviews, and an attempt to enforce health regulations through the Board of Health, the residents in Campbell's account were unable to end the exploitative practices of the manufacturers.

The settlement had only minor successes. According to Campbell's (1898) version, the neighborhood children flocked to the settlement house, the local women joined the settlement's Mothers Club, and several young men formed a Civic Club. But the "sweating industry" competed for the time and energy of the disadvantaged neighborhood residents. The limited successes of the settlement program were met with utter disinterest and lack of commitment by the "philistine" rich who also lived within the geographic boundaries of the ward.

There were also subtle lines of conflict within the settlement—between the self-trained and the college-educated residents. Campbell (1898: 595) criticized conservative university professors who avoided settlement work, and she described the young college woman, freshly degreed, as:

> a trifle overweighted by her new possession, with, at times, a slight flavor of superciliousness toward the women who having been born too soon for college training are training themselves; a little doubtful of any knowledge or opinion which has not the university cachet, and insisting upon the university as the chief guaranty of the value of an opinion.

As Gilman had no college degree, there was a basis for tension with the college-trained residents at Unity Settlement.

During her Chicago period, Gilman was less ridiculed than in California but, conversely, she became identified as a "good woman" in a way she disliked.[17] Gilman (1935: 184) discovered herself at meetings "introduced by sonorous ministers as 'one of those consecrated women who have given their lives to the service of the poor and needy.' " Unity Settlement, unlike Hull-House, was sponsored by a religious organization and this no doubt increased the frequency and intensity with which Gilman was cast in a "do-gooder" role. Despite personal despondency, practical difficulties and social tensions, Gilman (1935: 185) worked at Unity settlement and "lectured and preached, wherever I was asked, for my expenses or for what they could afford to give" from December 1895 to April 1896.

Gilman's vision of the ideal life meshed imperfectly with the applied sociology lived by the other Chicago women. Gilman admired their radical experiments in work, housing, and women-centered lifestyles (Deegan 1996), but—especially in light of her subsequent marriage to Houghton Gilman in 1900—she preferred marriage and relatively more traditional housing. Gilman came to see social settlement residents—including those at Hull-House—as narrower than herself. "My interest," she wrote, "was in all humanity, not merely in the under side of it; in sociology, not social pathology" (Gilman 1935: 184). This was, however, a relatively small disparity within a larger realm of shared sociological purpose. For example, Gilman later wrote a series on "social pathology" that reflected her intellectual concern with issues frequently identified as "women's work" in sociology. The Hull-House residents, moreover, were interested in their neighbors and friends, not just the social pathology of their lives and community.

Four Months of Indecision and Departure from Chicago: April–July, 1896: Gilman was restless and often at sea in settlement work. By April 1896, she resumed her lectures and travel. Although she returned to Chicago's social settlements periodically between April and July, 1896, and visited often between 1897 and 1899, her temperament and ideology were not suited to settlement living. On 8 July 1896, Gilman left Chicago, after living in Chicago as a resident in a social settlement for nearly a year, and traveled to England to attend the International Socialist and Labor Congress.

Gilman had worked intimately in the midst of the women's sociological network in Chicago, and she championed many of their ideas for the rest of her life. This remarkable community of women lived many of the communal goals she espoused in her writings. Gilman was drawn to this community, and it undoubtedly served as a model for the natives of Herland. Hull-House was the center of one of the most vibrant female institutions that has ever existed in America; and Gilman, despite her travels, maintained her ties to that community from 1897 to 1899.

Gilman's Chicago and Hull-House Visits from 1897 to 1900; From a Nomadic Existence to Marriage: Gilman lived a nomadic existence, traveling from town to town, home to home, lecturing and writing from 1897 to 1900. During this time, Chicago became one of Gilman's frequent lengthy stopovers, particularly in 1897 and 1898. She did not reside at Hull-House, but she was a frequent visitor. Gilman was attracted to the Chicago women's community and the settlement movement. Below, I briefly note the little-known Chicago-related events in Gilman's life from 1897 to 1900, events that were personally and intellectually important.

The Year 1897: In late January, 1897, Gilman was again in Chicago. On 23 January, for example, she went to the:

> Woman's Club meeting—Miss Anthony & Miss Shaw spoke. I read (at Miss A's request) "Mother to Child." All seem glad to see me. Go to Hull House to dinner. Settlement Federation meeting—dull, but I was glad to see them all at it. (Gilman 1994, II: 656)[18]

During these months, Gilman (M. A. Hill 1995, 201) "for the most part . . . would turn to Jane Addams' Hull House as the central focus of her work."

On 3 February, Gilman began living with Mrs. Marietta Dow in Chicago. Jennie Dow, Mrs. Dow's daughter, worked at Hull-House, where Addams and Jennie Dow became close friends (Addams 1932). Gilman remained at the Dow's home until July 16—almost half a year. During this time, Gilman's life was filled with lectures and periodic travels as well.

Throughout 1897, Gilman wrote on Fabian socialism and sociology. In fact, she wrote a humorous and insightful series on an imaginary classroom experience in sociology over the course of a succession of installments published in *The American Fabian* (Gilman 1897–1898). In these serialized, make-believe lectures in sociology, a male professor leads simultaneously didactic and amusing discussions on the merits of Fabian sociology. Satirically, the male narrator instructs groups such as "millionaires" and "the average woman." In Gilman's later Herland/Ourland novels, a female Herland native employs a similar format to teach "Herland knowledge" (i.e., female sociology) to a male sociologist. The Hull-House ties to Fabian socialism and sociology were strong in 1896, too, and were another link with Gilman's work (Deegan 1988a: 263–266).

After Gilman left Chicago, she visited a health resort in Wyoming, New York. Here she met many Chicago friends, including Addams, and Professor Ward (Gilman 1994, II: 685).[19] On 17 July, Gilman and Addams were both at the hotel, and two days later, they discussed Gilman's forthcoming work, *Women and Economics* (Gilman 1898). Gilman (1994, II: 685) recalled in her diary: "A good morning. Talk with Miss Addams. She is really impressed—with the new big idea. To have her see it is a great help." Addams left on July 19 and two days later Gilman finished her "Fabian 'Class' thing for August" (Gilman 1994, II: 685).

Throughout 1897, Addams and Gilman visited, talked, attended each other's lectures—and those of their friends, wrote, and shared ideas. This was a fruitful and important intellectual influence central to a significant part of Gilman's most provocative writing and social thought.

The Years 1898, 1899, and 1900: Gilman resumed her peripatetic lifestyle, but returned to Chicago as a base again in 1898. Her diary records a lengthy stay at Mrs. Dow's between 17 November 1897 and 15 January 1898. She returned again during the next November from the second to the twenty-fourth.

The year 1898 was filled with responses to her newly published *Women and Economics*, and the book was widely read at Hull-House. Thus, Florence

Kelley wrote to Gilman: " 'Ms. A' has carried off one copy to Rockford [Illinois, site of Addams's childhood home and collegiate alma mater], and given our wonted frugality, the residents are waiting in rows for her to come back with it."[20] Addams also wrote to Gilman. She deemed *Women and Economics* a "masterpiece" and announced that "it put perfectly clearly many things which I have been fumbling after" (Addams, in Sklar 1995: 305). Lane (1990: 7) also noted Addams's support of Gilman's book: "In a letter to Florence Kelley, Jane Addams described *Women and Economics* as the 'first real substantial contribution made by a woman to the science of economics.' " Gilman visited Hull-House or allies of the settlement numerous times throughout her stay.[21]

During the year of 1898—and earlier in 1895, 1896, and 1897—Gilman spent the time around the Christmas season in Chicago and near Hull-House. This emotionally-charged holiday time (Deegan 1989) provided Gilman with a "home" where she repeatedly returned. This was likely important to Gilman, as her daughter lived with her former husband and his second wife, Grace Channing. The female world of love and ritual (Smith-Rosenberg 1975) in Chicago was deeply meaningful and provided a needed haven for the nomadic Gilman.

Gilman's visits to Hull-House dramatically diminished in 1899 when she took to the road, although she briefly visited Chicago in November. Addams called on Gilman on 12 November, but there is only one reference to a Hull-House stop during the month (Gilman 1994, II: 799, 801).

In December, Gilman attended a Women's Congress in England where she met many compatible colleagues including E. A. Ross. She returned to the U.S.A. with Mr. and Mrs. Ross and spent the holidays with them in California. During the year, Gilman increasingly moved toward a commitment to marry Houghton, and it is striking that she now celebrated the holiday with a married couple rather than the women's community in Chicago.

Impressions of a dispirited visit to Hull-House in 1900 comprise one of Gilman's last comments on the settlement in her published letters to Houghton. Gilman (1995: 372) made this weary observation on 15 May:

> Went to Hull House to dine. Hull House always uses me up. Such a flux of disconnected people. Such a noisome neighborhood. And wonderful Miss Addams handling it all so well and meeting the thousand calls upon her so gently and effectively— it is magnificent, but it tires me very much.

Gilman was then seeing a doctor for an unspecified illness and feared a resurgence of her previous mental disability. She was in the throes of a significant decision: her upcoming marriage to Houghton (Gilman 1995: 372–373).

On 11 June 1900 Gilman traveled from Chicago to Detroit with "the Dow's man carrying my bags to the train." Her close association with Hull-House was ending, and she was breaking with its female world of love and ritual. She arrived in Detroit at six o'clock and, in an anticlimactic passage, Gilman (1994, II: 814) noted "Mr. Reed Stewart, Unitarian minister, arrives about 7:30, and we are married." Thus ends Gilman's years of wandering without a home and of her frequent visits to Hull-House and the community it engendered.

The four years that Gilman lived in Chicago or frequently visited were rarely mentioned in Gilman's formal writings and have been overlooked by most biographers. For example, despite the many months Gilman spent with Mrs. Dow in Chicago, Mrs. Dow was not mentioned in Gilman's (1935) autobiography. Hull-House and Addams receive but a few comments and her three-month stay as a resident is only briefly recalled. The bulk of Gilman's sociologically steeped Chicago years is neither reflexively examined by Gilman nor understood by her critics.

These years were vital to Gilman. But they did not fit well with her later married life. It was a time filled with strong emotions: these years challenged her ideas in creative ways, such as imagining a female world of love and ritual in Herland; and they were frightening, too, in making real the seemingly unsolvable problems of poverty, alienation, and despair. The Hull-House women, moreover, were successful in the professions, in public acceptance, in their friendships, and in their lives. Gilman's life, by contrast, was torn by doubt, anger, and hard times. All these women were on a sociological journey, however. For an important period, they traveled it together. When they separated, I do not believe that Gilman forgot them.

Although Gilman often portrayed herself as an outsider, and may have experienced herself as an outsider, she was warmly received and anchored in several professional relationships on a number of dimensions. These bonds helped construct her sociological identity, which she embraced, while her identification with the larger profession and community was distant. Her sociological imagination was brought to fruition in her stories of Herland.

GILMAN AND SOCIOLOGICAL KNOWLEDGE

Reconstructing the sociology of knowledge is more difficult when authors—and Gilman's case exemplifies this problem—did not systematically cite the sources they used in their work. Gilman apparently cared little about the interpretive problems created for subsequent scholars when she failed to carefully document the origins of her ideas. Gilman's partially published diaries document her extensive reading and reflection on the work of many scholars, but she consistently claimed that few of these ideas influenced her. Since fiction writers typically eschew footnotes, the documentation problem is compounded when Gilman's fiction works are included for analysis in a study of her intellectual resources.[22] Frustratingly for today's disciplinary historians, Gilman's lackadaisical citation style was not atypical in her era, particularly among women in sociology.

Gender bias complicates matters further. Male sociologists tended not to cite women writers whose ideas they sometimes appropriated as their own (Spencer 1913). Similarly, women writers occasionally neglected to formally cite their sisters. Gilman, for example, rarely, if ever, footnoted Addams's considerable influence on her scholarly works—although she did praise Addams's ideas and work in other contexts, such as her autobiography. Women writers, moreover, tended to give more formal credit to men who influenced their thinking. Gilman's effusive dedication to Ward (quoted above) is an excellent example. Thus, uncovering Gilman's reciprocal sociological influence requires looking beyond footnotes, bibliographies, and formal publications per se to autobiographies, diaries, personal correspondence, and archival resources (M. R. Hill 1993).

SOCIOLOGICAL THEORIES THAT INFLUENCED GILMAN

The sociological sources of Gilman's epistemological assumptions are located among the ideas and practices of Jane Addams, Lester F. Ward, Edward A. Ross, and Patrick Geddes. Each theorist participated in overlapping intellectual networks through which Gilman ran as a unifying thread. Within the intellectual milieu outlined in this section, three confluences of ideas and sociological networks are identified: (1) the cultural feminism shared by Addams, Ward, and Gilman; (2) the reform Darwinism shared by Ward, Geddes, and Gilman; and (3) the Fabian socialism of Geddes, Addams, and Gilman. From these sources, Gilman wove a distinctive theory of feminist reform Darwinism that set the logic and drove the narrative of the Herland/Ourland saga.

At least three major themes with sociological import animate the Herland/Ourland story. These assumptions include:

1. Assertion of the excellence of women's values and abilities,
2. Belief in the biological and evolutionary origin of women's superior attributes, and
3. A socialist vision of political and social equality between the sexes.

These assumptions are the central components of Gilman's feminist reform Darwinism, a distinctive perspective that called for social reform, the further development of the polity and social welfare, and the full participation of women in society.

Jane Addams and Cultural Feminism

Gilman and Jane Addams shared several theoretical assumptions about society. With respect to 1890s "cultural feminism," they assumed that traditionally defined feminine values are superior to traditionally accepted masculine values (Deegan 1988a: 25; Donovan 1985). This assumption, so visible in the nonfiction writings of Gilman and Addams, is fundamental to the Herland/Ourland saga—wherein Gilman animated this formal, sociological idea and gave it a sense of humor and satiric punch. Gilman and Addams promulgated the cultural feminist thesis, but each did so in her own way. Nonetheless, the commonalities between these two theorists are striking.

In framing her vision of cultural feminism, Addams (especially during the mid-1890s when Gilman was active at Hull-House) employed Otis Tufton Mason's (1894) *Woman's Share in Primitive Culture*. Mason's text was a radical statement on the role of women in the formation of culture and civilization. He attributed the development of many, if not all, major innovations in art, language, religion, and industry to women. He documented that, in general, women housed, fed, and clothed the species in early societies. Mason (1894: 240) stressed the uniqueness of women's abilities and nature, even in the areas of public governance and speech. Cultural feminism is a guide to the organizing logic of Herland and to Gilman's ideas on women's place in social evolution.

Johann Bachofen's (1861) groundbreaking work on early matriarchal societies was frequently cited as evidence that women were the earliest and most important members of society. Bachofen concluded that in matriarchal societies very different rules governed sexuality, marriage, property inheritance, and the distribution of power than typically operate in societies led by men. When women had greater social control than men, less stringent social sanctions were imposed on female sexual activities and the choice of partners. Illegitimacy was nil, inheritance and descent were organized through female ancestors. Matriarchal societies (excepting Amazons) were typically nonmilitaristic. Finally, religion, arts, and crafts were organized around female symbols of fertility and anatomy.

Josephine Donovan (1985: 31–63) documents that the scholarship of Bachofen and other men was employed by a wide range of feminists, including Elizabeth Cady Stanton, Margaret Fuller, and Matilda Joslyn Gage. These feminist intellectuals, particularly Gage, pointed to radical religious interpretations of cultural feminism that comprise one theme in Gilman's Herland/Ourland saga. Gilman constructed a feminist religious myth about the birth/rebirth of society that stands in sharp contrast to male-oriented accounts such as the Book of Genesis. The cultural feminist thesis in the Herland/Ourland saga was not restricted to religious symbolism, however.

The study of women took center stage in the works of both Addams and Gilman. Suffrage, the home, and working women were common concerns. Both sociologists studied "primitive" societies and ultimately concluded that women were increasingly oppressed as "civilization" spread. Despite these significant areas of overlapping interest and thought, however, they differed in emphasis and topics addressed.

Gilman advocated the idea of "maternal instinct" more strongly than Addams. For Gilman, "maternal instinct" was a sex-linked strength of women that was denied its full expression in patriarchal societies. This biological assumption permeated Herland's social rules and cultural meanings as well as Ellador's critiques of Ourland. In their writings, Gilman and Addams addressed the social origin of behavior and both writers were concerned with the theoretical and practical significance of social meaning and human interaction. However, Addams turned more frequently to symbolic interactionism for her interpretations, whereas Gilman drew more often on reform Darwinism.[23]

Addams stressed social justice for juvenile delinquents, immigrants, and prostitutes, but Gilman disclaimed a too narrow interest in "pathological" concerns in favor of normalcy and society as a whole. Thus, she emphasized the study of "normal" children (Gilman 1900), the home more than the social settlement (Gilman 1903), and marital relations per se (Gilman 1898).

Addams and Gilman wrestled differently with elitist tendencies that both inherited from childhood where intellectual achievement and "the finer things" were highly regarded. Addams, intently religious and clearly elitist as a young woman, became more tolerant and egalitarian as she matured, to the point that equality, compassion, and reverence for life became hallmarks of her career. Gilman, however, never quite shook loose the occasional ethnocentric lapses that stood in surprising contrast to her feminist ideals and support of Fabian socialism.

Of the two women, Addams was more politically active, more concerned with the plight of the poor and working classes, and more directly involved in applied sociology. Gilman was clearly more scholarly, more utopian, more influential in New York intellectual circles, and more radical in her study (but not practice) of marriage and motherhood. Addams was a public leader who acted concretely on her vision of a new world, whereas Gilman was an intellectual leader who systematically described her understanding and vision of the present. In their joint advocacy of cultural feminism, Gilman and Addams gave intellectual and applied life to a major intellectual tradition within which each drew attention to different foci.

Gilman consistently thought that women were biologically superior to men due to their maternal instincts. Addams sometimes shared this belief; and conversely both believed in the plasticity of human nature, with Addams emphasizing this more than Gilman. Gilman, in particular, practiced a female chauvinism based partially on a biological explanation. She did not see "parenting" as equally valued and "instinctual" for both sexes. She did see good parenting as a human potential and goal for everyone, as evidenced in the conclusion of *With Her in Ourland*. For men and women, however, Gilman assumed not only the superiority of the women's vision but also a biological advantage. To the extent that she relied upon such biological determinism, her arguments were weakened.

Cultural feminism has been interpreted as "essentialist" or assuming that unitary behavior and social forces shape all women. Although some cultural feminists employ a notion of "women's culture" that does inadequately address racial, religious, economic, and sexual preference diversity among different groups of women, this criticism does not apply to Addams or Gilman. Both addressed issues of diversity and difference. Although Gilman was sometimes a snob and a bigot, she did not assume all women had similar cultural ideas, behavior, or experience.

A more intractable difficulty with Gilman's theory was its lack of institutional, intellectual, and popular continuity. She was a leader of her time, but her ideas were not historically institutionalized or incorporated within American society or sociology. Although Gilman is enjoying a renaissance within the multidisciplinary study of women, such work often remains dissociated from mainstream influence. A major reason for this is the patriarchal structure of power and ideas, a barrier that Gilman understood and opposed.

Gilman's allegiance to cultural feminism was not unique among feminists (especially among feminist sociologists) in her era, but her union of cultural feminism with reform Darwinism was virtually singular. Addams assumed that feminine values were socially learned, defined, and transmitted through human interaction. That is, Addams adhered to "symbolic interactionism" or "critical pragmatism" (Deegan 1988a) then being formulated by male sociologists at the University of Chicago between 1894 and 1905 (James 1904). After 1909, Addams increasingly combined her work in cultural feminism with her ideas on critical pragmatism. Gilman was influenced by pragmatism, but tended to share the assumptions of male sociologists who subscribed to more material, biological ideas based in Darwin's theory of evolution.

Gilman and Social Darwinism

Social Darwinism flourished in the United States as a theory of society from the 1870s to 1900. Proponents applied Charles Darwin's model of biological evolution to the development of society. The most famous social Darwinist was Herbert Spencer. He combined belief in competitive "survival of the fittest" with support of the status quo, individualism, and capitalism. He opposed social intervention to improve society and advocated a natural progression of social changes (Hofstader 1959; Magner 1992). Although originally supportive of individual rights for women, Spencer increasingly opposed women's rights in the public sphere. He thought women's lives were driven by reproduction and that marriage was the suitable contract for their representation by men (Magner 1992).

Gilman was a firm adherent of Darwinist thought, but she employed several assumptions from Darwin to justify social intervention for improving the situation of women (Magner 1992). Gilman, like other social Darwinists, compared human society to a living organism that followed the laws of growth, mutation, and development that Darwin found so applicable in his studies of biology. Gilman, like many other "reform Darwinists" such as Ward and Geddes, advocated social planning to resolve social problems.

But, unlike many reform Darwinists, Gilman was a cultural feminist. She believed that women were the founders of human society, that women subsequently lost their power only after men gained ascendancy over them. Thus, Gilman challenged the male-oriented version of social Darwinism that stressed the natural origin of the status quo. She also challenged reform Darwinists who did not emphasize social change for women. Whereas Gilman's version remains largely unstudied, the more popular, male-oriented renditions of social and reform Darwinism are well documented and better understood (Goldman 1955; Hofstadter 1959; Magner 1978; Bannister 1979; Russett 1989).

Gilman's combination of cultural feminism and social Darwinism was shared by Ward, and this fundamental tie explains her fierce dedication to him. Ward's influence must be examined, therefore, to explicate Gilman's sociology and its application in *With Her in Ourland*.

Lester Ward's Reform Darwinism and "Gynaecocracy"

Reform Darwinism was first articulated with force by Henry George (1879) in *Progress and Poverty*. George attacked the support of economic exploitation implicit in conservative social Darwinism. In addition to a critique of the economic justification of inequality, George "went after conservative religion and the conservative conception of democracy" (Goldman 1955: 77).

Ward was influenced by reform Darwinism, but he extended it into its logical expression for women, and he did so in a manner sympathetic to feminism.[24] Gilman's interpretation of cultural feminism emerged directly from the writings of Ward. Her deep admiration for Ward is reflected in numerous points of similarity between her work and Ward's. Ward (1888: 266) not only contended "that in the economy of organic nature the female sex is the primary, and the male a secondary element," but also criticized patriarchal colleagues who argued for male organic superiority. Unlike Ward, most social Darwinists thought women were inferior to men in terms of intelligence, physical strength, and mental skills. That is to say, biology destined that the great genius and the great criminal would both be male.

Ward's discussions of "gynaecocracy" and "parthenogenesis," his systems model approach, and his five-stage theory of societal revolution, were applied in Gilman's Herland/Ourland saga. Early on, Ward (1888: 272) explored "parthenogenesis" (i.e., virgin reproduction in vegetables). In *Applied Pure Sociology*, Ward (1906b) further detailed his feminist reform Darwinist theory of "gynaecocracy" (wherein women were the "central, steady branch" of human evolution). Ellador's alert attention to a complex of interrelated social forces reflected Ward's focus.

Ward's systems theory of social evolution is particularly germane to the Herland/Ourland story. Ward not only thought that women were the basis of early social formations, but also that continued restrictions on women in industrial society impeded social evolution. Ward (1888: 275) asserted that: "Woman is the unchanging trunk of the great genealogic tree; while man with all his vaunted superiority, is but a branch, a grafted scion, as it were, whose acquired qualities die with the individual, while those of woman are handed up to futurity." Building on this assumption, Ward (1906a: 544) outlined five major revolutions in human society:

> First, the transition from asexuality to sexuality thru the origin of the male sex; second, the passage of the male from the condition of a minute fertilizing adjunct to a condition of superiority in size, power and beauty to the organism proper, then called the female; and third, the change during the early human period of female dominance, or matriarchy, to male dominion, or patriarchy.

The fourth revolution was monogamous heterosexuality (i.e., the current state of affairs as Ward saw it). The fifth and highest stage would occur when women and men became truly equal. This as yet unrealized revolution structures the conclusion of *With Her in Ourland*. Ward's feminist reform Darwinism fit the logic of the Herland/Ourland saga—and Gilman's *Women and Economics* (1898).

REFORM MOVEMENTS SHAPING THE PRAXIS OF GILMAN'S IDEAS

Patrick Geddes's Reform Darwinism and Fabian Socialism

When Gilman traveled to England in July 1896, she met many Fabians at the International Socialist and Labor Congress. She also met the Russian scholar and activist Petr Kropotkin, another close friend of Addams (Deegan 1988a: 262–263). Thus, although no longer living in Chicago, another common interest between Addams and Gilman emerged: Gilman's attraction to Fabian socialism, a socialist and sociological vision that flourished in England. Both Addams and Gilman endorsed Fabian policies of increased public ownership of community goods and labor's right to

organize. Fabian sociologists Beatrice and Sydney Webb formed an interpersonal and professional network along with Addams and Gilman
(Deegan 1988a: 263–266).

In England, the ideas of Patrick Geddes—and those of Fabian sociologists Beatrice and Sydney Webb—were of considerable moment. Geddes,
however, was not steeped in cultural feminist ideas as were Addams and
Gilman. Geddes and his student, Arthur Thompson, wrote about sex,
however, in their influential text *The Evolution of Sex* (Geddes and
Thompson 1889) and employed a social Darwinist model to interpret
Victorian gendered behavior. The book borders on the inane, but it was
nonetheless a major inspiration for Gilman in *Women and Economics*.

At the cellular level, argued Geddes and Thompson (1889: 44–45), male
cells dissipated energy in a "katabolic" pattern whereas female cells exhibited abundant supplies of energy in a conservative "anabolic" pattern.
Conway (1972: 144) summarized their position: "By making sperm and
ovum exhibit the qualities of male katabolism or female anabolism Geddes
was able to deduce a dichotomy between the temperaments of the sexes
which was easily accommodated to the romantic idea of male rationality
and female intuition." This model dovetailed with Gilman's and Ward's
general epistemological notions. The "steady trunk" of women's biology
was fundamental to Ward's theoretical system, and Geddes's reform Darwinism fit the feminism of Ward and Gilman.[25]

Simultaneously, Geddes's applied work tied Geddes and Addams together in an increasingly complex network of sociological ideas. Geddes
developed an elaborate "applied sociology" that included planned cities, a
social settlement in Scotland, and public education that parallelled Addams's ideas (Conway 1972: 150–151). Addams became one of Geddes's
closest sociological colleagues, but she never adopted his model of reform
Darwinism. Gilman, however, did. Gilman also drew on Utopian literature,
an interest she developed in childhood.

Charlotte Perkins Gilman and American Utopias

Multitudes of utopian schemes have found a home in the U.S.A. and
Gilman's life was structured by such dreams and activities (Kanter 1972;
Turner 1982). As a young adolescent, from June 1874 through February
1876, Gilman lived with her mother in one such community, the Sweden-
borgians:

> Here was a group of religious nonconformists, a group of divor-
> cees at that, cooperating on housework, communing in their
> mystic faith, and forming what would seem to many a threaten-
> ing substitute for the traditional family model. (M. A. Hill 1980:
> 37)

The first utopian group that captured the mature imagination of Gilman
was Edward Bellamy's nationalism program. Gilman adopted a series of
political platforms embraced by the populists and later by the progressives.
Gilman's advocacy of these social reform schemes was rooted in her belief
in democracy and education. Her "liberal agenda" frequently involved a
radical application of these ideals, especially for women. Gilman's utopian
vision was intertwined with a liberal agenda and combined with her
feminist reform Darwinism. *With Her in Ourland* exemplifies the active use
of these assumptions.

Addams's Social Reforms as an Influence on Gilman:
Democracy and Critical Pragmatism

Gilman drew on an elaborate program of reforms to animate Ellador's
conversations with Van in Ourland. Ellador's suggestions often articulated
specific changes underlying the progressive politics she shared with Addams, Ward, Ross, Geddes, and Bellamy's Nationalists. Ellador in *With Her
in Ourland* combined cultural feminism with the progressive platforms that
Addams helped to write for the Progressive Party in 1912 and 1916.

Addams's theory of critical pragmatism was based on democracy to
ensure social equality, and education as the mechanism to guarantee that
right. Social interaction based on equal participation for all, however, was
stunted and blocked in American cities. Capitalism, immigration, and
changes in the home affecting primarily women, children, and the aged,
resulted in communication and interaction failures for the whole community. Democracy and education were the tools needed to improve social
institutions, develop community control, and infuse everyday life with
vitality. Gilman shared this view of stunted human potential, a theme
expressed throughout *With Her in Ourland*. Gilman, however, viewed the
situation primarily in social evolutionary terms rather than a symbolic
interactionist framework.

Addams and Education

Education was, to Addams, a continuous, lifelong process. It is potentially active in all situations and the key to responsible action and reflective thought. Human intelligence can be maximized through systematic knowledge, reflection, and analysis. Education can provide concrete information about everyday life and allow people to articulate their goals and needs. It opens cultural ideas and knowledge for all, not just the elite. The desire to know is an intrinsic part of being human. Gilman shared these beliefs with Addams. Gilman's lifework, and that of Ellador's in *With Her in Ourland*, was to educate others about society and women's inequality. Gilman, like Ellador, quickly absorbed new information and marshalled it logically when analyzing social inequalities, a mental faculty that perplexed male sociologists. Thus, Gilman has Van observe: "It must have been due to their entirely different education. . . . All the new facts we gave them they had promptly hung up in the rights places, like arranging things in a large well-planned, not over-filled closet, and they knew where to find them at once."

Addams espoused the goal of equality, leading her to break from the educational programs adopted by the academic pragmatists. Advocating ideals expressed in the works of Kropotkin and Tolstoy, she opposed elitist education that segregated people from their experiences, family, and labor. Gilman also opposed education that radically separated ideas from everyday life. Her own lack of formal education led to discrimination against her in a variety of settings, similar to those noted by Campbell (1898) in her criticism of college-trained workers in social settlements.

Addams and Democracy

Democracy was foundational to Addams's critical pragmatism. Democracy, Addams (1902: 6) wrote, was a central principle of all human action: "We are thus brought to a conception of Democracy not merely as a sentiment which desires the well-being of all men, nor yet as a creed which believes in the essential dignity and equality of all men, but as that which affords a rule of living as well as a test of faith." Democracy was a product of "diversified human experience and [its] resultant sympathy" (Addams 1902: 12). It was the method for discovering truth, combining rational thought with the equal participation of all citizens in community processes. Although democracy was flawed and often inoperative, "the cure for the ills of Democracy is more Democracy" (Addams 1902: 12).

Democracy was a way of living, of experiencing life, of finding out the meaning of action. Social interaction was the core of daily life, and science was a method for gathering information about it. Addams (1902: 7) averred that "We have come to have an enormous interest in human life as such, accompanied by confidence in its essential soundness." This democratic vision was found in Herland and a source of criticism for Ourland.

In Addams's ideal society, democracy emerged from the good judgment and spirit of the community. Humans were basically good but they lacked information needed for full community cooperation and participation. In their daily lives, people could learn to generate and accept barriers to cooperation and egalitarian ways of living. Citizens had to learn how to destroy such barriers and build more creative and life-giving skills.

Traditionally, Americans interpreted "democracy" to mean equality before the law (especially for literate white men). Most of the arguments concerning human rights in a democratic society have emphasized "suffrage" as the route to political participation and governance. This definition and practice of democracy was too restricted for Addams and Gilman. Democracy was a more holistic concept, encompassing the right of total equality—politically, socially, and economically. This definition of democracy radically assumes that all people are equal. Each component of Addams's understanding of democracy is outlined below.

Political Democracy: Both Gilman and Addams fought for women's suffrage for years, and Ellador supported it too. Women's right to vote was intrinsic to women's participation in society. Both Gilman and Addams supported the franchise as a means for women to instill their values into the political sphere. They did not support the achievement of this goal through the use of armed conflict and physical confrontations, but they were not docile or inactive. They marched in parades, delivered voluminous addresses, wrote articles, and became national leaders who were extremely influential in legitimating the right for women to vote. Access to the vote was only a limited reform goal, however (Addams 1902: 223).

Social Democracy: Gilman and Addams differed the most in their understanding of social democracy. When discussing problems of social democracy, Addams often focused on immigrant laborers and their children. For this populace, generational differences were amplified with their change of culture and country. Older immigrants lost in two ways: the art and history of their people were absent and often denigrated; while the worst values of American culture were emphasized, namely the search for money. Thus, Addams (1910: 234) noted that "this tendency upon the part of the older immigrants to lose the amenities of European life without sharing those of American" society was a consistent loss and strain to immigrants, their communities, and their families. Gilman saw the problems of all children with great sympathy, yet she sometimes criticized immigrant groups rather sharply.

Both Addams and Gilman despised the social problems that immigrants faced, but Addams understood the new community's role in creating these problems more than Gilman did. The immigrants' children, explained Addams, often found the rules enforced in the home to be too harsh. Their parents misunderstood their behaviors as being "loose" and "evil" instead of "normal" or "acceptable" in a new society. Further stress was caused by the poverty of the families and lack of fun at home. Frequently, the children's wages were needed and controlled by the parents. This parental dominance made their children angry, and the new generation sometimes turned to crime to get extra money and social freedom. Addams (1910: 251) compassionately described this situation as follows: "Most of these premature law breakers are in search of Americanized clothing and others are only looking for playthings. They are all distracted by the profusion and variety of the display, and their moral sense is confused by the general air of open-handedness." Thus, an understanding of the effort to be part of this society while another society had been lost provided a key to understanding the need for social democracy. The right to have one's lifestyle and ethnic culture understood and accepted was a major concern. Such social equality was necessary for the immigrants' participation in the community. Addams (1905: 204) chided Americans for not wanting to risk their "American" customs and values:

> I hope to be able to sustain the contention that such danger as exists arises from intellectual dearth and apathy; that we are testing our national life by a tradition too provincial and limited to meet its present motley and cosmopolitical character; that we lack mental energy, adequate knowledge, and a sense of the youth of the earth.

This criticism could sometimes be directed at Gilman.

Thus, social democracy was a cornerstone of Addams's concept of equality. Since social customs generated everyday life and its meaning, total acceptance of individuals and their local lifestyles led to an understanding of the community's shared system of thought and esthetics. Class differences, furthermore, were important causes of human suffering. Economic exploitation was a major source of this oppression, but other forms of exploitation were also significant. Restrictions on political rights, education, and social custom also needed elimination. Workers needed equality on three fronts: political, social, and economic. Gilman understood the pain of poverty better than the pain of prejudice.

Economic Democracy: Gilman and Addams were both committed to establishing minimal standards of living, good housing, and healthy food. Addams lived in the midst of poverty, and awareness of economic oppression filled her life. Gilman understood the realities of economic deprivation, and her experience of it at Unity Settlement precipitated a deep depression. She could write about it; she did not want to be overwhelmed by it. Lane (1990) depicts much of Gilman's adult life as on the edge of poverty due to her expenditures for her publications and her financial support of other family members. But this experience of financial constraint arose from Gilman's active choices about spending money and her ability to meet these financial obligations. As an adult, she was not ground down by the filth and oppression she saw in the neighborhood surrounding the Unity Settlement.

Providing minimal standards of living for all was a platform espoused by Addams, Gilman, and the Fabian sociologists. This form of socialism was compatible with women's values articulated in cultural feminism. The conflict model of Marxism was thereby eliminated. In *Hull-House Maps and Papers* (Residents of Hull-House 1895), just published when Gilman arrived at Hull-House, Addams set forth her early disenchantment with the conflict model. She saw society as based on both conflict and cooperation, but if peaceful relations were the goal of society then the means to reach that end should be congruent with the end itself.

Marxists also saw the world as based on material values. Rather than reenforcing this concept of the power of capital, both Gilman and Addams recognized the power of other resources and capacities. Art, literature, affection, and emotions were separate bases for being and acting in the world that had their own value and force. Marxist socialists who emphasized the power of the economy strengthened the ideology that the economy dominated society. Marxists thereby weakened other forms of proletariat and institutional resistance to capital.

Both Gilman and Addams remained partial to the socialist vision because it emphasized the primacy of economic exploitation and a program for its resolution. Nonetheless, their differences with conflict methods and underlying principles of addressing economic exploitation caused the two women to part company with Marxism. In particular, their support of democracy and education were major mechanisms for nonviolent cultural feminism to yield a society composed of political, social, and economic equals.

Applied Epistemology: Gilman, Ross, and Ward

Lester Ward and Edward A. Ross were also active in political programs promoting social change, a theme that reverberates in Gilman's writings. Ward was affected by Bellamy's (1888) *Looking Backward*, a book Ward called a "sugar-coated bomb" (Scott 1976: 33). It prompted him to become more involved in social action and, in turn, sociology. Ward was increasingly active in political action for social change, but this work was rarely evident in his sociological writings. Ward (1903) was an abstract theorist of applied sociology. As Fabian socialism became legitimated, however, he aligned increasingly with this cause:

> Socialism in the United States and Great Britain had almost become respectable, and reforms of all sorts were in the air. Individual socialists and a surge of Socialist educational forums paid court to Ward, and he spoke to various socialist groups in America and abroad. Eugene Debs and lesser organizers quoted Ward in speeches and pamphlets, and Ward even found himself at speakers' tables with Emma Goldman, the well-known anarchist. (Scott 1976: 39)

Gilman was also active in these circles.

Ward also advocated "education" as a major tool for social transformation. He had himself entered the wider social world through advanced education, and he believed it would lead to greater equality as it became more available. Ward believed in "scientific education" following Auguste Comte's model of "positivism," but Ward democratized and broadened the scope of the educated masses. This model fit the feminist reform Darwinism that Ward advanced. Instead of the elite private education supported by most social Darwinists, Ward wanted mass compulsory education. Gilman's popular lectures fit this scheme of mass education, and Ellador's education about Ourland reveals how self-teaching could occur. Gilman and Ward, therefore, saw the implementation of concrete proposals as part of their evolutionary model. Gilman clearly developed the role of women in her proposals more than Ward did, but their ideas here were complementary and not contradictory.

Edward A. Ross was more activist in his programs than was Ward. Ross, however, still wrote about his plans for social change more often than he led large groups of followers. Ross also supported more progressive, active proposals for women's rights than did Ward, and Gilman shared Ross's views here.

Ross, Ward, Addams, and Gilman displayed intellectual courage and leadership at various times in their lives. Ward dared to change specialties from botany to the untried social science of sociology (Chugerman 1939; Scott 1976). Ross struggled to obtain freedom of speech in the academy and helped institutionalize the tenure system as a result (Ross 1915). Addams endured the persecution of the "Red Scare" (Deegan 1988a). And, Gilman lived her life on the cutting edge of public debate on women. All these sociologists challenged a patriarchal society and profession. Their work provides the background for reading the Herland/Ourland saga as sociology.

Gilman was influenced by Addams, Ward, Ross, and others, but she nonetheless viewed sociology through her own special lens. Her brilliant synthesis of her ideas with those of her colleagues is illustrated in the Herland/Ourland saga. Herland itself is feminist reform Darwinism come alive—Ellador's journey through Ourland is a progressive critique of the world in 1915. Reading these volumes as sociological literature transforms our contemporary understanding of them. Further, they show contemporary feminist sociologists how a perceptive early scholar moved beyond masculinist literature in sociology to create a feminist language and myth of her own.

GILMAN'S TRANSFORMATIONAL RULES: FROM SOCIOLOGICAL NON-FICTION TO FICTION IN *HERLAND* AND *WITH HER IN OURLAND*

The Herland/Ourland saga is a sociological transformation of Gilman's female sociology from nonfiction to fiction. Gilman linked the languages of social science and systematic observation with creativity and the literary imagination. Her sociological innovation and imagination make unique contributions to the sociology of knowledge. Previous critics of the Herland/Ourland saga have not articulated Gilman's transformation rules and sociological intent together. Sociologists have used fiction as a pedagogical and methodological technique, but twentieth-century academic sociologists rarely recognize fiction as a legitimate mode of discourse. Literary scholars employ literary rules—rather than sociological criteria—to evaluate texts. Hence, Gilman's achievement in *With Her in Ourland* is misunderstood by both sociologists and literary critics.

Gilman transformed sociology into fiction by using her feminist episte-
mology to generate a "media frame"—that is, a set of principles for ordering
action in her writings (Deegan 1989: 110). Her transformational leap from
nonfiction to fiction was accomplished through eight interrelated strategies, discussed below. Understanding the transformational rules in Gilman's media frame allows us to better appreciate Gilman's sociological
fiction. These tales are fictional representations of Gilman's sociology. The
fictional dialogues between Ellador and Van represent the two sides in a
feminist versus patriarchal discourse. The complex Gilman formula underlies this otherwise simple narrative. Understanding this formula, in turn,
transforms our reading of the Herland/Ourland stories.

Sociological Authority

First, Gilman wrote as an authority in sociology. Acknowledging this
expertise is crucial to the Herland adventures. This legitimation contra-
dicts the interpretations of Gilman and the Herland texts developed by
Ann Lane, the major Gilman scholar on *Herland* and *With Her in Ourland*.
Lane (1990: 230) describes Gilman as an outsider in the history of ideas:
"She suffered, as all outsiders do, from lack of engagement with the trained,
critical intelligentsia of her day." And further:

> Although she lived on the margin of intellectual life—she was
> never an accepted member of the intellectual establishment
> except through some personal contact with those who were—
> she was a part of the intellectual currents and movements that
> shaped the new ideas of her time. (Lane 1990: 230)

Others offer similar analyses (Degler 1989). In fact, Gilman was *not* an
outsider in sociology.

Embodied Sociological Experience

Second, Gilman wrote as an embodied sociologist who drew on her
female experience. Gilman's life in communal groups, especially Hull-
House and the Chicago female world of love and ritual, provided her with
lived experience of successful female communities outside traditional
family structures and homes.

Given this experience, Ellador represents Gilman and other female
sociologists. Their "female sociological labor" was enacted by dozens of

female sociologists and was supported by a few male sociologists, represented by Van. The collective female voice addressed male colleagues who genuinely labored to understand society but were blinded by androcentric culture (Gilman 1911). Those biased, but otherwise well-intentioned, male social scientists had the potential to learn from their female colleagues. As Van explained (Gilman 1979: 26): "I always flattered myself I had the scientific imagination, which, incidentally, I considered the highest sort. One has a right to a certain amount of egotism if founded on fact." The willingness of a few male sociologists to study and learn made them an appreciative audience for Gilman's work.

Gilman's male sociologist does not blindly idolize women as does Jeff, the physician. Nor does Gilman draw her sociologist in the manner of the brutish misogynist, Terry. For Gilman, male sociologists are the vanguard of their sex, men who can change for the better despite their initial patriarchal biases. Vandyke Jennings is the collective representative of the males in the sociological establishment who are sensitive and sympathetic to women's ideas and are malleable to instruction. Thus, Ellador literally explains female culture and work to Van, a male sociologist. This is not an obscure reading of *Herland* and *With Her in Ourland*, but one obviously intended by Gilman.

Cultural Feminism

Third, Gilman depicted the female culture through the lens of her cultural feminism. Gilman scholarship, however, sometimes misreads Gilman's commitment to cultural feminism. Thus, Ann Lane (1990: 252) wrote:

> Unlike many women reformers and social critics of her time, Gilman acknowledged but did not seriously value the importance of a powerful female culture. She did not envision the domestic role as generating effective power for most women. She stressed, instead, the condition of servitude imposed on women and the servile personality that resulted from that condition. Gilman saw male contributions to civilization as superior.

In fact, Gilman strongly supported the ideas of many female sociologists who lived in female environments in social settlements—one of the living models for Herland.

With Her in Ourland is a dialogue between female sociologists and male sociologists. They discuss active social programs that could help humans step up to the next stage in evolution. But Ellador must show Van how flawed the entire world is—and that America is a failed democracy. Women are enslaved by lack of suffrage, by their economic dependency, and by dysfunctional housing and ridiculous clothing. Ellador is a coherent voice for Gilman's sociological work up to 1916. The Herland/Ourland saga is a consummate performance that addresses Gilman's colleagues and public in an entertaining and humorous way about the serious societal issues analyzed by cultural feminists.

Societal Vision

Fourth, Gilman envisioned a new society emerging from pragmatism, populism, and nationalism. She proposed institutional modifications in economics, child care, the home, and the marketplace. Democracy and education are portrayed as cornerstones of this new society. For example, in response to Van's question of what Ellador would like to see changed in Ourland, Ellador replied:

> Definite training in democratic thought, feeling and action, from infancy. An economic administration of common resources under which the home would cease to be a burden and become an *unconscious* source of happiness and comfort. And, of course, the socialization of home industry.

She defends Fabian socialism and minces no words with capitalists:

> Talk of blood-suckers! You have oil-suckers and coal-suckers, water-suckers and wood-suckers, railroad-suckers and farm-suckers—this splendid young country is crawling with them— and has not the intelligence, the energy, to shake them off.

Ellador presents many examples of nationalist/populist/ progressive ideas that are not yet fully adopted. Indeed, her predictions of poverty, human suffering, and waste—in the absence of the requisite institutional changes—have come all too true.

Feminist Reform Darwinism

Fifth, Gilman based her arguments on feminist reform Darwinism and employed an evolutionary model of society based on instinctual, gendered behaviors. Gilman opened up a new possibility for women in Herland: They were the group who could advance all society up the evolutionary scale. This gendered superiority was the obverse of patriarchal reform Darwinism, particularly its links to patriarchal religions. Ellador even recommended reading Lester Ward to understand this theory: "No one can study biology and sociology much and not see that on the first physiological lines the female is the whole show, so to speak, or at least most of it." The biological superiority of women was not intended to conquer men, however. It was a tool to change all societies and all their members. Ellador tells Van: "Don't be too hard on Mr. Man." Both sexes are needed for the new stage in social advancement.

Contradictions Between Racism and Anti-Racism

Sixth, Gilman was simultaneously racist and anti-racist. Her struggle to transcend her own society and personal fears are reflected in Ellador's occasional ambivalence. Sensitive readers will understandably wince at some passages in *With Her in Ourland.* For example, Ellador disapproves of letting "the poor and oppressed" enter the U.S.A. and deplores the "crowding injections of alien blood, by vast hordes of low-grade laborers." Her backhanded compliments to Jews were, often as not, egregious affronts.

But Gilman also opposed racism and narrow-minded thinking. For example, Gilman/Ellador thought that white people were racist against all people of color, an insight Van protested but could not thoroughly deny. She decried slavery and the continued oppression of African Americans. Ellador could not fathom the slaughter of Native Americans. "All of them?" the shocked Ellador asked when told of the genocide by a "democratic civilization." Similarly, she cannot understand the brutal destruction of the people of Hawaii. Van sulked: "We wanted to Christianize them." But Ellador responds by wondering if this was what Christ would have done.

The larger part of Gilman's critique of religion was rooted in her dismay with belief systems that kept women in traditional family roles and defined women as less sacred than men (Gilman 1923). Thus, from the point of view of women's emancipation, her critiques of religion are progressive; seen from the perspective of religious toleration, however, she sometimes appears insensitive and ethnocentric. Such difficulties, of course, are no less problematic today, as evidenced by our own perplexities over political correctness and identity politics (Grossberg 1992).

Gilman was bigoted and ethnocentric at times, but she was also frequently insightful, timely, courageous, and a brilliant sociologist. She was often humorous—and occasionally pedantic. This composite picture deserves understanding and analysis. Gilman was not a perfect woman; she was, however, one of the most astute analysts of women's oppression. This is her legacy, stripped of mythical legends.

In defense of Gilman's occasional lapses, I argue that the far more severe patriarchal biases of Karl Marx, Max Weber, Sigmund Freud, and Emile Durkheim, as well as most other male theorists, should not automatically disqualify their works from inclusion on standard reading lists. If scholars only read theorists without errors and without flaws, scholars and scholarship would disappear! The literate public would evaporate, and our entire cultural heritage would be destroyed. *With Her in Ourland* is flawed by Gilman's elitism and ethnocentrism, but ignoring Gilman's utopia because of her blemishes invites failure to examine her at all. Serious readers, I believe, want to understand the interaction of race, sex, and class in modern society—and in Gilman's work. The dilemma of reading masculinist literature while trying simultaneously to write from a perspective without bias is one that plagues all feminists, not just Gilman.

Critiques of "Masculinist Literature" in Sociology

Seventh, Gilman exhibited penetrating insight in her critique of the patriarchal discourses of sociology and "masculinist literature" wherein the male view is assumed to be the human voice (Gilman 1911: 88–89). Both *Herland* and *With Her in Ourland* are important alternate discourses on the nature of sociology. These fantasies can and should be read as critiques in the sociology of knowledge.

The thousands, perhaps millions, who have endured the pontifications of sexist sociologists—whether in published writings, speeches, or classrooms—will get a delightful "zing" when reading the Herland novels. Gilman gently, sometimes caustically, criticized these arrogant and ignorant males in a context of love as well as frustration.

What can we do with patriarchal men? This century-old question is addressed by all feminists, especially feminist sociologists. Gilman's criticism also applies today to the new media-augmented industry of social science experts who flood the mass media. The masculinist ideology undergirding many of these male interests percolates through their claims to facts, scientific theories, and truth. Ellador's arguments undermine this silly, "modern," social science nonsense.

Critiques of "Masculinist Literature" in Fiction

Finally, Gilman intentionally violated the norms of "good literature" in her Herland/Ourland stories. Ironically, her violation of these norms, particularly in *With Her in Ourland*, led to evaluations of the work as "inferior literature." But, Gilman's intentional transformation of the rules of masculinist literature must be considered in any evaluation of her work.

Gilman judged literature to be "the most powerful and necessary of the arts, and fiction is its broadest form" (Gilman 1911: 93). She held fiction, rather than nonfiction, in the highest regard. As a sociologist, she wanted to transform the "facts" of sociology into the "art" of fiction. In this way, she intended to shape culture itself. Fiction was severely circumscribed, however, because of men's interests, their control over publishing and distribution, and their control over readers' consciousness.

Fiction was channeled through two types of stories: "the Story of Adventure, and the Love Story" (Gilman 1911: 94). "It is surely something more than coincidence that these are the two essential features of masculinity—Desire and Combat—Love and War" (Gilman 1911: 95). Ninety percent of fiction concentrates on love and stops at marriage—just as *Herland* ends. Gilman tells us this is where masculinist literature ends (Gilman 1911: 95, 102). New fields of human fiction are explored by Gilman in the Herland/Ourland stories. She presents a dramatic reversal of the myth of Adam and Eve. This is the future-oriented story of *Herland* and *With Her in Ourland*: Ellador/Eve saves Adam/Van.

TOWARD THE RENEWAL OF OURLAND

At the conclusion of *With Her in Ourland*, the women of Herland open themselves to the possibilities of the outside world They actively bring men into their community in order to help both men and women in the wider world. Ellador suggests a series of concrete steps to solve the world's most pressing problems. And, with great optimism, the closing words of the novel are: " 'And then—the other new Hope, too—perhaps— perhaps—a son!' And in due time a son was born to us." This auspicious ending of *With Her in Ourland* reverses the ending of *Herland*, whereat two of the three men depart the feminist society and Herland remains in splendid isolation. Gilman did not propose an irreconcilable, biological distinction between the sexes, a frequent interpretation of Herland. Rather, Gilman proposed that strong women could resocialize violent and self-destructive men so that they would become nurturant, cooperative, and just. Androcentric culture could contribute its technological and material knowledge to improve everyday life in Herland, as well. This united, female and male, vision is Gilman's utopia. It assumes mythic proportions with the rebirth of society through women's culture. *With Her in Ourland* is important today because it celebrates the power of women to change the world, "Ourland."

Charlotte Perkins Gilman was a great sociologist, and sometimes a great literary writer. One of her achievements as a sociologist was her journey through Ourland. She bridged a gap between men and women; experts and citizens; literature and social science. Like all great and daring treks, she made some mistakes on her journey, but her accomplishments far outweigh her flaws. Feminists are often criticized, and Gilman endured a life of public and private censure. She was an optimistic theorist in the face of incredible opposition, including her own struggle against despair. Gilman focused on "the new attitude of the full-grown woman, who faces the demands of love with the high standards of conscious motherhood" (Gilman 1911: 95, 105). This new story is Ellador's journey through Ourland.

With Her in Ourland is a vital book. It challenges several major interpretations of Gilman scholarship; it signals a re-reading of Herland as a utopian society; it informs us about gendered work in sociology and the history of ideas; it locates Gilman's life as a sociologist within a professional network and an intellectual discourse; it exemplifies a method for linking nonfiction and fiction through a formulaic transformation; and, most importantly— from a reader's perspective—it is often witty, insightful, and entertaining. Through our imaginations, we travel with Ellador in Ourland and absorb her instructive lessons and gracious humor. Perhaps, too, we have progressed a bit further in our understanding of liberation and utopian futures since Gilman wrote this book. After all, that is precisely what she predicted.

Finally, a note on the editing and preparation of this edition. We correct several obvious typographical/typesetting errors appearing in the 1916 serialized version. Similarly, we standardize spellings in those few places where the effect is unobtrusive and contributes to readability and consistency. The more peculiar time-bound spellings of Gilman's era, however, such as "Burmah" and "Thibet," and her sometimes archaic word choices, we always allow to stand. All of the ellipses, dashes, and strings of asterisks found in our edition are, to the best of our ability, reproduced exactly as they stood replete in *The Forerunner*. In no case does an ellipse or other such device indicate that we deleted anything from Gilman's text. Where Gilman failed to supply chapter titles (i.e., Chapters 9–12) we supply descriptive headings within square brackets.

NOTES

1. The republication of *Herland* was widely and favorably reviewed, for example, in the *Atlantic*, *The New York Times Book Review*, *The New Yorker*, and the *Christian Science Monitor*. Favorable dust jacket blurbs were garnered from Susan Brownmiller, Alix Kates Shulman, Joanna Russ, Eve Merriam, Ernest Callenbach, and Marge Piercy. For complete references, see Scharnhorst (1985: 72–73).

2. More recently, a few critics have fired salvos at *Herland* directly (e.g., Lant 1990; Peyser 1992). The extreme rhetoric of these attacks bears little relevance to Gilman's actual text.

3. *Cultural feminism* is a term possessing currency among scholars in several disciplines. This theory assumes that traditionally-defined feminine values are superior to traditionally-defined masculine values (Deegan 1988a: 25, 225–246). *Critical pragmatism* is my own construct and is developed in my study of Jane Addams (Deegan 1988a: 247–308). *Feminist reform Darwinism* is introduced here for the first time. Jane Upin (1993) discusses similarities between Gilman and John Dewey and employs the concept *feminist pragmatism* in her analysis. My understanding of feminist pragmatism is presented below.

4. Two biographies, by Mary A. Hill (1980) and Ann J. Lane (1990), greatly expand our knowledge of Gilman's complicated life. Hill presents an exquisite analysis of Gilman's early life and career, from 1860 to 1896, while Lane presents a psychologically oriented examination of many significant people in Gilman's life. Both biographies are informative, but neither examines Gilman's sociological work in depth. The publication of Gilman's (1994) diaries and her letters to Houghton (Gilman 1995) are additional resources. Charles Stetson's (1985) published letters to Gilman may also interest the reader.

5. Readers are encouraged to peruse not only the text of *Herland*, but also *The Forerunner* as a whole. The latter task is eased by the issue of a reprint edition of all seven volumes of *The Forerunner* by Greenwood Press.

6. Gilman scholarship is flourishing in the humanities. In addition to the biographies noted above, a fascinating account of Gilman's ideas about space and women's work in the home is found in Allen (1988). Outstanding collections of articles are found in the volumes edited by Meyering (1989) and Karpinski (1992). In an exquisite article, Magner (1978) compared the influence of scientific language and concepts in the work of several feminists, including Gilman. Magner persuasively argues that Gilman was a notable social Darwinist, although her work has been systematically ignored by male theorists working on this topic. Magner (1992) also compares Gilman and Herbert Spencer in an informative

essay. A major but problematic text on feminist theory by Josephine Donovan (1985: 31–63) considers Gilman as both an individual theorist and as a representative of a distinct cultural feminist tradition that includes the sociologist Jane Addams.

In addition, several major male historians, for example, Degler (1966) and O'Neill (1972), wrote important introductions to Gilman's reprinted books. Magner (1978: 70, n.44) shows that Degler exhibits an apparent "compulsion to issue warnings about taking her [Gilman's] claims to scientific background too seriously," a flaw shared by many male commentators on Gilman's work. In a similar vein, O'Neill (1972: xviii) condescendingly wrote that "Mrs. Gilman was, in her prime, the cleverest phrasemaker among leading feminists." Andrew Sinclair (1966: 272), on the other hand, claimed that Gilman is the "Marx and Veblen" of the woman's movement. Despite their limitations, O'Neill and Degler made significant contributions to Gilman scholarship by incorporating her in their other writings. O'Neill (1967) analyzed Gilman's role in changing ideas about divorce, the family, and the home. Degler (1989), it must be appreciated, reintroduced Gilman's social thought to a new generation of scholars.

7. Käsler devised his criteria in reconstructing the history of German sociology and I adapt them to the American scene (Deegan 1988a: 9–13).

8. Ross to Gilman, quoted from Gale (1935: xvii). Ross's reference is to Gilman's (1911) book, *The Man-Made World*.

9. Ward to Gilman, 9 February 1907, quoted in M. A. Hill (1980: 267).

10. Ward to Gilman, quoted in Gale (1935: xvi).

11. Addams to Campbell, cited in Lane (1990: 183).

12. Newspaper clipping, Hull-House Scrapbooks, Vol. III, 1895–1897: 15, Swarthmore College Peace Collection.

13. Ibid.

14. Ibid.

15. The precise dates of Gilman's Hull-House residency are not known and there is no extant diary for this period. Gilman (1935: 184) recalled having lived three months at Hull-House. She departed California in late July and spent "a month" visiting in Wisconsin, suggesting an arrival in Chicago in late August or early September 1895. Her lectures at the Hull-House Social Science Club were scheduled to begin on 1 October 1895. Unity Settlement in Chicago, to which Gilman moved from Hull-House, was established in November 1895. See also M. A. Hill (1980: 272–282).

16. Florence Kelley to Charlotte Gilman, 28 July 1898, Gilman Papers, Schlesinger Library, Radcliffe College.

17. Jane Addams (1910: viii) shared Gilman's disdain for the "good woman" label. Allen F. Davis (1973) suggests falsely that Addams manipulated and enjoyed this "heroine" image. His widely accepted text has seriously misled subsequent scholarship on Addams.

18. The referents here are, presumably, Susan B. Anthony, Anna Howard Shaw, and Jane Addams.

19. The referent is, presumably, Lester Ward.

20. 28 July 1898, Gilman Papers, 177, 138, one of two microfilms reels.

21. Gilman (1995: 198–223) logged visits on November 17, 18, 23, and 24, and on December 4, 5, 7, 8, 10, 11, 12, 13, 26, 27, and 30.

22. The tendency to segregate fiction and non-fiction into mutually exclusive categories artificially destroys the unifying purpose and logic that characterize Gilman's work as a whole. Wilson's (1989) insightful critique of *Herland* is an instructive exception to this trend.

23. Symbolic interaction defines society as a product of human meaning and interaction. It is strongly tied to the "Chicago sociology" developed by George H. Mead and William I. Thomas at the University of Chicago (Deegan and Hill 1987).

24. Patrick Geddes authored a reform Darwinist book on women's natural "anabolic" or passive energies that is a strange attempt to study women from a reform Darwinist perspective. Due to its curious theory of gendered energy, I do not consider it "feminist reform Darwinism." This book strongly influenced W. I. Thomas but he soon rejected its thesis. The connection between Thomas and Addams and cultural feminism is explored in Deegan (1988a: 202–208). See also Jill Conway's (1972) excellent discussion.

25. Geddes' assumption of increased variability among men (as opposed to less frequent variations among women) was decried by later feminists as intrinsically sexist and unfair to women. Gilman's role in "the variability debate" deserves separate analysis.

REFERENCES

Archival Sources

Arthur and Elizabeth Schlesinger Library on the History of Women in America, Radcliffe College, Cambridge, Massachusetts
— Charlotte Perkins Gilman Collection
University of Illinois at Chicago, University Library, Chicago, Illinois
— Jane Addams Memorial Collection
— Addams Papers
Wisconsin State Historical Society, Madison, Wisconsin
— Edward A. Ross Papers

Books and Articles

Adams, Phoebe-Lou. 1979. Review of *Herland. Atlantic Monthly* 243 (April): 99.
Addams, Jane. 1902. *Democracy and Social Ethics.* New York: Macmillan.

————. 1905. "Recent Immigration: A Field Neglected by the Scholar." *University Record* 9 (January): 274–284.

————. 1910. *Twenty Years at Hull-House*. New York: Macmillan.

————. 1932. *The Excellent Becomes the Permanent*. New York: Macmillan.

Addams, Jane, Emily Greene Balch, and Alice Hamilton. 1915. *The Women at the Hague*. New York: Macmillan.

Allen, Polly Wynn. 1988. *Building Domestic Liberty: Charlotte Perkins Gilman's Architectural Feminism*. Amherst: University of Massachusetts Press.

Bachofen, Johann Jakob. 1861. *Das Mutterrecht*. Stuttgart: Krais and Hoffman.

Bannister, Robert C. 1979. *Social Darwinism: Science and Myth in Anglo-American Thought*. Philadelphia: Temple University Press.

Bellamy, Edward. 1888. *Looking Backward*. Boston: Ticknor.

Bernikow, Louise. 1979. Review of *Herland*. *The New York Times Book Review* (April 8): 20–21.

Borgatta, Edgar F., and Henry J. Meyer, eds. 1959. Foreword, Preface, and Biographical Introduction, pp. iii, vi–xii in *Social Control and the Foundations of Sociology: Pioneer Contributions of Edward Alsworth Ross to the Study of Society*, by Edward A. Ross. Boston: Beacon Press.

Campbell, Helen. 1898. "Social Settlements and the Civic Sense." *Arena* 20 (November–December): 589–603.

Chugerman, Samuel. 1939. *Lester F. Ward*. Durham, NC: Duke University Press.

Conway, Jill. 1972. "Stereotypes of Femininity in a Theory of Sexual Evolution." Pp. 140–154 in *Suffer and Be Still: Women in the Victorian Age*, edited by Martha Vicinus. Bloomington: Indiana University Press.

Davis, Allen F. 1973. *American Heroine*. New York: Oxford University Press.

Deegan, Mary Jo. 1987. "Not a Sociologist: The Historical Redefinition of Early Women Activists and Humanist Sociologists." Keynote address, James B. McKee Symposium, Michigan State University.

————. 1988a. *Jane Addams and the Men of the Chicago School, 1892–1918*. New Brunswick, NJ: Transaction.

————. 1988b. "Transcending a Patriarchal Past: Teaching the History of Women in Sociology." *Teaching Sociology* 16 (April): 141–150.

————. 1989. *American Ritual Dramas: Social Rules and Cultural Meanings*. Westport, CT: Greenwood Press.

————, ed. 1991. *Women in Sociology: A Bio-Bibliographcal Sourcebook*. Westport, CT: Greenwood Press.

————. 1995. "The Second Sex and the Chicago School: Women's Accounts, Knowledge, and Work, 1945–1960." Pp. 322–364 in *A Second Chicago School?* edited by Gary A. Fine. Chicago: University of Chicago Press.

————. 1996. "Dear Love, Dear Love: Feminist Pragmatism and the Chicago Female World of Love and Ritual." *Gender & Society* 10 (October): 590–607.

Deegan, Mary Jo, and Michael R. Hill, eds. 1987. *Women and Symbolic Interaction.* Boston: Allen and Unwin.

Degler, Carl N., ed. 1966. Introduction, pp. vi–xxxv in *Women and Economics,* by Charlotte Perkins Gilman. New York: Harper and Row.

―――. 1989. "Charlotte Perkins Gilman on the Theory and Practice of Feminism," pp. 11–29 in *Charlotte Perkins Gilman: The Woman and Her Work,* edited by Sheryl L. Meyering. Ann Arbor, MI: UMI Research Press.

Donovan, Josephine. 1985. *Feminist Theory.* New York: Frederick Ungar.

Eagan, Maureen L. 1989. "Evolutionary Theory in the Social Philosophy of Charlotte Perkins Gilman." *Hypatia* 4 (Spring): 102–119.

Faris, Robert E. L. 1967. *Chicago Sociology, 1920–1932.* Chicago: University of Chicago Press.

Gale, Zona. 1935. Foreword, pp. xxiii–lii in *The Living of Charlotte Perkins Gilman: An Autobiography,* by Charlotte Perkins Gilman. New York: D. Appleton-Century.

Geddes, Patrick, and J. Arthur Thompson. 1889. *The Evolution of Sex.* London: W. Scott.

George, Henry. 1879. *Progress and Poverty.* New York: J. W. Lovell.

Gilman, Charlotte Perkins. 1890. "Similar Cases." *New England Magazine,* new series 3 (September): 134–135.

―――. 1892. "The Yellow Wall-Paper." *New England Magazine,* 5 (January): 647–656.

―――. 1897–1898. "First Class in Sociology." *American Fabian* 3 (January): 9–11; (March): 11–13; (May): 7–9; (June): 2–3; (September): 6–7; 4 (February): 6–8; (March): 6–7.

―――. 1898. *Women and Economics.* Boston: Small and Maynard.

―――. 1900. *Concerning Children.* Boston: Small and Maynard.

―――. 1903. *The Home: Its Work and Influences.* New York: McClure and Phillips. (Reprinted, with an introduction by William O'Neill, Urbana: University of Illinois Press, 1972.)

―――. 1904. *Human Work.* New York: McClure and Phillips.

―――. 1907a. "Social Consciousness." (Comment on a paper by Charles H. Cooley.) *American Journal of Sociology* 12 (March): 690–691.

―――. 1907b. "Social Darwinism." (Comment on a paper by D. Collin Wells.) *American Journal of Sociology* 12 (March): 713–714.

―――. 1910. Review of *Pure Sociology. Forerunner* 1 (October): 26–27.

―――. 1911. *The Man-Made World, or Our Androcentric Culture.* London: T. Fisher Unwin.

―――. 1912a. "The Socialist and the Suffragist." *Life and Labor* 2 (February): 61.

―――. 1912b. "We Stand as One." *Life and Labor* 2 (May): 153.

―――. 1912c. Review of *The Changing Chinese. Forerunner* 3 (February): 56.

―――. 1913. Memorial to Lester F. Ward. *Forerunner* 4 (June): 166.

———. 1915."Herland." *Forerunner* 6 (January): 12–17; (February): 38–44; (March): 65–72; (April): 94–100; (May): 123–129; (June): 150–155; (July): 181–187; (August): 207–213; (September): 237–243; (October): 265–270; (November): 287–293; (December): 318–325.

———. 1916. "With Her in Ourland." *Forerunner* 7 (January): 6–11; (February): 38–44; (March): 67–73; (April): 93–98; (May): 123–128; (June): 152–157; (July): 179–185; (August): 208–213; (September): 237–243; (October): 263–269; (November): 291–297; (December): 318–325.

———. 1923. *His Religion and Hers: A Study of the Faith of Our Fathers and the Work of Our Mothers*. New York: Century.

———. 1935. *The Living of Charlotte Perkins Gilman: An Autobiography*. With a foreword by Zona Gale. New York: D. Appleton-Century.

———. 1979. *Herland*. Introduced by Ann J. Lane. New York: Pantheon. (Originally published in *Forerunner*, 1915).

———. 1994. *The Diaries of Charlotte Perkins Gilman*, edited by Denise D. Knight. 2 vols. Charlottesville: University Press of Virginia.

———. 1995. *A Journey from Within: The Love Letters of Charlotte Perkins Gilman, 1897–1900*. Edited by Mary A. Hill. Lewisburg, PA: Bucknell University Press.

Goldman, Eric C. 1955. *Rendezvous with Destiny*. New York: Vintage Books.

Gotsch-Thomson, Susan. 1990. "The Integration of Gender into the Teaching of Classical Social Theory." *Teaching Sociology* 18 (January): 69–73.

Grossberg, Lawrence. 1992. *We Gotta Get Outta This Place*. New York: Routledge.

Hill, Mary A., ed. 1980. *Charlotte Perkins Gilman: The Making of a Radical Feminist, 1860–1896*. Philadelphia: Temple University Press.

———. 1995. Introduction, pp. 17–35 in *A Journey from Within: The Love Letters of Charlotte Perkins Gilman, 1897–1900*. Lewisburg, PA: Bucknell University Press.

Hill, Michael R. 1993. *Archival Strategies and Techniques*. Newbury Park, CA: Sage Publications.

———. 1996. "*Herland*." Pp. 251–254 in *Masterpieces of Women's Literature*, edited by Frank N. Magill. New York: HarperCollins.

———. Forthcoming. "Edward Alsworth Ross." In *American National Biography*, edited by John A. Garraty. Carey, NC: Oxford University Press.

Hobbs, Margaret. 1987. "The Perils of 'Unbridled Masculinity': Pacifist Elements in the Feminist and Socialist Thought of Charlotte Perkins Gilman." Pp. 149–169 in *Women and Peace: Theoretical, Historical and Practical Perspectives*, edited by Ruth Roach Pierson with the assistance of Joanne Thompson, Somer Brodribb, and Paula Bourne. London: Croom Helm.

Hofstader, Richard. 1959. *Social Darwinism in American Thought*. Revised edition. New York: G. Braziller.

James, William. 1904. "The Chicago School." *Psychological Bulletin* 1 (15 January): 1–5.

Kanter, Rosabeth Moss. 1972. *Commitment and Community: Communes and Utopias in Sociological Perspective*. Cambridge, MA: Harvard University Press.

Karpinski, Joanne B., ed. 1992. *Critical Essays on Charlotte Perkins Gilman*. New York: G. K. Hall.

Käsler, Dirk. 1981. "Methodological Problems of a Sociological History of Early German Sociology." Paper presented at the Department of Education, University of Chicago, 5 November.

Keith, Bruce. 1991. "Charlotte Perkins Gilman." Pp. 148–156 in *Women in Sociology: A Bio-Bibliographical Sourcebook*, edited by Mary Jo Deegan. Westport, CT: Greenwood Press.

Kurtz, Lester R. 1984. *Evaluating Chicago Sociology: A Guide to the Literature, with an Annotated Bibliography*. Chicago: University of Chicago Press.

Lane, Ann J. 1979. Introduction and editorial notes. Pp. v–xxiv, and ff. in *Herland*, by Charlotte Perkins Gilman. New York: Pantheon.

————. 1980, ed. "The Fictional World of Charlotte Perkins Gilman." Pp. ix–xlii in *The Charlotte Perkins Gilman Reader: "The Yellow Wallpaper" and Other Fiction*, by Charlotte Perkins Gilman. New York: Pantheon.

————. 1990. *To Herland and Beyond: The Life and Work of Charlotte Perkins Gilman*. New York: Pantheon.

Lant, Kathleen Margaret. 1990. "The Rape of the Text." *Tulsa Studies in Women's Literature* 9 (Fall): 291–308.

Lemert, Charles C., ed. 1993. *Social Theory: Multicultural and Classic Readings*. Boulder, CO: Westview Press.

Lengermann, Patricia, and Jill Niebrugge-Brantley. 1996. "Engendering Social Theory: Early Women Sociologists Theorize Domestic Service." Paper presented at the Midterm Conference, International Sociological Association, Research Committee on the History of Sociology, Amsterdam, The Netherlands.

Magner, Lois N. 1978. "Women and the Scientific Idiom: Textual Episodes from Wollstonecraft, Fuller, Gilman, and Firestone." *Signs: Journal of Women in Culture and Society* 4 (Autumn): 61–80.

————. 1992. "Darwinism and the Woman Question: The Evolving Views of Charlotte Perkins Gilman." Pp. 115–128 in *Critical Essays on Charlotte Perkins Gilman*, edited by Joanne B. Karpinski. New York: G. K. Hall.

Mason, Otis Tufton. 1894. *Woman's Share in Primitive Culture*. New York: D. Appleton-Century.

Meyering, Sheryl L., ed. 1989. *Charlotte Perkins Gilman: The Woman and Her Work*. Ann Arbor, MI: UMI Research Press.

O'Neill, William L. 1967. *Divorce in the Progressive Era*. New Haven, CT: Yale University Press.

————. 1972. Introduction. In *The Home: Its Work and Influences*, by Charlotte Perkins Gilman. Urbana: University of Illinois Press.

Peyser, Thomas Galt. 1992. "Reproducing Utopia." *Studies in American Fiction* 20 (Spring): 1–16.

Residents of Hull-House. 1895. *Hull-House Maps and Papers: A Presentation of Nationalities and Wages in a Congested District of Chicago, Together with Comments and Essays on Problems Growing Out of the Social Conditions.* New York: Thomas Y. Crowell.

Ross, Edward A. 1911. *The Changing Chinese: The Conflict of Oriental and Western Cultures in China.* New York: Century.

———. 1913. "Lester Frank Ward." *American Journal of Sociology* 19 (July): 64–67.

———. 1915. "Freedom of Comunication and the Struggle for Right." *Publications of the American Sociological Society* 9: 1–10.

———. 1922. *The Social Trend.* New York: Century.

———. 1936. *Seventy Years of It: An Autobiography.* New York: D. Appleton-Century.

Russett, Cynthia Eagle. 1989. *Sexual Science: The Victorian Construction of Woman.* Cambridge, MA: Harvard University Press.

Scharnhorst, Gary. 1985. *Charlotte Perkins Gilman: A Bibliography.* Metuchen, NJ: Scarecrow.

Scott, Clifford H. 1976. *Lester Frank Ward.* Boston: Twayne.

Sinclair, Andrew. 1966. *The Emancipation of the American Woman.* New York: Harper and Row.

Sklar, Kathryn Kish. 1995. *Florence Kelley and the Nation's Work.* New Haven: Yale University Press.

Smith, Marsha A. 1989. "The Disoriented Male Narrator and Societal Conversion: Charlotte Perkins Gilman's Feminist Utopian Vision." *American Transcendental Quarterly*, New Series, 3 (March): 123–133.

Smith-Rosenberg, Carroll. 1975. "The Female World of Love and Ritual." *Signs: Journal of Women in Culture and Society* 1 (Autumn): 1–29.

Spencer, Anna Garlin. 1913. *Woman's Share in Social Culture.* New York: Mitchell Kennerly.

Stern, Bernhard J., ed. 1938–1949. "The Ward-Ross Correspondence, 1891–1912." *American Sociological Review* 3 (June): 362–401; 11 (October): 593–605; (December): 734–748; 12 (December): 703–720; 13 (February): 82–94; 14 (February): 88–119.

Stetson, Charles Walter. 1985. *Endure: The Diaries of Charles Walter Stetson*, edited by Mary A. Hill. Philadelphia: Temple University Press.

Terry, James L. 1983. "Bringing Women . . . In: A Modest Proposal." *Teaching Sociology* 10 (January): 251–261.

Turner, Victor, ed. 1982. *Celebration: Studies in Festivity and Ritual.* Washington, DC: Smithsonian Institution Press.

Upin, Jane S. 1993. "Charlotte Perkins Gilman: Instrumentalism Beyond Dewey." *Hypatia* 8 (Spring): 38–63.

Ward, Lester F. 1883. *Dynamic Sociology*. New York: D. Appleton.

———. 1888. "Our Better Halves." *Forum* 6 (November): 266–275.

———. 1903. *Pure Sociology: A Treatise on the Origin and Spontaneous Development of Society*. New York: Macmillan.

———. 1906a. "The Past and Future of the Sexes." *Independent* 60 (March 8): 541–545.

———. 1906b. *Applied Pure Sociology: A Treatise on the Conscious Improvement of Society by Society*. Boston: Ginn.

Weinberg, Julius. 1972. *Edward Alsworth Ross and the Sociology of Progressivism*. Madison: State Historical Society of Wisconsin.

Wilson, Christopher P. 1989. "Charlotte Perkins Gilman's Steady Burghers: The Terrain of *Herland*." Pp. 173–190 in *Charlotte Perkins Gilman: The Woman and Her Work*, edited by Sheryl L. Meyering. Ann Arbor, MI: UMI Research Press.

Woods, Robert A., and Albert J. Kennedy, eds. 1911. *Handbook of Settlements*. New York: Charities Publications Committee, Russell Sage Foundation.

With Her in Ourland

1

The Return

(*Synopsis of* Herland: *Three American young men discover a country inhabited solely by women, who were Parthenogenetic, and had borne only girl children for two thousand years; they marry three of the women. Two of the men and one woman leave the country of Herland to return to America; Jeff Margrave remaining with his wife, Celis, a willing citizen; Terry O. Nicholson being expelled for bad conduct; and Ellador electing to go with her husband, Vandyck Jennings.*)

THE THREE OF US, all with set faces of high determination, sat close in the big biplane as we said good-bye to Herland and rose whirring from the level rock on that sheer edge. We went up first, and made a wide circuit, that my wife Ellador might have a view of her own beloved land to remember. How green and fair and flower-brightened it lay below us! The little cities, the thick dotted villages, the scattered hamlets and wide parks of grouped houses lay again beneath our eyes as when we three men had first set our astonished masculine gaze on this ultra-feminine land.

Our long visit, the kind care, and judicious education given us, even though under restraint, and our months of freedom and travel among them, made it seem to me like leaving a second home. The beauty of the place was borne in upon me anew as I looked down on it. It was a garden, a great cultivated park, even to its wildest forested borders, and the cities were ornaments to the landscape, thinning out into delicate lace-like tracery of scattered buildings as they merged into the open country.

Terry looked at it with set teeth. He was embittered through and through, and but for Ellador I could well imagine the kind of things he would have said. He only made this circuit at her request, as one who said: "Oh, well—an hour or two more or less—it's over, anyhow!"

Then the long gliding swoop as we descended to our sealed motor-boat in the lake below. It was safe enough. Perhaps the savages had considered it some deadly witch-work and avoided it; at any rate save for some dents and scratches on the metal cover, it was unhurt.

With some careful labor, Terry working with a feverish joyful eagerness, we got the machine dissembled and packed away, pulled in the anchors, and with well-applied oiling started the long dis-used motor, and moved off toward the great river.

Ellador's eyes were on the towering cliffs behind us. I gave her the glass, and as long as we were on the open water her eyes dwelt lovingly on the high rocky border of her home. But when we shot under the arching gloom of the forest she turned to me with a little sigh and a bright, steady smile.

"That's good-bye," she said. "Now it's all looking forward to the Big New World—the Real World—with You!"

Terry said very little. His heavy jaw was set, his eyes looked forward, eagerly, determinedly. He was polite to Ellador, and not impolite to me, but he was not conversational.

We made the trip as fast as was consistent with safety; faster, sometimes; living on our canned food and bottled water, stopping for no fresh meat; shooting down the ever-widening river toward the coast.

Ellador watched it all with eager, childlike interest. The freshness of mind of these Herland women concealed their intellectual power. I never quite got used to it. We are so used to seeing our learned men cold and solemn, holding themselves far above all the "enthusiasm of youth," that it is hard for us to associate a high degree of wisdom and intellectual power with vivid interest in immediate events.

Here was my Wife from Wonderland, leaving all she had ever known,—a lifetime of peace and happiness and work she loved, and a whole nation of friends, as far as she knew them; and starting out with me for a world which I frankly told her was full of many kinds of pain and evil. She was not afraid. It was not sheer ignorance of danger, either. I had tried hard to make her understand the troubles she would meet. Neither was it a complete absorption in me—far from it. In our story books we read always of young wives giving up all they have known and enjoyed "for his sake." That was by no means Ellador's position. She loved me—that I knew, but by no means with that engrossing absorption so familiar to our novelists and their readers. Her attitude was that of some high ambassador sent on an important and dangerous mission. She represented her country, and that with a vital intensity we can hardly realize. She was to meet and learn a whole new world, and perhaps establish connections between it and her own dear land.

As Terry held to his steering, grim and silent, that feverish eagerness in his eyes, and a curb on his usually ready tongue, Ellador would sit in the bow, leaning forward, chin on her hand, her eyes ahead, far ahead, down the long reaches of the winding stream, with an expression such as one could imagine on Columbus. She was glad to have me near her. I was not only her own, in a degree she herself did not yet realize, but I was her one link with the homeland. So I sat close and we talked much of the things we saw and more of what we were going to see. Her short soft hair, curly in the moist air, and rippling back from her bright face as we rushed along, gave the broad forehead and clear eyes a more courageous look than ever. That finely cut mobile mouth was firmly set, though always ready to melt into a tender smile for me.

"Now Van, my dear," she said one day, as we neared the coast town where we hoped to find a steamer, "Please don't worry about how all this is going to affect me. You have been drawing very hard pictures of your own land, and of the evil behavior of men; so that I shall not be disappointed or shocked too much. I won't be, dear. I understand that men are different from women—must be, but I am convinced that it is better for the world to have both men and women than to have only one sex, like us. We have done the best we could, we women, all alone. We have made a nice little safe clean garden place and lived happily in it, but we have done nothing whatever for the rest of the world. We might as well not be there for all the good it does anyone else. The savages down below are just as savage, for all our civilization. Now you, even if you were, as you say, driven by greed and sheer love of adventure and fighting—you have gone all over the world and civilized it."

"Not all, dear," I hastily put in. "Not nearly all. There are ever so many savages left."

"Yes I know that, I remember the maps and all the history and geography you have taught me."

It was a never-ending source of surprise to me the way those Herland women understood and remembered. It must have been due to their entirely different system of education. There was very much less put into their minds, from infancy up, and what was there seemed to grow there—to stay in place without effort. All the new facts we gave them they had promptly hung up in the right places, like arranging things in a large well-planned, not over-filled closet, and they knew where to find them at once.

"I can readily see," she went on, "that our pleasant collective economy is like that of bees and ants and such co-mothers; and that a world of fathers does not work as smoothly as that. We have observed, of course, among animals, that the instincts of the male are different from those of the female, and that he likes to fight. But think of all you have *done!*"

That was what delighted Ellador. She was never tired of my stories of invention and discovery, of the new lands we had found, the mountain ranges crossed, the great oceans turned into highways, and all the wonders of art and science. She loved it as did Desdemona the wild tales of her lover, but with more understanding.

"It must be nobler to have Two," she would say, her eyes shining. "We are only half a people. Of course we love each other, and have advanced our own little country, but it is such a little one—and you have The World!"

We reached the coast in due time, and the town. It was not much of a town, dirty and squalid enough, with lazy half-breed inhabitants for the most part. But this I had carefully explained and Ellador did not mind it, examining everything with kind impartial eyes, as a teacher would examine the work of atypical children.

Terry loved it. He greeted that slovenly, ill-built, idle place with ardor, and promptly left us to ourselves for the most part.

There was no steamer. None had touched there for many months, they said; but there was a sailing vessel which undertook, for sufficient payment, to take us and our motor-boat with its contents, to a larger port.

Terry and I had our belts with gold and notes; he had letters of credit too, while Ellador had brought with her not only a supply of gold, but a little bag of rubies, which I assured her would take us several times around the world, and more. The money system in Herland was mainly paper, and their jewels, while valued for decoration, were not prized as ours are. They had some historic treasure chests, rivalling those of India, and she had been amply supplied.

After some delay we set sail.

Terry walked the deck, more eager as the days passed. Ellador, I am sorry to say, proved a poor sailor, as was indeed to be expected, but made no fuss about her disabilities. I told her it was almost inescapable, unpleasant but not dangerous, so she stayed in her berth, or sat wrapped mummy fashion on the deck, and suffered in patience.

Terry talked a little more when we were out of her hearing.

"Do you know they say there's a war in Europe?" he told me.

"A war? A real one—or just the Balkans?"

"A real one, they say—Germany and Austria against the rest of Europe apparently. Began months ago—no news for a long time."

"Oh well—it will be over before we reach home, I guess. Lucky for us we are Americans."

But I was worried for Ellador. I wanted the world, my world, to look its best in her eyes. If those women, alone and unaided, had worked out that pleasant, peaceful, comfortable civilization of theirs, with its practical sisterliness and friendliness all over the land, I was very anxious to show her that men had done at least as well, and in some ways better—men and women, that is. And here we had gotten up a war—a most undesirable spectacle for an international guest.

There was a missionary on board, a thin, almost emaciated man, of the Presbyterian denomination. He was a most earnest person, and a great talker, naturally.

"Woe unto me," he would say, "if I preach not this gospel!" And he preached it "in season and out of season."

Ellador was profoundly interested. I tried to explain to her that he was an enthusiast of a rather rigid type, and that she must not judge Christianity too harshly by him, but she quite re-assured me.

"Don't be afraid, my dear boy—I remember your outline of the various religions—all about how Christianity arose and spread; how it held to-gether in one church for a long time, and then divided, and kept on dividing—naturally. And I remember about the religious wars, and perse-cutions, that you used to have in earlier ages. We had a good deal of trouble with religion in our first centuries too, and for a long time people kept appearing with some sort of new one they had had 'revealed' to them, just like yours. But we saw that all that was needed was a higher level of mentality and a clear understanding of the real Laws—so we worked toward that. And, as you know, we have been quite at peace as to our religion for some centuries. It's just part of us."

That was the clearest way of putting it she had yet thought of. The Herland religion was like the manners of a true aristocrat, a thing inborn and inbred. It was the way they lived. They had so clear and quick a connection between conviction and action that it was well nigh impossible for them to know a thing and not do it. I suppose that was why, when we had told them about the noble teachings of Christianity, they had been so charmed, taking it for granted that our behavior was equal to our belief.

The Reverend Alexander Murdock was more than pleased to talk with Ellador—any man would be, of course. He was immensely curious about her too, but even to impertinent questions she presented an amiable but absolute impermeability.

"From what country do you come, Mrs. Jennings?" he asked her one day, in my hearing. He did not know I was within earshot, however.

Ellador was never annoyed by questions, nor angry, nor confused. Where most people seem to think that there is no alternative but to answer correctly or, to lie, she recognized an endless variety of things to say or not say. Sometimes she would look pleasantly at the inquirer, with those deep kind eyes of hers, and ask: "Why do you wish to know?" Not sarcastically, not offensively at all, but as if she really wanted to know why they wanted to know. It was generally difficult for them to explain the cause of their curiosity, but if they did; if they said it was just interest, a kindly human interest in her, she would thank them for the interest, and ask if they felt it about every one. If they said they did, she would say, still with her quiet gentleness: "And is it customary, when one feels interested in a stranger, to ask them questions? I mean is it a—what you call a compliment? If so, I thank you heartily for the compliment."

If they drove her—some people never will take a hint—she would remain always quite courteous and gentle, even praise them for their perseverance, but never say one word she did not choose to. And she did not choose to give to anyone news of her beloved country until such time as that country decided it should be done.

The missionary was not difficult to handle.

"Did you not say that you were to preach the gospel to all nations— or all people—or something like that?" she asked him. "Do you find some nations easier to preach to than others? Or is it the same gospel to all?"

He assured her that it was the same, but that he was naturally interested in all his hearers, and that it was often important to know something of their antecedents. This she agreed might be an advantage, and left it at that, asking him if he would let her see his Bible. Once he was embarked on that subject, she had only to listen, and to steer the conversation, or rather the monologue.

I told her I had overheard this bit of conversation, begging her pardon for listening, but she said she would greatly enjoy having me with her while he talked. I told her I doubted if he would talk as freely if there were three of us, and she suggested in that case that if I was interested I was quite welcome to listen as far as she was concerned. Of course I wasn't going to be an eavesdropper, even on a missionary trying to convert my wife, but I heard a good bit of their talk as I strolled about, and sat with them sometimes.

He let her read his precious flexible Oxford Bible at times, giving her marked passages, and she read about a hundred times as much as he thought she could in a given time. It interested her immensely, and she questioned him eagerly about it:

"You call this 'The Word of God'?"

"Yes," he replied solemnly. "It is His Revealed Word."

"And every thing it says is true?"

"It is Truth itself, Divine Truth," he answered.

"You do not mean that God wrote it?"

"Oh, no. He revealed it to His servants. It is an Inspired Book."

"It was written by many people, was it not?"

"Yes—many people, but the same Word."

"And at different times?"

"Oh yes—the revelation was given at long intervals—the Old Testament to the Jews, the New Testament to us all."

Ellador turned the pages reverently. She had a great respect for religion, and for any sincere person.

"How old is the oldest part?" she asked him.

He told her as best he could, but he was not versed in the latest scholarship and had a genuine horror of "the higher criticism." But I supplied a little information on the side, when we were alone, telling her of the patchwork group of ancient legends which made up the first part; of the very human councils of men who had finally decided which of the ancient writings were inspired and which were not; of how the Book of Job, the oldest of all, had only scraped in by one vote, and then, with rather a malicious relish, of that most colossal joke of all history—how the Song of Songs—that amorous, not to say salacious ancient love-lyric, had been embraced with the others and interpreted as a mystical lofty outburst of devotion with that "black but comely" light-o'-love figuring as The Church.

Ellador was quite shocked.

"But Van!—he ought to know that. You ought to tell him. Is it generally known?"

"It is known to scholars, not to the public as a whole."

"But they still have it bound in with the others—and think it is holy—when it isn't."

"Yes," I grinned, "the joke is still going on."

"What have the scholars done about it?" she asked.

"Oh, they have worked out their proof, shown up the thing—and let it go at that."

"Wasn't there any demand from the people who knew to have it taken out of the Bible?"

"There is one edition of the Bible now printed in all the separate books—a whole shelf full of little ones, instead of one big one."

"I should think that would be much better," she said, "but the other one is still printed—and sold?"

"Printed and sold and given away by hundreds of thousands—with The Joke going right on."

She was puzzled. It was not so much the real outside things we did which she found it hard to understand, but the different way our minds worked. In Herland, if a thing like that had been discovered, the first effort of all their wisest students would have been to establish the facts. When they were sure about it, they would then have taken the rather shameful old thing out of its proud position among the "sacred" books at once. They would have publicly acknowledged their mistake, rectified it, and gone on.

"You'll have to be very patient with me, Van dearest. It is going to take me a long time to get hold of your psychology. But I'll do my best."

Her best was something amazing. And she would have come to her final conclusions far earlier but for certain firm preconceptions that we were somehow better, nobler, than we were.

The Reverend Murdock kept at her pretty steadily. He started in at the beginning, giving her the full circumstantial account of The Temptation, The Fall, and The Curse.

She listened quietly, with no hint in her calm face of what she might be thinking. But when he came to the punishment of the serpent: "Upon thy belly shalt thou go, and dust shalt thou eat all the days of thy life," she asked a question.

"Will you tell me please—how did the serpent 'go' before?"

Mr. Murdock looked at her. He was reading in a deep sorrowful voice, his mind full of the solemn purport of the Great Tragedy.

"What was his method of locomotion before he was cursed?" asked Ellador.

He laid down the book in some annoyance. "It is believed that the serpent walked erect, that he stood like a man, that he was Satan himself," he replied.

"But it says: 'Now the serpent was more subtile than any of the beasts of the field,' doesn't it? And the picture you showed me is of a snake, in the tree."

"The picture is, as it were, allegorical," he replied. "It is not reverent to question the divine account like this."

She did not mind this note of censure, but asked further: "As a matter of fact, do snakes eat dust? Or is that allegorical too? How do you know which is allegorical and which is fact? Who decides?"

They had a rather stormy discussion on that point; at least the missionary was stormy. He was unable to reconcile Ellador's gentle courtesy with her singular lack of reverence for mere statements.

But our theological discussions were summarily ended, and Ellador reduced to clinging to her berth, by a severe storm. It was not a phenomenal hurricane by any means; but a steady lashing gale which drove us far out of our course, and so damaged the vessel that we could do little but drive before the wind.

"There's a steamer!" said Terry on the third day of heavy weather. And as we watched the drift of smoke on the horizon we found it was nearing us. And none too soon! By the time they were within hailing distance our small vessel ran up signals of distress, for we were leaking heavily, and we were thankful to be taken off, even though the steamer, a Swedish one, was bound for Europe instead of America.

They gave us better accommodations than we had had on the other, and eagerly took on board our big motor-boat and biplane—too eagerly, I thought.

Ellador was greatly interested in the larger ship, the big blond men, and in their talk. I prepared her as well as I could. They had good maps of Europe, and I filled in her outlines of history as far as I was able, and told her of the war. Her horror at this was natural enough.

"We have always had war," Terry explained. "Ever since the world began—at least as far as history goes, we have had war. It is human nature."

"Human?" asked Ellador.

"Yes," he said, "human. Bad as it is, it is evidently human nature to do it. Nations advance, the race is improved by fighting. It is the law of nature."

Since our departure from Herland, Terry had rebounded like a rubber ball from all its influences. Even his love for Alima he was evidently striving to forget, with some success. As for the rest, he had never studied the country and its history as I had, nor accepted it like Jeff; and now he was treating it all as if it really was, what he had often called it to me, a bad dream. He would keep his word in regard to telling nothing about it; that virtue was his at any rate. But in his glad reaction, his delighted return, "a man in a world of men," he was now giving information to Ellador in his superior way, as if she was a totally ignorant stranger. And this war seemed almost to delight him.

"Yes," he repeated, "you will have to accept life as it is. To make war is human activity."

"Are some of the soldiers women?" she inquired.

"Women! Of course not! They are men; strong, brave men. Once in a while some abnormal woman becomes a soldier, I believe, and in Dahomey—that's in Africa—one of the black tribes have women soldiers. But speaking generally it is men—of course."

"Then why do you call it 'human' nature?" she persisted. "If it was human wouldn't they both do it?"

So he tried to explain that it was a human necessity, but it was done by the men because they could do it—and the women couldn't.

"The women are just as indispensable—in their way. They give us the children—you know—men cannot do that."

To hear Terry talk you would think he had never left home.

Ellador listened to him with her grave gentle smile. She always seemed to understand not only what one said, but all the back-ground of sentiment and habit behind.

"Do you call bearing children 'human nature'?" she asked him.

"It's woman nature," he answered. "It's her work."

"Then why do you not call fighting 'man nature'—instead of human?"

Terry's conclusion of an argument with Ellador was the simple one of going somewhere else. So off he went, to enjoy himself in the society of those sturdy Scandinavians, and we two sat together discussing war.

2

War

FOR A LONG TIME my wife from Wonderland, as I love to call her, used to the utmost the high self-restraint taught by her religion, her education, the whole habit of her life. She knew that I should be grieved by her distresses, that I expected the new experiences would be painful to her and was watching to give what aid and comfort I could; and further she credited me with a racial sensitiveness and pride far beyond the facts.

Here again was one of the differences between her exquisitely organized people and ours. With them the majority of their interests in life were communal; their love and pride and ambition was almost wholly for the group, even motherhood itself was viewed as social service, and so fulfilled. They were all of them intimately acquainted with their whole history, that was part of their beautiful and easy educational system; with their whole country, and with all its industries.

The children of Herland were taken to all parts of the country, shown all its arts and crafts, taught to honor its achievements and to appreciate its needs and difficulties. They grew up with a deep and vital social consciousness which not one in a thousand of us could approach.

This kind of thing does not show; we could not see it externally, any more than one could see a good housewife's intimate acquaintance with and pride in the last detail of her *menage*. Further, as our comments on their country had been almost wholly complimentary (they had not heard Terry's!), we had not hurt this national pride; or if we had they had never let us see it.

Now here was Ellador, daring traveler, leaving her world for mine, and finding herself, not as we three had been, exiled into a wisely ordered, peaceful and beautiful place, with the mothering care of that group of enlightened women; but as one alone in a world of which her first glimpse was of hideous war. As one who had never in her life seen worse evil than misunderstanding, or accident, and not much of these; one to whom universal comfort and beauty was the race habit of a thousand years, the sight of Europe in its present condition was far more of a shock than even I had supposed.

She thought that I felt as she did. I did feel badly, and ashamed, but not a thousandth part as she would have felt the exposure of some fault in Herland; not nearly as badly as she supposed.

I was constantly learning from her to notice things among us which I had never seen before, and one of the most conspicuous of my new impressions was the realization of how slightly socialized we are. We are quite indifferent to public evils, for the most part, unless they touch us personally; which is as though the housewife was quite indifferent to having grease on the chairs unless she happened to spoil her own dress with it. Even our "reformers" seem more like such a housewife who should show great excitement over the greasy chairs, but none over the dusty floor, the grimy windows, the empty coal-bin, the bad butter, or the lack of soap. Special evils rouse us, some of us, but as for a clean, sanitary, effortless housekeeping—we have not come to want it—most of us.

But Ellador, lovely, considerate soul that she was, had not only the incessant shock of these new impressions to meet and bear, but was doing her noble best to spare my feelings by not showing hers. She could not bear to blame my sex, to blame my country, or at least my civilization, my world; she did not wish to cast reproach on me.

I was ashamed, to a considerable degree. If a man has been living in the pleasant atmosphere of perfect housekeeping, such as I have mentioned, and is then precipitated suddenly into foul slovenliness, with noise, confusion and ill-will, he feels it more than if he had remained in such surroundings from the first.

It was the ill-will that counted most. Here again comes the psychic difference between the women of Herland and us. People who grow up amid slang, profanity, obscenity, harsh contradiction and quarrelling, do not particularly note or mind it. But one reared in an atmosphere of the most subtle understanding, gracious courtesy, and a loving use of language as an art, is very sharply impressed if someone says: "Hold yer jaw, yer son of a ——!," or even by a glowering roomful of silent haters.

That's what was heavy on Ellador all the time,—the atmosphere, the social atmosphere of suspicion, distrust, hatred, of ruthless self-aggrandizement and harsh scorn.

There was a German officer on this ship. He tried to talk to Ellador at first, merely because she was a woman and beautiful. She tried to talk to him, merely because he was a human being, a member of a great nation.

But I, watching, saw how soon the clear light of her mind brought out the salient characteristics of his, and of how, in spite of all her exalted philosophy, she turned shuddering away from him.

We were overhauled by an English vessel before reaching our destination in Sweden, and all three of us were glad to be transferred because we could so reach home sooner. At least that was what we thought. The German officer was not glad, I might add.

Ellador hailed the change with joy. She knew more about England than about the Scandinavian countries, and could speak the language. I think she thought it would be—easier there.

We were unable to get away as soon as we expected. Terry indeed determined to enlist, or to join the service in some way, and they were glad to use him and his aeroplane. This was not to be wondered at. If Terry had the defects of his qualities he also had the qualities of his defects, and he did good work for the Allies.

Ellador, rather unexpectedly asked to stay awhile: "It is hard," she said, "but we may not come again perhaps, and I want to learn all I can."

So we stayed and Ellador learned. It did not take her long. She was a rapid reader, and soon found the right books. She was a marvelous listener, and many were glad to talk to her, and to show her things.

We investigated in London, Manchester, Birmingham; were entertained in beautiful country places; went motoring up into Scotland and in Ireland; visited Wales, and then, to my great surprise, she urged that we go to France.

"I want to see, to know," she said. "To really *know*——"

I was worried about her. She had a hard-set fixity of expression. Her unfailing gentleness was too firm of surface, and she talked less and less with me about social conditions.

We went to France.

She visited hospitals, looking at those broken men, those maimed and blinded boys, and grew paler and harder daily. Day by day she gathered in the new language, till soon she could talk with the people.

Then we ran across Terry, scouting about with his machine; and Ellador asked to be taken up—she wanted to see a battlefield. I tried to dissuade her from this, fearing for her. Even her splendid health seemed shaken by all she had witnessed. But she said: "It is my duty to see and know all I can. This is not, they tell me—exceptional? This—war?"

"Not at all," said Terry. "It's only bigger than usual, as most things are now. Why, in all our history there have only been about three hundred years without war."

She looked at him, her eyes widening, darkening. "When was that?" she said. "After Jesus came?"

Terry laughed. "Oh no," he said. "It wasn't any one time. It's three hundred years here and there, scattering. So you see war is really the normal condition of human life."

"So," she said. "Then I ought to see it. Take me up, please."

He didn't want to; said it was dangerous; but it was very hard to say no to Ellador, and she had her way. She saw the battle lines of trenches. She saw the dead men; she saw and heard the men not dead, where there had been recent fighting. She saw the ruins, ruins everywhere.

That night she was like a woman of marble, cold, dumb, sitting still by the window where she could rest her eyes on the far stars. She treated me with a great poignant tenderness, as one would treat a beloved friend whose whole family had become lepers.

We went back to England, and she spent the last weeks of our stay there finding out all she could about Belgium.

That was the breaking point. She locked the door of her room, but I heard her sobbing her heart out—Ellador, who had never in all her splendid young life had an experience of pain, and whose consciousness was mainly social. We feel these horrors as happening to other people; she felt them as happening to herself.

I broke the lock—I had to get to her. She would not speak, would not look at me, but buried her face in the pillow, shuddering away from me as if I, too, were a German. The great sobs tore her. It was, I suddenly felt, not like the facile tears of an ordinary woman, but like the utter breakdown of a strong man. And she was as ashamed of it.

Then I had enough enlightenment to see some little relief for her, not from the weight of horrible new knowledge, but from the added burden of her self-restraint.

I knelt beside her and got her into my arms, her head hidden on my shoulder.

"Dear," said I, "Dear—I can't help the horror, but at least I can help you bear it—and you can let me try. You see you're all alone here—I'm all you've got. You'll have to let it out somehow—just say it all to me."

She held me very close then, with a tense, frightened grip. "I want—I want—my Mother!" she sobbed.

Ellador's mother was one of those wise women who sat in the Temples, and gave comfort and counsel when needed. They loved each other more than I, not seeing them always together, had understood. Yet her mother had counseled her going, had urged it, for the sake of their land and its future.

"Mother! Mother! Mother!" she sobbed under her breath. "Oh—Mother! Help me bear it!"

There was no Mother and no Temple, only one man who loved her, and in that she seemed to find a little ease, and slowly grew quieter.

"There is one thing we know more about than you do," I suggested. "That is how to manage pain. You mustn't keep it to yourself—you must let it out—let the others help bear it. That's good psychology, dear."

"It seems so—unkind," she murmured.

"Oh, no, it's not unkind; it's just necessary. 'Bear ye one another's burdens,' you know. Also we have a nice proverb about marriage. 'It makes joy double and halveth trouble.' Just pile it on me, dearest—that's what a husband is for."

"But how can I say to you the things I feel? It seems so rude, so to reflect on your people—your civilization."

"I think you underrate two things," I suggested. "One is that I'm a human creature, even if male; the other that my visit to Herland, my life with you, has had a deep effect on me. I see the awfulness of war as I never did before, and I can even see a little of how it must affect you. What I want you to do now is to relieve the pressure of feeling which is hurting so, by putting it into words—letting it out. Say it all. Say the very worst. Say—'This world is not civilized, not human. It is worse than the humble savagery below our mountains.' Let out, dear—I can stand it. And you'll feel better."

She lifted her head and drew a long, shuddering breath.

"I think you are right—there must be some relief. And here are You!" Suddenly she threw her arms around me and held me close, close.

"You *do* love me—I can feel it! A little—a very little—like mother love! I am so grateful!"

She rested in my arms, till the fierce tempest of pain had passed somewhat, and then we sat down, close together, and she followed my advice, seeking to visualize, to put in words, to fully express, the anguish which was upon her.

"You see," she began slowly, "it is hard for me to do this because I hate to hurt you. You must care so—so horribly."

"Stop right there, dear," I told her. "You overestimate my sensitiveness. What I feel is nothing at all to what you feel—I can see that. Remember that in our race-traditions war is a fine thing, a splendid thing. We have idealized war and the warrior, through all our history. You have read a good deal of our history by now."

She had, I knew, and she nodded her head sadly. "Yes, it's practically all about war," she agreed. "But I didn't—I couldn't visualize it."

She closed her eyes and shrank back, but I went on steadily: "So you see this is not—to us—wholly a horror; it is just more horrible than other wars on account of the infamous behavior of some combatants, and because we really are beginning to be civilized. Now this pain that you see is no greater than the same pain all the way back in history—always. And you are not being miserable about that, surely?"

No, she admitted, she wasn't.

"Very well," I hurried on, "we, the human race, outside of Herland, have been fighting one another for all the ages, and we are here yet; some of these military enthusiasts say because of war—some of the pacifists say in spite of it, and I'm beginning to agree with them. With you, Ellador, through you, and because of you, and because of seeing what human life can be, in your blessed country, I see things as I never did before. I'm growing."

She smiled a little at that, and took my hand again.

"You are the most important ambassador that ever was," I continued. "You are sent from your upland island, your little hidden heaven, to see our poor blind bleeding world and carry news of it to your people. Perhaps that vast storehouse of mother-love can help to set us straight at last. And you can't afford to *feel* our sorrow—you'd die of it. You must think—and talk it off, remorselessly, to me."

"You Amazing Darling!" she answered at last, drawing a deep breath. "You are right—wholly right. I'm afraid I have—a little—underrated your wisdom. Forgive me!"

I forgave her fast enough, though I knew it was an impossible offence, and she began to free her mind.

"First as to Christianity," she said. "That gave me great hopes—at first. Not the mythology of course, but the spirit; and when that missionary man enlarged on the spread of Christianity and its countless benefits I began to feel that here was a lovely thing it would do us good to know about—something very close to Motherhood."

"Motherhood," always reverently spoken, was the highest, holiest word they knew in Herland.

"But as I've read and talked and studied all these weeks, I do not find that Christianity has done one thing to stop war, or that Christian countries fight any less than heathen ones—rather more. Also they fight among themselves. Christianity has not brought peace on earth—not at all."

"No," I admitted, "it hasn't, but it tries to—ameliorate, to heal and save."

"That seems to me simply—foolish," she answered. "If there is a house on fire, the only true way to check the destruction is to put the fire out. To sit about trying to heal burned skin and repair burned furniture is—foolish."

"Especially when the repaired furniture serves as additional fuel for more fire," I added.

"You see it!" she exclaimed joyfully. "Then why don't you—but, I see—you are only one. You alone cannot change it."

"Oh no, I'm not alone in that," I answered cheerfully. "There are plenty more who see it."

"Then why—" she began, but checked herself, and paused a little, continuing slowly. "What I wish to get off my mind is this spectacle of measureless suffering which human beings are deliberately inflicting on one another. It would be hard enough to bear if the pain was unavoidable— that would be pure horror, and the eager rush to help. But here there is not only horror but a furious scorn—because they do not have to have it at all."

"You're quite right, my dear," I agreed. "But how are you going to make them stop?"

"That's what I have to find out," she answered gravely. "I wish Mother was here—and all the Over-Mothers. They would find a way. There must *be* a way. And you are right—I must not let myself be overcome by this—"

"Put it this way," I suggested. "Even if three quarters of the world should be killed there would be plenty left to refill, as promptly as would be wise. You remember how quickly your country filled up?"

"Yes," she said. "And I must remember that it is the race-progress that counts, not just being alive."

Then, wringing her hands in sudden bitterness, she added: "But this stops all progress! It is not merely that people are being killed. Half the world might die in an earthquake and not do this harm! It is the Hating I mind more than the killing—the perversion of human faculty. It's not humanity dying—it is humanity going mad!"

She was shivering again, that black horror growing in her eyes.

"Gently dear, gently," I told her. "Humanity is a large proposition. You and I have a whole round world to visit—as soon as it is safe to travel. And in the meantime I want to get you to my country as soon as possible. We are not at war. Our people are good-natured and friendly. I think you'll like us."

It was not unnatural for an American, in war-mad Europe, to think of his own land with warm approval, nor for a husband to want his wife to appreciate his people and his country.

"You must tell me more about it," she said eagerly. "I must read more too—study more. I do not do justice to the difference, I am sure. I am judging the world only by Europe. And see here, my darling—do you mind if we see the rest first? I want to know The World as far as I can, and as quickly as I can. I'm sure that if I study first for awhile, in England—they seem so familiar with all the world—that we might then go east instead of west, and see the rest of it before we reach America—leave the best to the last."

Except for the danger of traveling there seemed no great objection to this plan. I would rather have her make her brief tour and then return with me to my own dear country at the end, than to have her uneasy there and planning to push on.

We went back to a quiet place in England, where we could temporarily close our minds to the Horror, and Ellador, with unerring judgment, found an encyclopedic young historian with the teaching gift, and engaged his services for a time.

They had a series of maps—from old blank "terra incognita" ones, with its bounding ocean of ancient times, to the spread of accurate surveying which now gives us the whole surface of the earth. She kissed the place where her little homeland lay hidden—but that was when he was not looking.

The rapid grasp she made at the whole framework of our history would have astonished anyone not acquainted with Herland brains and Herland methods of education. It did astonish the young historian. She by no means set herself to learn all that he wanted to teach her; on the contrary she continually checked his flow of information, receiving only what she wanted to know.

A very few good books on world evolution—geological, botanical, zoological, and ethnic, gave her the background she needed, and such a marvel of condensation as Winwood Reade's *Martyrdom of Man* supplied the outline of history.

Her own clear strong uncrowded and logical mind, with its child-fresh memory, saw, held and related the facts she learned, with no apparent effort. Presently she had a distinct view of what we people have been up to on earth for the few ages of our occupancy. She had her estimate of time taken and of the rate of our increased speed. I had never realized how long, how immeasurably long and slow, were the years "before progress," so to speak, or the value of each great push of new invention. But she got them all clearly in place, and, rigidly refusing to be again agonized by the ceaseless wars, she found eager joy in counting the upward steps of social evolution.

This joy increased as the ages came nearer to our own. She became fascinated with the record of inventions and discoveries and their interrelative effects. Each great religion as it entered, was noted, defined in its special power and weakness, and its consequences observed. She made certain map effects for herself, "washing in" the different areas with various colors, according to the different religions, and lapping them over where they had historically lapped, as for instance, where the "mañana" of the Spaniard marks the influence following Oriental invasion, and where Buddhism produces such and such effects according to its reception by Hindu, Chinese, or Japanese.

"I could spend a lifetime in these details," she eagerly explained again, "but I'm only after enough to begin on. I must get them *placed*—so that I can understand what each nation is *for*, what they have done for one another, and for the world; which of them are going on, and how fast; which of them are stopping—or sinking back—and why. It is *profoundly* interesting."

Ellador's attitude vaguely nettled me, just a little, in that earlier consciousness I was really outgrowing so fast. She seemed like an enthusiastic young angel "slumming." I resented—a little—this cheerful and relentless classification—just as poor persons resent being treated as "cases."

But I knew she was right after all, and was more than delighted to have her so soon triumph over the terrible influence of the war. She did not, of course, wholly escape or forget it. Who could? But she successfully occupied her mind with other matters.

"It's so funny," she said to me. "Here in all your history books, the whole burden of information is as to who fought who—and when; and who 'reigned' and when—especially when. Why are your historians so morbidly anxious about the exact date?"

"Why it's important, isn't it?" I asked.

"From certain points of view, yes; but not in the least from that of the general student. The doctor wants to know at just what hour the fever rises, or declines; he has to have his 'chart' to study. But the public ought to know how fever is induced and how it is to be avoided. People in general ought to know the whole history of the world in general; and what were the most important things that happened. And here the poor things are required to note and remember that this king 'came to the throne' at such a date and died at such another—facts of no *historic* importance whatever. And as to the wars and wars and wars—and all these 'decisive battles of history' "—Ellador had the whole story so clearly envisaged now that she could speak of war without cringing—"why that isn't history at all!"

"Surely it's part of history, isn't it?" I urged.

"Not even part of it. Go back to your doctor's chart—his 'history of the case.' That history treats of the inception, development, success or failure of the disease he is treating. To say that 'At four-fifteen p.m. the patient climbed into another patient's bed and bit him,' is no part of that record of tuberculosis or cancer."

"It would be if it proved him delirious, wouldn't it?" I suggested.

Ellador lifted her head from the chart she was filling in, and smiled enchantingly. "Van," she said, "I'm proud of you. That's splendid!

"It would then appear," she pursued, glancing over her papers, "as if the patient had a sort of intermittent fever—from the beginning; hot fits of rage and fury, when he is practically a lunatic, and cold fits, too," she cried eagerly, pursuing the illustration, "cold and weak, when he just lies helpless and cannot do anything."

We agreed that as a figure of speech this was pretty strong and clear, with its inevitable suggestion that we must study the origin of the disease, how to cure, and still better, prevent it.

"But there is a splendid record behind all that," she told me. "I can't see that your historians have ever seen it clearly and consecutively. You evidently have not come to the place where all history has to be consciously revised for educational purposes."

"Ours is more complex than yours, isn't it?" I offered. "So many different nations and races, you know?"

But she smiled wisely and shook her head, quoting after her instructor: " 'And history, with all her volumes vast, hath but one page.' "

"They all tell about the same things," she said. "They all do the same things, and not one of them ever sees what really matters most—ever gives 'the history of the case' correctly. I truly think, dear, that we could help you with your history."

She had fully accepted the proposition I made that day when the Horror so overthrew her, and now talked to me as freely as if I were one of her sisters. She talked about men as if I wasn't one, and about the world as if it was no more mine than hers.

There was a strange exaltation, a wonderful companionship, in this. I grew to see life as she saw it, more and more, and it was like rising from some tangled thorny thicket to take a bird's eye view of city and farmland, of continent and ocean. Life itself grew infinitely more interesting. I thought of that benighted drummer's joke, that "Life is just one damn thing after another," so widely accepted as voicing a general opinion. I thought of our pathetic virtues of courage, cheerfulness, patience—all so ridiculously wasted in facing troubles which need not be there at all.

Ellador saw human life as a thing in the making, with human beings as the makers. We have always seemed to regard it as an affliction—or blessing—bestowed upon us by some exterior force. Studying, seeing, understanding, with her, I grew insensibly to adopt her point of view, her scale of measurements, and her eager and limitless interest. So when we did set forth on our round-the-world trip to my home, we were both fairly well equipped for the rapid survey which was all we planned for.

3

A Journey of Inspection

IT WAS FORTUNATE for Ellador's large purposes that her fat little bag of jewels contained more wealth than I had at first understood, and that there were some jewel-hungry millionaires left in the world. In India we found native princes who were as much athirst for rubies and emeralds as ever were their hoarding ancestors, and who had comfortable piles of ancient gold wherewith to pay for them. We were easily able to fill snug belts with universally acceptable gold pieces, and to establish credit to carry us wherever there were banks.

She was continually puzzled over our money values. "Why do they want these so much?" she demanded. "Why are they willing to pay so much for them?"

Money she understood well enough. They had their circulating medium in Herland in earlier years; but it was used more as a simple method of keeping accounts than anything else—like tickets, and finally discontinued. They had so soon centralized their industries, that the delay and inconvenience of measuring off every item of exchange in this everlasting system of tokens became useless, to their practical minds. As an "incentive to industry" it was not necessary; motherhood was their incentive. When they had plenty of everything it was free to all in such amounts as were desired; in scarcity they divided. Their interest in life was in what they were doing—and what they were going to do, not in what they were to get. Our point of view puzzled her.

I remember this matter coming up between Ellador and a solemn college professor, an economist, as we were creeping through the dangerous Mediterranean. She questioned and listened, saying nothing about her country—this we had long since found was the only safe way; for the instant demand: "Where is it?" was what we did not propose to answer.

But having learned what she could from those she talked with, and sped searchingly through the books they offered her, she used to relieve her mind in two ways; by talking with me, and by writing.

"I've simply got to," she told me. "I'm writing a book—in fact, I'm writing two books. One is notes, quotations, facts, and pictures—pictures—pictures. This photography is a wonderful art!"

She had become quite a devotee of said art, and was gathering material right and left, to show her people.

"We'll have to go back and tell them, you know," she explained, "and they'll be *so* interested, I shall have to go about lecturing, as you men did."

"I wish you'd go about lecturing to us," I told her. "We have more to learn than you have—of the really important matters in living."

"But I couldn't, you see, without quoting always from home—and then they'd want to know—they'd have a right to know. Or else they wouldn't believe me. No, all I can do is to ask questions; to make suggestions, perhaps, here and there; even to criticize a little—when I've learned a lot more, and if I'm very sure of my hearers. Meanwhile I've got to talk it off to you, you poor boy—and just write. You shall read it, if you want to, of course."

Her notes were a study in themselves.

Ships and shipping interested her at once, as something totally new, and her first access to encyclopedias had supplied background to what she learned from people. She had set down, in the briefest possible manner, not mere loose data as to vessels and navigation, but an outlined history of the matter, arranged like a genealogical tree.

There were the rude beginnings—log, raft, skin-boat, basket-boat, canoe; and the line of paddled or oared boats went on to the great carved war-canoes with outriggers, the galleys of Romans and Norsemen, the delicate birchbarks of our American Aborigines, and the neat manufactured ones on the market. A bare sentence covered it, and another the evolution of the sailing craft; then steam.

"Navigation is an exclusively masculine process," she noted. "Always men, only men. Oared vessels of large size required slave labor; status of sailors still akin to slavery; rigid discipline, miserable accommodations, abusive language and personal violence." To this she added in parenthesis: "Same holds true of armies. Always men, only men. Similar status, but somewhat better provision for men, and more chance of promotion, owing to greater danger to officers."

Continuing with ships, she noted: "Psychology: a high degree of comradeship, the habit of obedience—enforced; this doubtless accounts for large bodies of such indispensable men putting up with such wretched treatment. Obedience appears to dull and weaken the mind; same with soldiers—study further. Among officers great personal gallantry, a most exalted sense of duty, as well as brutal and unjust treatment of inferiors. The captain in especial is so devoted to his concept of duty as sometimes to prefer to 'go down with his ship' to being saved without her. Why? What social service is there in being drowned? I learn this high devotion is found also in engineers and in pilots. Seems to be a product of extreme responsibility. Might be developed more widely by extending opportunity."

She came to me with this, asking for more information on our political system of "rotation in office."

"Is that why you do it?" she asked eagerly. "Not so much as to get the work done better, as to make all the people—or at least most of them—feel greater responsibility, a deeper sense of duty?"

I had never put it that way to myself, but I now agreed that that was the idea—that it must be. She was warmly interested; said she knew she should love America. I felt sure she would.

There was an able Egyptologist on board, a man well acquainted with ancient peoples, and he, with the outline she had so well laid down during her English studies, soon filled her mind with a particularly clear and full acquaintance with our first civilizations.

"Egypt, with its One River; Asia Minor, with the Valley of the Two Rivers and China with its great rivers—" she pored over her maps and asked careful eager questions. The big black bearded professor was delighted with her interest, and discoursed most instructively.

"I see," she said. "I see! They came to places where the soil was rich, and where there was plenty of water. It made agriculture possible, profitable— and then the surplus—and then the wonderful growth—of course!"

That German officer, who had made so strong and disagreeable an impression while we were on the Swedish ship, had been insistent, rudely insistent, on the advantages of difficulty and what he called "discipline." He had maintained that the great races, the dominant races, came always from the north. This she had borne in mind, and now questioned her obliging preceptor, with map outspread and dates at hand.

"For all those thousands of years these Mediterranean and Oriental peoples held the world—were the world?"

"Yes, absolutely."

"And what was up here?" she pointed to the wide vacant spaces on the northern coasts.

"Savages—barbarians—wild, skin-clad ferocious men, madam."

Ellador made a little diagram, a vertical line, with many ages marked across it.

"This is The Year One—as far back as you can go," she explained, pointing to the mark at the bottom. "And here we are, near the top—this is Now. And these Eastern peoples held the stage and did the work all the way up to—here, did they?"

"They certainly did, madam."

"And were these people in these northern lands there all the time? Or did they happen afterward?"

"They were there—we have their bones to prove it."

"Then if they were there—and as long, and of the same stock—you tell me that all these various clans streamed out, westward, from a common source, and became in time, Persians, Hindus, Pelasgians, Etruscans, and all the rest—as well as Celts, Slavs, Teutons?"

"It is so held, roughly speaking." He resented a little her sweeping generalizations and condensations; but she had her own ends in view.

"And what did these northern tribes contribute to social progress during all this time?"

"Practically nothing," he answered. "Their arts were naturally limited by the rigors of the climate. The difficulties of maintaining existence prevented any higher developments."

"I see, I see," she nodded gravely. "Then why is it, in the face of these facts, that some still persist in attributing progress to difficulties, and cold weather."

This professor, who was himself Italian, was quite willing to question this opinion.

"That theory you will find is quite generally confined to the people who live in the colder climates," he suggested.

When Ellador discussed this with me, she went further. "It seems as if, when people say—'The World' they mean their own people," she commented. "I've been reading history as written by the North European races. Perhaps when we get to Persia, India, China and Japan, it will be different."

It was different. I had spent my own youth in the most isolated of modern nations, the one most ignorant of and indifferent to all the others; the one whose popular view of foreigners is based on the immigrant classes, and whose traveling rich consider Europe as a play-ground, a picture gallery, a museum, a place wherein to finish one's education. Being so reared, and associating with similarly minded persons, my early view of history was a great helter-skelter surging background to the clear, strong, glorious incidents of our own brief national career; while geography consisted of the vivid large scale familiar United States, and a globe otherwise covered with more or less nebulous maps; and such political evolution as I had in mind consisted of the irresistible development of our own "institutions."

All this, of course, was my youthful attitude. In later studies I had added a considerable knowledge of general history, sociology and the like, but had never realized until now how remote all this was to me from the definite social values already solidly established in my mind.

Now, associating with Ellador, dispassionate and impartial as a visiting angel, bringing to her studies of the world, the triple freshness of view of one of different stock, different social development, and different sex, I began to get a new perspective. To her the world was one field of general advance. Her own country held the foreground in her mind, of course, but she had left it as definitely as if she came from Mars, and was studying the rest of humanity in the mass. Her alien point of view, her previous complete ignorance, and that powerful well-ordered mind she brought to bear on the new knowledge so rapidly amassed, gave her advantages as an observer far beyond our best scientists.

The one special and predominant distinction given to her studies by her supreme femininity, was what gave me the most numerous, and I may say, unpleasant surprises. In my world studies I had always assumed that humanity did thus and so, but she was continually shearing through the tangled facts with her sharp distinction that this and this phenomenon was due to masculinity alone.

"But Ellador," I protested, "why do you say—'the male Scandinavians continually indulged in piracy,' and 'the male Spaniards practiced terrible cruelties,' and so on? It sounds so—invidious—as if you were trying to make out a case against men."

"Why, I wouldn't do that for anything!" she protested. "I'm only trying to understand the facts. You don't mind when I say 'the male Phoenicians made great progress in navigation,' or 'the male Greeks developed great intelligence,' do you?"

"That's different," I answered. "They did do those things."

"Didn't they do the others, too?"

"Well—yes—they did them, of course; but why rub it in that they were exclusively males?"

"But weren't they, dear? Really? Did the Norse women raid the coasts of England and France? Did the Spanish women cross the ocean and torture the poor Aztecs?"

"They would have if they could!" I protested.

"So would the Phoenician women and Grecian women in the other cases—wouldn't they?"

I hesitated.

"Now my Best Beloved," she said, holding my hand in both hers and looking deep into my eyes—"Please, oh *please*, don't mind. The facts are there, and they are immensely important. Think, dearest. We of Herland have known no men—till now. We, alone, in our tiny land, have worked out a happy, healthy life. Then you came—you 'Wonderful Three.' Ah! You should realize the stir, the excitement, the Great Hope that it meant to us! We knew there was more world—but nothing about it, and you meant a vast new life to us. Now I come to see—to learn—for the sake of my country.

"Because, you see, some things we gathered from you made us a little afraid. Afraid for our children, you see. Perhaps it was better, after all, to live up there, alone, in ignorance, but in happiness, we thought. Now I've come—to see—to learn—to really understand, if I can, so as to tell my people.

"You *mustn't* think I'm against men, dear. Why, if it were only for your sake, I would love them. And I'm sure—we are all sure at home (or at least most of us are) that two sexes, working together, must be better than one.

"Then I can see how, being two sexes, and having so much more complex a problem than ours, and having all kinds of countries to live in—how you got into difficulties we never knew.

"I'm making every allowance. I'm firm in my conviction of the superiority of the bisexual method. It *must* be best or it would not have been evolved in all the higher animals. But—but you can't expect me to ignore facts."

No, I couldn't. What troubled me most was that I, too, began to see facts, quite obvious facts, which I had never noticed before.

Wherever men had been superior to women we had proudly claimed it as a sex-distinction. Wherever men had shown evil traits, not common to women, we had serenely treated them as race-characteristics.

So, although I did not enjoy it, I did not dispute any further Ellador's growing collection of facts. It was just as well not to. Facts are stubborn things.

We visited a little in Tunis, Algiers, and Cairo, making quite an excursion in Egypt, with our steamship acquaintance, whose knowledge was invaluable to us. He translated inscriptions; showed us the more important discoveries, and gave condensed accounts of the vanished civilizations.

Ellador was deeply impressed.

"To think that under one single city, here in Abydos, there are the remains of five separate cultures. Five! As different as can be. With a long time between, evidently, so that the ruins were forgotten, and a new people built a new city on the site of the old one. It is wonderful."

Then she turned suddenly on Signor Armini. "What did they die of?" she demanded.

"Die of? Who, madam?"

"Those cities—those civilizations?"

"Why, they were conquered in war, doubtless; the inhabitants were put to the sword—some carried away as slaves, perhaps—and the cities razed to the ground?"

"By whom?" she demanded. "Who did it?"

"Why, other peoples, other cultures, from other cities."

"Do you mean other peoples, or just other men?" she asked.

He was puzzled. "Why, the soldiers were men, of course, but war was made by one nation against another."

"Do you mean that the women of the other nations were the governing power and sent the men to fight?"

No, he did not mean that.

"And surely the children did not send them?"

Of course not.

"But people are men, women and children, aren't they? And only the adult men, about one-fifth of the population, made war?"

This he admitted perforce, and Ellador did not press the point further.

"But in these cities were all kinds of people, weren't there? Women and children, as well as men?"

This was obvious, also; and then she branched off a little: "What made them want to conquer a city?"

"Either fear—or revenge—or desire for plunder. Oftenest that. The ancient cities were the centers of production, of course." And he discoursed on the beautiful handicrafts of the past, the rich fabrics, the jewels and carved work and varied treasures.

"Who made them," she asked.

"Slaves, for the most part," he answered.

"Men and women?"

"Yes—men and women."

"I see," said Ellador. She saw more than she spoke of, even to me.

In ancient Egypt she found much that pleased her in the power and place of historic womanhood. This satisfaction was shortlived as we went on eastward.

With a few books, with eager questioning of such experts as we met, and what seemed to me an almost supernatural skill in eliciting valuable and apposite information from unexpected quarters, my lady from Herland continued to fill her mind and her note-books.

To me, who grew more and more to admire her, to reverence her, to tenderly love her, as we traveled on together, there now appeared a change in her spirit, more alarming even than that produced by Europe's war. It was like the difference between the terror roused in one surrounded by lions, and the loathing experienced in the presence of hideous reptiles, this not in the least at the people, but at certain lamentable social conditions.

In visiting our world she had been most unfortunately first met by the hot horrors of war; and I had thought to calm her by the static nations, the older peoples, sitting still among their ruins, richly draped in ancient and interesting histories. But a very different effect was produced. What she had read, while it prepared her to understand the sequence of affairs, had in no case given what she recognized as the really important events and their results.

"I'm writing a little history of the world," she told me, with a restrained smile. "Just a little one, so that I can have something definite to show them."

"But how can you, dearest—in this time, with what data you have? I know you are wonderful—but a history of the world!"

"Only a little one," she answered. "Just a synopsis. You know we are used to condensing and simplifying for our children. I suppose that is where we get the 'grasp of salient features' you have spoken of so often. These historians I read now certainly do not have it."

She continued tender to me, more so if anything. Of two things we talked with pleasure: of Herland and my land, and always of the beauty of nature. This seemed to her a ceaseless source of strength and comfort.

"It's the same world," she said, as we leaned side by side on the rail at the stern, and watched the white wake run uncoiling away from us, all silver-shining under the round moon. "The same sky, the same stars, some of them, the same blessed sun and moon. And the dear grass—and the trees—the precious trees."

Being by profession a forester, it was inevitable that she should notice trees; and in Europe she found much to admire, though lamenting the scarcity of food-bearing varieties. In Northern Africa she had noted the value of the palm, the olive, and others, and had readily understood the whole system of irrigation and its enormous benefits. What she did not easily grasp was its disuse, and the immeasurable futility of the fellaheen, still using the shadoof after all these ages of progress.

"I don't see yet," she admitted, "what makes their minds so—so impervious. It can't be because they're men, surely. Men are not duller than women, are they, dear?"

"Indeed they are not!" I cried, rather stung by this new suggestion. "Men are the progressive sex, the thinkers, the innovators. It is the women who are conservative and slow. Even you will have to admit that."

"I certainly will if I find it so," she answered cheerfully. "I can see that these women are dull enough. But then—if they do things differently there are penalties, aren't there?"

"Penalties?"

"Why, yes. If the women innovate and rebel the least that happens to them is that the men won't marry them—isn't that so?"

"I shouldn't think *you* would call that a penalty, my dear," I answered.

"Oh, yes, it is; it means extinction—the end of that variety of woman. You seem to have quite successfully checked mutation in women; and they had neither education, opportunity, or encouragement in other variation."

"Don't say 'you,' " I urged. "These are the women of the Orient you are talking about, not of all the world. Everybody knows that their position is pitiful and a great check to progress. Wait till you see my country!"

"I shall be glad to get there, dearest, I'm sure of that," she told me. "But as to these more progressive men among the Egyptians—there was no penalty for improving on the shadoof, was there? Or the method of threshing grain by the feet of cattle?"

Then I explained, trying to show no irritation, that there was a difference in the progressiveness of nations, of various races; but that other things being equal, the men were as a rule more progressive than the women.

"Where are the other things equal, Van?"

I had to laugh at that; she was a very difficult person to argue with; but I told her they were pretty near equal in our United States, and that we thought our women fully as good as men, and a little better. She was comforted for a while, but as we went on into Asia, her spirit sank and darkened, and that change I spoke of became apparent.

Burmah was something of a comfort, and that surviving matriarchate in the island hills. But in our rather extended visit to India, guided and informed by both English and native friends, and supplied with further literature, she began to suffer deeply.

We had the rare good fortune to be allowed to accompany a scientific expedition up through the wonder of the Himalayas, through Thibet, and into China. Here that high sweet spirit drooped and shrunk, with a growing horror, a loathing, such as I had never seen before in her clear eyes. She was shocked beyond words at the vast area of dead country; skeleton country, deforested, deshrubbed, degrassed, wasted to the bone, lying there to burn in the sun and drown in the rain, feeding no one.

"Van, Van," she said. "Help me to forget the women a little and talk about the land! Help me to understand the—the holes in the minds of people. Here is intelligence, intellect, a high cultural development—of sorts. They have beautiful art in some lines. They have an extensive literature. They are old, very old, surely old enough to have learned more than any other people. And yet here is proof that they have never mastered the simple and obvious facts of how to take care of the land on which they live."

"But they still live on it, don't they?"

"Yes—they live on it. But they live on it like swarming fleas on an emaciated kitten, rather than careful farmers on a well-cultivated ground. However," she brightened a little, "there's one thing; this horrible instance of a misused devastated land must have been of one great service. It must have served as an object lesson to all the rest of the world. Where such an old and wise nation has made so dreadful a mistake—for so long, at least no other nation need to make it."

I did not answer as fully and cheerfully as she wished, and she pressed me further.

"The world has learned how to save its trees—its soil—its beauty—its fertility, hasn't it? Of course, what I've seen is not all—it's better in other places?"

"We did not go to Germany, you know, my dear. They have a high degree of skill in forestry there. In many countries it is now highly thought of. We are taking steps to preserve our own forests, though, so far, they are so extensive that we rather forgot there was any end of them."

"It will be good to get there, Van," and she squeezed my hand hard. "I must see it all. I must 'know the worst' and surely I am getting the worst first! But you have free education—you have every advantage of climate—

you have a mixture of the best blood on earth, of the best traditions. And you are brave and free and willing to learn. Oh, Van! I am so glad it was America that found us!"

I held her close and kissed her. I was glad, too. And I was proud clear through to have her speak so of us. Yet, still—I was not as perfectly comfortable about it as I had been at first.

She had read about the foot-binding process still common in so large a part of China, but somehow had supposed it was a thing of the past, and never general. Also, I fancy she had deliberately kept it out of her mind, as something impossible to imagine. Now she saw it. For days and days, as we traveled through the less known parts of the great country, she saw the crippled women; not merely those serenely installed in rich gardens and lovely rooms, with big-footed slaves to do their bidding; or borne in swaying litters by strong Coolies; but poor women, working women, toiling in the field, carrying their little mats to kneel on while they worked, because their feet were helpless aching pegs.

Presently, while we waited in a village, and were entertained by a local magnate who had business relations with one of our guides, Ellador was in the women's apartment, and she heard it—the agony of the bound feet of a child. The child was promptly hushed, struck and chided; made to keep quiet, but Ellador had heard its moaning. From a woman missionary she got details of the process, and was shown the poor little shrunken stumps.

That night she would not let me touch her, come near her. She lay silent, staring with set eyes, long shudders running over her from time to time.

When it came to speech, which was some days later, she could still but faintly express it.

"To think," she said slowly, "that there are on earth men who can do a thing like that to women—to little helpless children!"

"But their men don't do it, dearest," I urged. "It is the women, their own mothers, who bind the feet of the little ones. They are afraid to have them grow up 'big-footed women!' "

"Afraid of what?" asked Ellador, that shudder passing over her again.

4

Nearing Home

WE STAYED SOME LITTLE TIME IN CHINA, meeting most interesting and valuable people, missionaries, teachers, diplomats, merchants, some of them the educated English-speaking Chinese.

Ellador's insatiable interest, her exquisite courtesy and talent as a listener, made anyone willing to talk to her. She learned fast, and placed in that wide sunlit mind of hers each fact in due relation.

"I'm beginning to understand," she told me sweetly, "that I mustn't judge this—miscellaneous—world of yours as I do my country. We were just ourselves—an isolated homogeneous people. When we moved, we all moved together. You are all kinds of people, in all kinds of places, touching at the edges and getting mixed. And so far from moving on together, there are no two nations exactly abreast—that I can see; and they mostly are ages apart; some away ahead of the others, some going far faster than others, some stationary."

"Yes," I told her, "and in the still numerous savages we find the beginners, and the back-sliders—the hopeless back-sliders—in human progress."

"I see—I see—" she said reflectively. "When you say 'the civilized world' that is just a figure of speech. The world is not civilized yet—only spots in it, and those not wholly."

"That's about it," I agreed with her. "Of course, the civilized nations think of themselves as the world—that's natural."

"How does it compare—in numbers?" she inquired. "Let's look!"

So we consulted the statistics on the population of the earth, chasing through pages of classification difficult to sift, until we hit upon a little table: "Population of the earth according to race."

"That ought to do, roughly speaking," I told her. "We'll call the white races civilized—and lump the others. Let's see how it comes out."

It came out that the total of Indo-Germanic, or Aryan—White, for Europe, America, Persia, India and Australia, was 775,000,000; and the rest of the world, black, red, brown and yellow, was 788,000,000.

"Do you mean that the majority of mankind is still uncivilized?" she asked.

She didn't ask it unpleasantly. Ellador was never sarcastic or bitter. But the world was her oyster—to study, and she was quite impartial.

I, however, felt reproached by this cool estimate. "No indeed," I said, "you can't call China uncivilized—it is one of the very oldest civilizations we have. This is only by race you see, by color."

"Oh, yes," she agreed, "and race or color do not count in civilization? Of course not—how stupid I was!"

But I laid down the pencil I was using to total up populations, and looked at her with a new and grave misgiving. She was so world-innocent. Even the history she had so swiftly absorbed had not changed her, any more than indecent novels affect a child; the child does not know the meaning of the words.

In the light of Ellador's colossal innocence of what we are accustomed to call "life," I began to see that process in a wholly new perspective. Her country was but one; her civilization was one and indivisible; in her country the women and children lived as mothers, daughters, sisters, in general tolerance, love, education and service. Out of that nursery, school, garden, shop, and parlor, she came into this great scrambling world of ours, to find it spotted over with dissimilar peoples, more separated by their varying psychology than by geography, politics, or race; often ignorant of one another, often fearing, despising, hating one another; and each national group, each racial stock, assuming itself to be "the norm" by which to measure others. She had first to recognize the facts and then to disentangle the causes, the long lines of historic evolution which had led to these results. Even then it was hard for her really to grasp the gulfs which divide one part of the human race from the others.

And now I had the unpleasant task of disabusing her of this last glad assumption, that race and color made no difference.

"Dear," I said slowly, "you must prepare your mind for another shock—though you must have got some of it already, here and there. Race and color make all the difference in the world. People dislike and despise one another on exactly that ground—difference in race and color. These millions who are here marked 'Aryan or White' include Persians and Hindus, yet the other white races are averse to intermarrying with these, whose skins are indeed much darker than ours, though they come of the same stock."

"Is the aversion mutual?" she asked, as calmly as if we had been discussing insects.

I assured her that, speaking generally, it was; that the flatter-faced Mongolians regarded us as hawklike in our aquiline features; and that little African children fled screaming from the unnatural horror of a first-seen white face.

But what I was thinking about was how I should explain to her the race prejudice in my own country, when she reached it. I felt like a housekeeper bringing home company, discovering that the company has far higher and more exacting standards than herself, and longing to get home first and set the house in order before inspection.

We spent some little time in Japan, Ellador enjoying the fairy beauty of the country, with its flower-worshipping, sunny-faced people, and the plump happy children everywhere.

But instead of being content with the artistic beauty of the place; with that fine lacquer of smiling courtesy with which their life is covered, she followed her usual course of penetrating investigation. It needed no years of study, no dreary tables of figures. With what she already knew, so clearly held in mind, with a few questions each loaded with implications, she soon grasped the salient facts of Japanese civilization. Its conspicuous virtues gave her instant joy. The high honor of the Samurai, the unlimited patriotism of the people in general, the exquisite politeness, and the sincere love of beauty in nature and art—these were all comforting, and the free-footed women also, after the "golden lilies" of China.

But presently, piercing below all these, she found the general poverty of the people, their helplessness under a new and hard-grinding commercial-ism, and the patient ignominy in which the women lived.

"How is it, dear," she asked me, "that these keenly intelligent people fail to see that such limited women cannot produce a nobler race?"

I could only say that it was a universal failing, common to all races—except ours, of course. Her face always lighted when we spoke of America.

"You don't know how I look forward to it, dear," she said. "After this painful introduction to the world I knew so little of—I'm so glad we came this way—saving the best to the last."

The nearer we came to America and the more eagerly she spoke of it, the more my vague uneasiness increased. I began to think of things I had never before been sensitive about and to seek for justification.

Meanwhile Ellador was accumulating heart-ache over the Japanese women, whose dual duty of child-bearing and man-service dominated all their lives.

"It is so hard for me to understand, Van; they aren't people at all, somehow—just wives—or worse."

"They are mothers, surely," I urged.

"No—not in our sense, not consciously. Look at this ghastly crowding! Here's a little country, easy to grasp and manage, capable of supporting about so many people—not more. And here they are, making a 'saturated solution' of themselves." She had picked up that phrase from one of her medical friends, a vigorous young man who told her much that she was eager to know about the health and physical development of the Japanese. "Can't they see that there are too many?" she went on. "If a people increases beyond its means of support it has to endure miserable poverty—or what is that the Germans demand?—expansion! They have to have somebody else's country. How strangely dull they are!"

"But, my dear girl, please remember that this *is* life," I told her. "This *is* the world. This *is* the way people live. You expect too much of them. It is a law of nature to increase and multiply. Of course, Malthus set up a terrified cry about over-populating the earth, but it has not come to that yet, not near. Our means of subsistence increase with the advance of science."

"As to the world, I can see that; but as to a given country, and especially as small a one as this—what does become of them?" she asked suddenly.

This started her on a rapid study of emigration, in which, fortunately, my own knowledge was of some use; and she eagerly gathered up and arranged in her mind that feature of our history on which hangs so much, the migration and emigration of peoples. She saw at once how, when most of the earth's surface was unoccupied, people moved freely about in search of the best hunting or pasturage; how in an agricultural system they settled and spread, widening with the increase of population; how ever since they met and touched, each nation limited by its neighbors, there had been the double result of over-crowding inside the national limits, and warfare in the interests of "expansion."

"I can see now the wonderful advantage you have," she said eagerly. "Humanity got its 'second wind' with the discovery of the 'new world'— didn't it?"

It always delighted me to note the speed and correctness with which she picked up idioms and bits of slang. They were a novelty to her, and a constant delight.

"You had a big new country to spread out in, and no competitors—there were no previous inhabitants, were there?"

"Nothing but Indians," I said.

"Indians?"

"Yes, savages, like those in the forests below your mountain land, though more advanced in some ways."

"How did you arrange with them?" she asked.

"I hate to tell you, Ellador. You see you have—a little—idealized my country. We did not 'arrange' with those savages. We killed them."

"All of them? How many were there?" She was quite calm. She made no movement of alarm or horror, but I could see the rich color fade from her face, and her dear gentle mouth set in harder lines of control.

"It is a long story, and not a nice one, I'm sorry to say. We left some, hemming them in in spots called 'reservations.' There has been a good deal of education and missionary work; some Indians have become fully civilized—as good citizens as any; and some have intermarried with the whites. We have many people with Indian blood. But speaking generally this is one of our national shames. Helen Hunt wrote a book about it, called 'A Century of Dishonor.' "

Ellador was silent. That lovely far-off homesick look came into her eyes.

"I hate to disillusion you, dear heart," I said. "We are not perfect in America. I truly think we have many advantages over any other country, but we are not blameless."

"I'll defer judgment till I get there," she presently answered. "Let's go back to what we were discussing—the pressure of population."

Rather sadly we took it up again, and saw how, as long as warfare was the relief, nations continually boiled over upon one another; gaining more land by the simple process of killing off the previous owners, and having to repeat the process indefinitely as soon as the population again pressed against its limits. Where warfare was abandoned and a settled boundary established, as when great China walled itself in from marauding tribes, then the population showed an ingrowing pressure, and reduced the standard of living to a ghastly minimum. Then came the later process of peaceful emigration, by which the coasts and islands of the Pacific became tinged with the moving thousands of the Yellow Races.

She saw it all as a great panorama, an endless procession, never accepting a static world with the limitations of parti-colored maps, but always watching the movement of races.

"That's what ails Europe now, isn't it?" she said at last. "That's why those close-packed fertile races were always struggling up and down among one another, and making room, for awhile, by killing people?"

"That's certainly a good part of it," I agreed. "Every nation wants more land to accommodate its increasing population."

"And they want an increase of population in order to win more land—don't they?"

This, too, was plain.

"And there isn't any way out of it—on a limited earth—but fixed boundaries with suicidal crowding inside, or the 'fortunes of war?' "

That, too, was plain, unfortunately.

"Then why do not the women limit the population, as we did?"

"Oh, Ellador, Ellador—you cannot seem to realize that this world is not a woman's world, like your little country. This is a man's world—and they did not want to limit the population."

"Why not?" she urged. "Was it because they did not bear the children? Was it because they would rather fight than live in peace? What *was* the reason?"

"Neither of those," I said slowly. "The real reason is that neither men nor women have been able to see broadly enough, to think deeply enough, sufficiently to visualize these great racial questions. They just followed their instincts and obeyed their ancient religions, and these things happened without their knowing why."

"But the women!" protested Ellador. "Surely the women could see as simple a thing as that. It's only a matter of square miles; how many people to a mile can live healthfully and pleasantly. Are these women willing to have their children grow up so crowded that they *can't* be happy, or where they'll have to fight for room to live? I can't understand it."

Then she went determinedly to question a Japanese authority, to whom we were introduced by one of our friends, as to the status of women in Japan. She was polite; she was meek; she steeled herself beforehand to hear without surprise; and the authority, also courteous to a degree, gave her a brief outline with illustrative story and quotation, of the point of view from which women were regarded in that country. She grasped it even more thoroughly than she had in India or China.

We left Japan for Home, via Hawaii, and for days she was silent about the subject. Then, as the wide blue sea, the brilliant days spinning by, the smooth magnificence of our progress comforted her, she touched on it once more.

"I'm trying not to *feel* about these particularly awful things, and not to judge, even, till I know more. These things are *so*; and my knowing them does not make them any worse than they were before."

"You're a brave girl—and a strong one," I assured her. "That's the only way to do. I'm awfully sorry you had to have such a dose at first—this war, of all things; and then women in the East! I ought to have prepared you better."

"You could not have, dearest—it would have been impossible. No mere words could have made me visualize the inconceivable. And no matter how I came to it, slow or fast, the horror would have been the same. It is as impossible for me to make you see how I feel it now, as it would have been for you to make me feel it beforehand."

The voyage did her great good. She loved the sea, and gloried in the ships, doing her best to ignore the pitiful labor conditions of those who made the glory possible. Always she made friends—travelers, missionaries, business men, and women, wherever she found them. Yet, strangely enough, she seemed more at a loss with the women than with the men; seemed not to know, quite, how to approach them. It was not for lack of love and sympathy—far from it; she was eager to make friends with them. I finally worked out an explanation like this: She made friends with the men on the human side rather than attracting them by femininity; and as human beings they exchanged ideas and got on well together. The women were not so human; had a less wide outlook, less experience, as a rule. When she did get near enough to one of them for talk at all intimate, then came the ultra-feminine point of view, the different sense of social and moral values, the peculiar limitations of their position.

I saw this, as reflected by Ellador, as I had never seen it for myself before. What I did not understand, at first, was why she seemed to flag in interest and in patience, with the women, sooner than with the men. She never criticized them, but I could see a puzzled grieved look come over her kind face and then she would withdraw.

There were exceptions, marked ones. A woman doctor who had worked for years in China was going home for a long needed vacation, and Ellador was with her day after day, "learning," she told me. And there was another, once a missionary, now a research worker in biology, who commanded her sincere admiration.

We came to the lovely Hawaiian Islands, quite rested and refreshed, and arranged to stay there awhile and enjoy the splendor of those sea-girt mountains. Here her eager social interest was again aroused and she supplied herself with the history of this little sample of "social progress" most rapidly. There were plenty to teach her, a few excellent books to read, and numbers of most self-satisfied descendants of missionaries to boast of the noble work of their fathers.

"This is very illuminating," she told me. "It is a—what's that nice word Professor Whiting used?—a microcosm—isn't it?"

By this time my dear investigator had as clear an idea of general human history as any one, not a specialist could wish; and had it in a very small note-book. While in England someone had given her Winwood Reade's wonderful "Martyrdom of Man," as good a basis for historical study as could be asked; and all the facts and theories she had been collecting since were duly related to her general views.

"Here you have done it so quickly—inside of a century. Only 1820—and these nice gentle golden-colored people were living here by themselves."

"They weren't always gentle—don't idealize them too much!" I interrupted. "They had wars and quarrels, and they had a very horrid taboo religion—particularly hard on women."

"Yes—I know that—they weren't 'perfect, as we are,' as Professor Boynton used to say; but they were beautiful and healthy and happy; they were courteous and kind; and oh, how splendidly they could swim! Even the babies, they tell me."

"I've understood a child can swim earlier than it can walk—did they tell you that?"

"Yes—why not? But look here, my dear. Then came the missionaries and—interfered. Now these natives and owners of the land are only 15 per cent. of the population, with 20 per cent. of the deaths. They are dispossessed and are being exterminated."

"Yes," I said. "Well?"

Ellador looked at me. One could watch the expressions follow one another over her face, like cloud shadows and sunlight over a landscape. She looked puzzled; she evidently saw a reason. She became stern; then a further reason was recognized, and then that heavenly mother-look came over her, the one I had grown to prize most deeply.

But all she said was: "I love you, Van."

"Thank Heaven for that, my dear. I thought you were going to cast me out because of the dispossessed Hawaiians. *I* didn't do it—you're not blaming me, are you?"

"Did not—America—do it?" she asked, quietly. "And do you care at all?"

Then I embarked on one of those confined and contradictory explanations by which the wolf who has eaten the lamb seeks to show how unavoidable—if not how justifiable it all was.

"Do you feel like that about England's taking the Boers' country?" she asked gently.

I did not. I had always felt that a particularly inexcusable piece of "expansion."

"And your country is not packed very close yet—is it? Having so much—why did you need these?"

"We wanted to Christianize them—to civilize them," I urged rather sulkily.

"Do you think Christ would have had the same effect on them? And does civilization help dead people?"

She saw I was hurt, and stopped to kiss me. "Let's drop it, dear—I was wrong to press the point. But I've become so used to saying everything to you, just as if you were one of my sisters—I forget that things must look differently when one's own country is involved."

She said no more about the vanishing Hawaiians, but I began to look at them with a very different feeling from what I had ever had before. We had brought them syphilis and tuberculosis. The Chinese brought them leprosy. One of their lovely islands was now a name of horror from that ghastly disease, a place where noble Christians strive to minimize the evil—too late.

The missionaries, nobly purposed, no doubt, to begin with, had amassed great fortunes in land given to them by these careless children who knew so little of land ownership; and the children and grandchildren of the missionaries lived wealthy and powerful, proud of the "great work" of their forefathers, and apparently seeing no evil in the sad results. Perhaps they thought it was no matter how soon the natives died, so that they died Christians.

And the civilization we have brought them means an endless day of labor, long hours of grinding toil for other people's profit, in place of the clean ease and freedom of their own old life. Hard labor, disease, death; and the lasting consciousness of all this among their dwindling ranks; exclusion, social dissemination, industrial exploitation, approaching extermination—it is no wonder their music is mournful.

I was glad to leave the lovely place; glad to put aside a sense of national guilt, and to see Ellador freshen again as the golden days and velvet nights flowed over us as we steamed toward the sunrise—and Home.

There were plenty of Californians on board, both wise and unwise, and I saw my wife, with a constantly increasing ease and skill, extracting information from each and all she talked with. It is not difficult to extract information about California from a Californian. Not being one myself; and having more definite knowledge about my own country than I had had about most of the others we had visited, I was able to check off this triumphant flood of "boosting" with somewhat colder facts.

Ellador liked it. "It does my heart good," she said, "both to know that there is such a country on earth, and that people can care for it like that."

She particularly revelled in Ina Coolbrith's exquisite poem "California," so rich with tender pride, with vivid appreciation. Some devotee had the book with her, and poured forth a new torrent of praise over a fine list she had of "Californian authors."

This annoyed me rather more than real estate, climate, fruit or flowers; and having been somewhat browbeaten over Hawaii, I wanted to take it out of somebody else. I am not as good as Ellador; don't pretend to be. At moments like that I don't even want to be. So I said to this bubbling enthusiast: "Why do you call all these people 'Californian authors?'"

She looked at me in genuine surprise.

"Were they born there?" I inquired. "Are they native sons or daughters?"

She had to admit they were not, save in a few cases. We marked those who were—it was a most insufficient list.

"But they lived in California," she insisted.

"How long?" I asked. "How long a visit or residence does it take to make an author a 'Californian'—like Mark Twain, for instance? Is he 'a Connecticut author' because he lived more years than that in Connecticut, or 'a New York author' because he lived quite a while in New York?"

She looked much annoyed, and I was not a bit sorry, but went on ruthlessly: "I think California is the only state in the Union that is not content with its own crop—but tries to claim everything in sight."

5

My Country

IN THROUGH THE GOLDEN GATE we steamed at last, one glorious morning; calm Tamalpais basking on the northern side, and the billowing city rising tumultously on the southern, with the brilliant beauty of "The Fair" glowing on the water's edge.

I had been through before, and showed her through the glass as we passed, the Seal Rocks and the Cliff House with the great Sutro Baths beside it; and then the jewelled tower, the streaming banners of that wonder-city of a year.

It was in February. There had been rain, and now the luminous rich green of the blazing sudden spring was cloaking every sloping shore. The long bay stretched wide on either hand; the fair bay cities opposite embroidered the western shore for miles; San Francisco rose before us.

Ellador stood by my side, holding my arm with tense excitement. "Your country, dear!" she said. "How beautiful it is! I shall love it!"

I was loving it myself, at that moment, as I never had before.

Behind me was that long journey of us three adventurous explorers; our longer imprisonment, and then these travels of ours, through war-torn Europe, and the slow dark reaches of the Oriental civilization.

"It certainly looks good to me!" I told her.

We spent many days at the great Exposition, and others, later, at the still lovelier, smaller one at San Diego,—days of great happiness to both of us, and real pride to me. Later on I lost this feeling—replacing it with a growing discomfort.

I suppose everyone loves and honors his own country—practically everyone. And we Americans, so young a people, so buoyantly carried along on the flood of easy geographical expansion, so suddenly increased in numbers, not by natural growth of our own stock but by crowding injections of alien blood, by vast hordes of low-grade laborers whose ignorant masses made our own ignorant masses feel superior to all the earth—we Americans are almost as boastful as the still newer Federation of Germany.

I had thought myself a sociologist, an ethnologist, one able to judge fairly from wide knowledge. And yet, with all my knowledge, with all my lucid criticism of my country's errors and shortcomings, I had kept an unshaken inner conviction of our superiority.

Ellador had shaken it.

It was not that she had found any fault with the institutions of my beloved land. Quite the contrary. She believed it faultless—or nearly so. She expected too much. Knowing her as I now did, becoming more and more familiar with the amazing lucidity and fairness of her mind, with its orderly marshalling of well-knit facts and the swinging searchlight of perception which covered every point in her field of vision, I had a strange helpless sense of coming to judgment.

In Herland I had never fully realized the quality of mind developed by their cultural system. Some of its power and clarity was of course plain to us, but we could no more measure that mind than a child can measure its teacher's. I had lived with it now, watched it work, seen it in relation to others, to those of learned men and women of various nations. There was no ostentation about Ellador's intellectual processes. She made no display of learning, did not contradict and argue. Sometimes, in questions of fact, if it seemed essential to the matter under discussion, she would quote authority in opposition, but for the most part she listened, asking a few questions to satisfy herself as to the point of view of her interlocutor. I used to note with appreciative delight how these innocent, almost irrelevant questions would bring out answers each one of which was a branching guide-post as to the mind of the speaker. Sometimes just two would show him to be capable of believing flat contradictions, or merely one would indicate a limitation of knowledge or an attitude of prejudice which "placed" the man at once. These were not "smart" questions, with a flippantly triumphant and all-too-logical demand at the end, leaving the victim confused and angry. He never realized what was being done to him.

"How do you have patience with these chumps?" I asked her. "They seem like children in your hands—and yet you don't hurt them a bit."

"Perhaps that is why," she answered gravely. "We are so used to children, at home—— And when a whole country is always, more or less, teaching children—why it makes us patient, I suppose. What good would it do to humiliate these people? They all know more than I do—about most things."

"They may know more, about some things, but it's their mental processes that seem so muddy—so sticky—so slow and fumbling somehow."

"You're right there, Van. It impresses me very much. There is an enormous fund of knowledge in the minds of your people—I mean any of these people I have met, but the minds themselves are—to me—astonishing. The Oriental mind is far more highly developed than the Occidental—in some lines; but as serenely unconscious of its limits as—as the other is. What strikes me most of all is the lack of connection between all this knowledge they have accumulated, and the way they live. I'm hoping to find it wholly different here. You Americans, I understand, are the people who do things."

Before I go on with Ellador's impressions of America I want to explain a little further, lest my native-born fellow-citizens resent too bitterly her ultimate criticisms. She perhaps would not have published those criticisms at all; but I can—now.

The sensitiveness I felt at first, the hurt pride, the honest pain, as my pet ideals inexorably changed color under that searchlight of hers, do what I would to maintain them in their earlier glory—all this is outgrown. I love my country, better than I ever did before. I understand it better—probably that accounts for the increased tenderness and patience. But if ever a country needed to wake up and look itself in the face, it is this one.

Ellador, in that amazing little pocket history she compiled, had set up the "order of exercises" in our development, and placed the nations in due sequence as contributors. Running over its neat pages, with the outline maps, the charts with their varied washes of color, showing this or that current of tendency and pressure of condition, one gathered at once a clear bird's eye view of what humanity had been doing all this time. She speculated sagely, with me, as to what trifling deflection of type, what variation in environment, was responsible for the divagation of races; especially those of quite recent common stock. But in the little book was no speculation, merely the simple facts.

Referring to it she could show in a few moments what special influences made Egypt Egypt, and differentiated Assyria from Chaldea. She shook her head sadly over those long early ages.

"They *were* slow to learn, weren't they?" she'd say; "Never seemed to put two and two together at all. I suppose that peculiar arrest of the mental processes was due first to mere social inertia, with its piled up weight of custom, and then much more to religion. That finality, that 'believing,' seemed to put an end to real thinking and learning."

"But, my dear," I interposed, "they were learned, surely. The ancient priests had practically all the learning, and in the Dark Ages, the Church in Europe was all that kept learning alive at all."

"Do you mean 'learning,' dear, or just 'remembering'?" she asked. "What did the Mediaeval Church 'learn'?"

This was a distinction I had never thought of. Of course what we have always called "learning" was knowing what went before—long before—and mostly what people had written. Still I made out something of a case about the study of alchemy and medicine—which she gravely admitted.

It remained true that the Church, any church, in any period, had set its face like a flint against the people's learning anything new; and, as we commonly know, had promptly punished the most progressive.

"It is a wonder to me," said Ellador, tenderly, "that you have done as well as you have—with all these awful handicaps. But you—America!—you have a different opportunity. I don't suppose you quite realize yourselves what a marvelous difference there is between you and every other people on earth."

Then she pointed out, briefly, how by the start in religious rebellion we had set free the mind from its heaviest shackles; by throwing off the monarchy and aristocracy we had escaped another weight; how our practically unlimited area and fluctuating condition made custom but a name; and how the mixture of races broke the current of heredity.

All this we had gone over on the steamer, sitting by the hour in our long chairs, watching the big smooth swells roll by, and talking of my country.

"You have reason to be proud," she would say. "No people on earth ever had such a chance."

I used to feel misgivings then, especially after Hawaii. I tried to arrange some satisfying defense for our treatment of the Asiatics, the Negroes, Mexico. I thought up all that I could to excuse the open evils that I knew—intemperance, prostitution, graft, lynching. I began to see more holes in the bright fabric of Columbia's robe than I had ever noticed before—and bigger ones. But at that I did not anticipate——.

We spent several weeks in California. I took her to see Shasta, the Yosemite, the cedars of Monterey, the Big Trees, the Imperial Valley. All through the country she poured out constant praises of the boundless loveliness of the land, the air, the sunshine, even the rain. Rain did not depress Ellador—she was a forester.

And she read, avidly. She read John Muir with rapture. "How I should have *loved* him!" she said. She read the brief history of the state, and some books about it—Ramona, for instance. She visited and talked with some leading Japanese—and Chinamen. And she read steadily, with a fixed non-committal face, the newspapers.

If I asked her anything about it all she would pour forth honest delight in the flowers and fruit, the beauty and brightness of the land. If I pressed for more, she would say: "Wait, Van dear—give me time. I've only just come—I don't know enough yet to talk!"

But, I knowing how quickly she learned, and how accurately she related new knowledge to old, watched her face with growing dismay. In Europe I had seen that beautiful face pale with horror; in Asia, sicken with loathing; now, after going around the world; after reaching this youngest land, this land of hope and pride, of wealth and power, I saw that face I loved so well, set in sad lines of disappointment—fairly age before my eyes.

She was still cheerful, with me, still happy out of doors; and her heart rose as I had hoped it would among the mountains, on the far-spread lustrous deserts, in that wordless wonder, the Grand Canyon of the Colorado.

But as she read, as she sat thinking, I could see the light die out of her face and a depressing look creep over it; a look of agonized disappointment, yet of patience too—and a courageous deep determination. It was as if a mother had learned that her baby was an idiot. * * *

As we drew eastward and the cities grew larger, noisier, blacker, her distress increased. She began to urge me to play games with her; to read aloud from books she loved; and especially to talk of Herland.

I was willing; more than willing. As I saw my country through her eyes—as I saw its effect on her—I became less and less inclined, indeed less able, to discuss it with her. But the tension grew; her suffering increased; until I told her as I had that terrible night in Europe, that she must talk to me about it.

"You see you will have to, whether you want to or not," I argued. "You cannot take all America to task about itself—you would get yourself disliked. Besides—if you don't want to tell them about your country—and if you pitch into theirs, they will insist on knowing where you come from, quite naturally. I can't bear to see you getting more and more distressed and saying nothing about it. Besides—it is barely possible that I might offer some palliation, or explanation, of some of the worst things."

"What do you consider 'the worst things'?" she asked casually enough.

But I was already wise enough to see at once that we might not agree on definition.

"Suppose we do this," I suggested. "Here are you, as extramundane as a Martian. You are like an Investigating Committee from another world. Quite apart from my love for you, my sympathy with you, my admiration for you—yes, all serious and sincere, my dear—I do appreciate this unparalleled opportunity to get a real outsider's point of view.

"This is something that never happened before, you see; Marco Polo came nearest to it, perhaps, when he went poking into the Asiatic wonderland. But these old adventurers of ours, whatever their hardships, never took it so hard as you do. They enjoyed satisfying their curiosity; they always thought their own birthplace infinitely superior, and the more inferior they found other places the more they enjoyed it. Now with you—it seems to hurt your feelings most horribly. I wish you could somehow detach yourself from it—so that you could learn, and not suffer."

"You are quite right, dear boy—it is most unphilosophical of me. I suppose it is largely a result of our long period of—lovingness—at home, that things strike so harshly on my mind."

"And partly your being a woman, don't you think?" I urged. "You see yours is a feminine culture and naturally more sensitive, isn't it?"

"Perhaps that is it," she said, pondering. "The very first thing that strikes me in this great rich lovely land of yours is its *unmotherliness*. We are of course used to seeing everything taken care of."

"But surely, it was worse—far worse—in the other countries wasn't it?"

She smiled tenderly and sadly. "Yes, Van, it was—but here—well, doubtless I expected too much."

"But isn't there some comfort in the contrast?" I asked eagerly. "Here is not the petrified oppression, the degradation of women, that so sickened you in Asia; and here is not the wild brutality of war that so horrified you in Europe."

"No—not either of those," she slowly agreed. "But you see I had warning that Europe was at war, and had read about it a little. It was like going into a—a slaughter-house, for the first time.

"Then all I learned in my studies in Europe prepared me to find what I did find in Asia—Asia was in some ways better than I had been told—in some ways worse. But here! * * * Oh, Van!" That look of gray anguish had settled on her face again. She seized my arms, held me fast, searched my face as if I was withholding something. Big slow tears welled over and dropped. "This is the top of the tree, Van; this is the last young nation, beginning over again in a New World—a New World! Here was everything to make life richly happy—everything. And you had all the dreadful record of the past to guide you, to teach you at least what not to do. You had courage; you had independence; you had intelligence, education, opportunity. And such splendid principles to start with—such high ideals. And then all kinds of people coming! Oh, surely, surely, surely this should be the Crown of the World!

"Why, Van—Europe was like a man with—with delirium tremens. Asia was like something gnarled and twisted with hopeless age. But America is a Splendid Child . . . with . . ." She covered her face with her hands.

I couldn't stand this. I was an American, and she was my wife. I took her in my arms.

"Look here, you blessed Herlander," I said, "I'm not going to have my country wiped off the map in disgrace. You must remember that all judgment is comparative. You cannot compare any other country with your country for two reasons; first your long isolation, and second that miraculous manlessness of yours.

"This world of ours has been in more or less intercourse and exchange for many more thousands of years than Herland has lived. We Americans were not a new created race—we were just English and Dutch and French and Scandinavian and Italian, and so on—just everybody. We brought with us our inherited tendencies, of course—all of them. And while we did make a clean break with some of the old evils, we had no revelation as to a perfect social method. You are expecting too much . . .

"Don't you see," I went on, for she said nothing, "that a Splendid Child may be a pretty bad child, sometimes, and may have the measles pretty hard—and yet not be hopeless?"

She raised her wet face from my shoulder and her own warm loving smile illuminated it once more.

"You're right, Van, you're wholly right," she agreed. "I was most unreasonable, most unwise. It is just a piece of the same world—a lot of pieces—mixed samples—on a new piece of ground. And it was a magnificent undertaking—I can see that—and you *are* young, aren't you? Oh, Van dear, you do make it easier."

I held her very close for awhile. This journey among strange lands had brought me one deep joy. Ellador had grown to need me as she never did in her own peaceful home.

"You see, dearest," I said, "you have a dual mission. You are to study all about the world and take your knowledge back with you—but all you need of it there is to decide whether you'll come out and play with us or not—or let any more of us come in. Then you have what I, as a citizen of the rest of the world—rather the biggest part of it, consider a more important duty. If that Herland mind of yours can find out what ails us—and how we are to mend it; if your little country with its strange experiment can bring aid in solving the problems of the world—that is what I call a Historic Mission! How does that strike you, Mrs. Jennings?"

It was good to see her rise to it. That wonderful motherheart, which all those women had, seemed to shine out like a sunrise. I went on, delighted with my success.

"I'll just forget I'm an American," I said. "This country is The Child. I'm not its father or anything—I'm just a doctor, a hygienist, an investigator. You're another—and a bigger one. Now I understand that you find The Child is in a bad way—worse off than I thought it was. To judge from your expression, dear, on several occasions, you think it is a very dirty child, a careless child, a wasteful child, with a bad temper and no manners—am I right?"

"Not about the temper, dear. Pettish at times, but not vindictive, and very, very kind. . . . Van . . . I think I've been too hard on The Child! I'm quite ashamed. Yes, we are two investigators—I'm so glad there are two!"

She stopped and looked at me with an expression I never saw enough of, that I used to long for in vain, at first; that look as if she *needed* me.

"No matter what we have in Herland," she said slowly, "we miss this—this united feeling. It grows, Van; I feel more and more as if—somehow or other—we were really *blended*. We have nothing just like it."

"No, you haven't—with all your Paradise. So let's allow some good things in your 'case,' and particularly in this case of the bad child. And we'll pitch in and work out a diagnosis—won't we? And then prescribe."

We pitched in.

First she had insisted on knowing the whole country. We made a sort of spiral, beginning on the outside, and circulated south, east, north, west, and so over again; till we wound ourselves up in Topeka. By that time we had been in every state, in all the principal cities, and in many of those tiny towns which are more truly indicative of the spirit of the community than the larger ones.

When we were interested in a given place we would stay awhile—there was nothing to hurry us; and when Ellador showed signs of wear and tear there was always some sweet wild country to fly to, and rest. She sampled both sea-coasts, the Great Lakes, and some little ones, many a long winding river, mountains wooded and mountains bare; the restful plains, the shadowy cypress swamps.

Her prompt reaction to the beauty of the real country was always beneficial, and, to my great delight she grew to love it, and even to feel a pride in its vast extent and variety—just as I did. We both admitted that it was a most illegitimate ground for pride, but we both felt it.

As she saw more of the cities, and of the people, by mere usage she grew accustomed to what had grieved her most at first. Also I suggested a method which she gladly used, and found most comforting, in which we classified all the evils as "transient," and concerned ourselves merely with finding out how they came there and how to remove them.

"Some of these things you'll just outgrow," she said relievedly. "Some are already outgrown. America is not nearly so—cocky—as Dickens found her. She is now in an almost morbid attitude of self-distrust and condemnation—but she'll outgrow that too."

It was a great relief to me to have her push through that period of shocked disappointment so readily. But of course the vigor of her mental constitution made it possible for her to throw off a trouble like that more easily than we can do it.

She soon devised methods of her own of acquiring further information. In her capacity of a traveler, and recently come from the seat of war, to say nothing of the Orient, she found frequent opportunity for addressing women's clubs, churches and forums of various kinds, and so coming in touch with large bodies of people; and their reactions.

"I am learning to realize 'the popular mind,' " she said. "I can already distinguish between the different parts of the country. And, oh, Van——" she laughed a little, caught her breath over, and added with an odd restraint: "I'm getting to know the—women."

"Why do you say it like that?" I inquired.

She looked at me in what I might describe as "forty ways at once." It was funny. There was such an odd mixture of pride and shame, of hope and disillusionment; of a high faith and a profound distrust.

"I can stand it," she protested. "The Child is by no means hopeless—in fact I begin to think it is a very promising child, Van. But, oh, how it does behave!"

And she laughed.

I was a little resentful. We were such good chums by this time; we had played together such a lot, and studied together so widely; we had such a safe foundation of mutual experience that I began to dare to make fun of my strange Princess now and then, and she took it most graciously.

"There's one thing I won't stand for," I told her solemnly. "You can call my country a desert, my people incompetent, dishonest, wasteful and careless to a degree; you can blackguard our agriculture, horticulture, aboriculture, floriculture, viticulture, and—and—("Apiculture," she suggested, with a serious face.)—you can deride our architecture and make trivial objections to the use of soot as a civic decoration; but there is one thing I, as an American Man, will not stand—you mustn't criticize our Women!"

"I won't," she said meekly, a twinkle in her eye. "I won't say one word about them, dear—until you ask me to!"

Whereat I knew that my doom was sealed once more. Could I rest without knowing what she thought of them?

6

The Diagnosis

"HOW ARE YOU GETTING ON WITH 'THE CASE,' MRS. J.?" I asked Ellador one evening when she seemed rather discouraged. "What symptoms are worrying you most now?"

She looked at me with wide anxious eyes, too much in earnest to mind the "Mrs. J.," which usually rather teased her.

"It's an awfully important case, Van dear," she answered soberly, "and a serious one—very serious, I think. I've been reading a lot, had to, to get background and perspective, and I feel as if I understood a good deal better. Still———. You helped me ever so much by saying that you were not new people, just mixed Europeans. But the new country and the new conditions began to make you all into a new people. Only———."

"These pauses are quite terrifying," I protested. "Won't you explain your ominous 'still,' and sinister 'only'?"

She smiled a little. "Why the 'still' should have been followed by the amount I did not understand, and the 'only'———." She stopped again.

"Well, out with it, my dear. Only what?"

"Only you have done it too fast and too much in the dark. You weren't conscious you see."

"Not conscious—America not conscious?"

"Not self-conscious, I mean, Van."

This I scouted entirely, till she added patiently: "Perhaps I should say nationally conscious, or socially conscious. You were plunged into an enormous social enterprise, a huge swift, violent experiment; the current of social evolution burst forth over here like a subterranean river finding an outlet. Things that the stratified crust of Asia could not let through, and the heavy shell of European culture could not either, just burst forth over here and swept you along. Democracy had been—accumulating, through all the centuries. The other nations forced it back, held it down. It boiled over in France, but the lid was clapped on again for awhile. Here it could pour forward—and it poured. Then all the people of the same period of social development wanted to come too, and did,—lots of them. That was inevitable. All that 'America' means in this sense is a new phase of social development, and anyone can be an American who belongs to it."

"Guess you are right so far, Mrs. Doctor. Go ahead!"

"But while this was happening to you, you were doing things yourselves, some of them in line with your real position and movement, some dead against it. For instance, your religion."

"Religion against what? Expound further."

"Against Democracy."

"You don't mean the Christian religion, do you?" I urged, rather shocked.

"Oh, no, indeed. That would have been a great help to the world if they had ever taken it up."

I was always entertained and somewhat startled by Ellador's detached view. She knew the same facts so familiar to us, but they had not the same connotations.

"I think Jesus was simply wonderful," she went on. "What a pity it was he did not live longer!"

This was a new suggestion to me. Of course I no longer accepted that pitiful old idea of his being a pre-arranged sacrifice to his own father, but I never deliberately thought of his having continued alive, and its possible effects.

"He is supposed to have been executed at about the age of thirty-three, was he not?" she went on. "Think of it—hardly a grown man! He should have had thirty or forty more years of teaching. It would all have become clearer, more consistent. He would have worked things out, explained them, made people understand. He would have made clear to them what they were to *do*. It was an awful loss."

I said nothing at all, but watched the sweet earnest face, the wise far-seeing eyes, and really agreed with her, though in my mind rose a confused dim throng of horrified objections belonging not to my own mind, but to those of other people.

"Tell me how you mean that our religion was against democracy," I persisted.

"It was so personal," she said, "and so unjust. There must have crept into it, in early times, a lot of the Buddhist philosophy, either direct or filtered, the 'acquiring merit' idea, and asceticism. The worst part of all was the idea of sacrifice—that is *so* ancient. Of course what Jesus meant was social unity, that your neighbor *was* yourself—that we were all one humanity—'many gifts, but the same spirit.' He must have meant that—for that is So.

"What I mean by 'your religion' is the grade of Calvinism which dominated young America, with the still older branches, and the various small newer ones. It was all so personal. My soul—*my* salvation. My conscience—*my* sins. And here was the great living working truth of democracy carrying you on in spite of yourselves—*E Pluribus Unum*.

"Your economic philosophy was dead against it too—that foolish *laissez-faire* idea. And your politics, though what was new in it started pretty well, has never been able to make much headway against the highest religious sanction, the increasing economic pressure, and the general drag of custom and tradition—inertia."

"You are somewhat puzzling, my fair Marco Polo," I urged. "So you mean to extol our politics, American politics?"

"Why of course!" she said, her eyes shining. "The principles of democracy are wholly right. The law of federation, the method of rotation in office, the stark necessity for general education that the people may understand clearly, the establishment of liberty—that they may act freely—it is splendidly, gloriously right! But why do I say this to an American!"

"I wish you could say it to every American man, woman, and child," I answered soberly. "Of course we used to feel that way about it, but things have changed somehow."

"Yes, yes," she went on eagerly. "That's what I mean. You started right, for the most part, but those high-minded brave old ancestors of yours did not understand sociology—how should they? it wasn't even born. They did not know how society worked, or what would hurt it the most. So the preachers went on exhorting the people to save their own souls, or get it done for them by imputed virtues of someone else—and no one understood the needs of the country.

"Why, Van! Vandyke Jennings! As I understand more and more how noble and courageous and high-minded was this Splendid Child, and then see it now, bloated and weak, with unnatural growth, preyed on by all manner of parasites inside and out, attacked by diseases of all kinds, sneered at, criticized, condemned by the older nations, and yet bravely stumbling on, making progress in spite of it all—I'm getting to just *love* America!"

That pleased me, naturally, but I didn't like her picture of my country as bloated and verminous. I demanded explanation.

"Do you think we're too big?" I asked. "Too much country to be handled properly?"

"Oh, *no!*" she answered promptly. "Not too big in land. That would have been like the long lean lines of youth, the far-reaching bones of a country gradually rounding out and filling in as you grow. But you couldn't wait to grow, you just—swelled."

"What on earth do you mean, Ellador?"

"You have stuffed yourself with the most ill-assorted and unassimilable mass of human material that ever was held together by artificial means," she answered remorselessly. "You go to England, and the people are English. Only three per cent. of aliens even in London, I understand. And in France the people are French—bless them! And in Italy, Italian. But here—it's no wonder I was discouraged at first. It has taken a lot of study and hard thinking, to see a way out at all. But I do see it. It was simply awful when I began.

"Just look! Here you were, a little band of really promising people, of different nations, yet of the same general stock, and *like-minded*—that was the main thing. The real union is the union of idea; without that—no nation. You made settlements, you grew strong and bold, you shook off the old government, you set up a new flag, and then——!"

"Then," said I proudly, "we opened our arms to all the world, if that is what you are finding fault with. We welcomed other people to our big new country—'the poor and oppressed of all nations!'" I quoted solemnly.

"That's what I mean by saying you were ignorant of sociology," was her cheerful reply. "It never occurred to you that the poor and oppressed were not necessarily good stuff for a democracy."

I looked at her rather rebelliously.

"Why, just study them," she went on, in that large sweeping way of hers. "Hadn't there been poor and oppressed enough in the past? In Chaldaea and Assyria and Egypt and Rome—in all Europe—everywhere? Why, Van, it is the poor and oppressed who make monarchy and despotism—don't you see that?"

"Hold on, my dear—hold on! This is too much. Are you *blaming* the poor helpless things for their tyrannical oppression?"

"No more than I blame an apple-tree for bearing apples," she answered. "You don't seriously advance the idea that the oppressor began it, do you? Just one oppressor jumping on the necks of a thousand free men? Surely you see that the general status and character of a people creates and maintains its own kind of government?"

"Y-e-es," I agreed. "But all the same, they are *human*, and if you give them proper conditions they can all rise—surely we have proved that."

"Give them proper conditions, and give them time—yes."

"Time! They do it in one generation. We have citizens, good citizens, of all races, who were born in despotic countries, all equal in our democracy."

"How many Chinese and Japanese citizens have you?" she asked quietly. "How are your African citizens treated in this 'equal' democracy!"

This was rather a facer.

"About the first awful mistake you made was in loading yourself up with those reluctant Africans," Ellador went on. "If it wasn't so horrible, it would be funny, awfully funny. A beautiful healthy young country, saddling itself with an antique sin every other civilized nation had repudiated. And here they are, by millions and millions, flatly denied citizenship, socially excluded, an enormous alien element in your democracy."

"They are not aliens," I persisted stoutly. "They are Americans, loyal Americans; they make admirable soldiers——"

"Yes, and servants. You will let them serve you and fight for you—but that's all, apparently. Nearly a tenth of the population, and not part of the democracy. And they never asked to come!"

"Well," I said, rather sullenly. "I admit it—everyone does. It was an enormous costly national mistake, and we paid for it heavily. Also it's there yet, an unsolved question. I admit it all. Go on please. We were dead wrong on the blacks, and pretty hard on the reds; we may be wrong on the yellows. I guess this is a white man's country, isn't it? You're not objecting to the white immigrants, are you?"

"To legitimate immigrants, able and willing to be American citizens, there can be no objection, unless even they come too fast. But to millions of deliberately imported people, not immigrants at all, but victims, poor ignorant people scraped up by paid agents, deceived by lying advertisements, brought over here by greedy American ship owners and employers of labor—there are objections many and strong."

"But, Ellador—even granting it is as you say, they too can be made into American citizens, surely?"

"They can be, but are they? I suppose you all tacitly assume that they are; but an outsider does not see it. We have been all over the country now, pretty thoroughly. I have met and talked with people of all classes and all races, both men and women. Remember I'm new to 'the world,' and I've just come here from studying Europe, and Asia, and Africa. I have the hinterland of history pretty clearly summarized, though of course I can't pretend to be thorough, and I tell you, Van, there are millions of people in your country who do not belong to it at all."

She saw that I was about to defend our foreign born, and went on: "I do not mean the immigrants solely. There are Bostonians of Beacon Hill who belong in London; there are New Yorkers of five generations who belong in Paris; there are vast multitudes who belong in Berlin, in Dublin, in Jerusalem; and there are plenty of native Sons and Daughters of the Revolution who are aristocrats, plutocrats, anything but democrats."

"Why of course there are! We believe in having all kinds—there's room for everybody—this is the 'melting-pot,' you know."

"And do you think that you can put a little of everything into a melting-pot and produce a good metal? Well fused and flawless? Gold, silver, copper and iron, lead, radium, pipe clay, coal dust, and plain dirt?"

A simile is an untrustworthy animal if you ride it too hard. I grinned and admitted that there were limits to the powers of fusion.

"Please understand," she urged gently. "I am not looking down on one kind of people because they are different from others. I like them all. I think your prejudice against the black is silly, wicked, and—hypocritical. You have no idea how ridiculous it looks, to an outsider, to hear your Southern enthusiasts raving about the horrors of 'miscegenation' and then to count the mulattos, quadroons, octoroons and all the successive shades by which the black race becomes white before their eyes. Or to see them shudder at 'social equality' while the babies are nourished at black breasts, and cared for in their most impressionable years by black nurses—their *children*!"

She stopped at that, turned away from me and walked to the opposite window, where she stood for some time with her hands clenched and her shoulders heaving.

"Where was I?" she asked presently, definitely dropping the question of children. "Black—yes, and how about the yellow? Do they 'melt'? Do you want them to melt? Isn't your exclusion of them an admission that you think some kinds of people unassimilable? That democracy must pick and choose a little?"

"What would you have us do?" I asked rather sullenly. "Exclude everybody? Think we are superior to the whole world?"

Ellador laughed, and kissed me. "I think *you* are," she whispered tenderly. "No—I don't mean that at all. It would be too great a strain on the imagination! If you want a prescription—far too late—it is this: Democracy is a psychic relation. It requires the intelligent conscious co-operation of a great many persons all 'equal' in the characteristics required to play that kind of a game. You could have safely welcomed to your great undertaking people of every race and nation who were individually fitted to assist. Not by any means because they were 'poor and oppressed,' nor because of that glittering generality that 'all men are born free and equal,' but because the human race is in different stages of development, and only some of the races—or some individuals in a given race—have reached the democratic stage."

"But how could we discriminate?"

"You mustn't ask me too much, Van. I'm a stranger; I don't know all I ought to, and, of course I'm all the time measuring by my background of experience in my own country. I find you people talk a good bit about the Brotherhood of Man, but you haven't seemed to think about the possibilities of a sisterhood of women."

I looked up alertly, but she gave a mischievous smile and shook her head. "You do not want to hear about the women, I remember. But seriously, dear, this is one of the most dangerous mistakes you have made; it complicates everything. It makes your efforts to establish democracy like trying to make a ship go by steam and at the same time admitting banks of oars, masses of sails and cordage, and mere paddles and outriggers."

"You can certainly make some prescription for this particularly dreadful state, can't you?" I urged. "Sometimes 'an outsider' can see better than those who are—being melted."

She pondered awhile, then began slowly: "Legitimate immigration is like the coming of children to you,—new blood for the nation, citizens made, not born. And they should be met like children, with loving welcome, with adequate preparation, with the fullest and wisest education for their new place. Where you have that crowded little filter on Ellis Island, you ought to have Immigration Bureaus on either coast, at ports so specified, with a great additional department to definitely Americanize the newcomers, to teach them the language, spirit, traditions and customs of the country. Talk about offering hospitality to all the world! What kind of hospitality is it to let your guests crowd and pack into the front hall, and to offer them neither bed, bread nor association? That's what I mean by saying that you are not conscious. You haven't taken your immigration seriously enough. The consequence is that you are only partially America, an America clogged and confused, weakened and mismanaged, for lack of political compatibility."

"Is this all?" I asked after a little. "You make me feel as if my country was a cross between a patchwork quilt and a pudding stone."

"Oh, dear, no!" she cheerfully assured me. "That's only a beginning of my diagnosis. The patient's worst disease was that disgraceful out-of-date attack of slavery, only escaped by a surgical operation, painful, costly, and not by any means wholly successful. The second is this chronic distension from absorbing too much and too varied material, just pumping it in at wild speed. The third is the most conspicuously foolish of all—to a Herlander."

"Oh—leaving the women out?"

"Yes. It's so—so—well, I can't express to you how *ridiculous* it looks."

"We're getting over it," I urged. "Eleven states now, you know—it's getting on."

"Oh, yes, yes, it's getting on. But I'm looking at your history, and your conditions, and your loud complaints, and then to see this great mass of fellow-citizens treated as if they weren't there—it is unbelievable!"

"But I told you about that before we came," said I. "I told you in Herland—you knew it."

"I knew it, truly. But, Van, suppose anyone had told you that in Herland women were the only citizens—would that have prevented your being surprised?"

I looked back for a moment, remembering how we men, after living there so long, after "knowing" that women were the only citizens, still never got over the ever recurring astonishment of *realizing* it.

"No wonder it surprises you, dear,—I should think it would. But go on about the women."

"I'm not touching on the women at all, Van. This is only in treating of democracy—of your country and what ails it. You see——"

"Well, dear? See what?"

"It is so presumptuous of me to try to explain democracy to you, an American citizen. Of course you understand, but evidently the country at large doesn't. In a monarchy you have this one allowed Ruler, and his subordinate rulers, and the people submit to them. Sometimes it works very well, but in any case it is something done for and to the people by someone they let do it.

"A democracy, a real one, means the people socially conscious and doing it themselves—doing it *themselves*! Not just electing a Ruler and subordinates and submitting to them—transferring the divine right of kings to the divine right of alderman or senators. A democracy is a game everybody has to play—*has* to—else it is not a democracy. And here you people deliberately left out half!"

"But they never had been 'in'; you know, in the previous governments."

"Now, Van—that's really unworthy of you. As subjects they were the same as men, and as queens they were the same as kings. But you began a new game—that you *said* must be 'by the people'—and so on, and left out half."

"It was—funny," I admitted, "and unfortunate. But we're improving. Do go on."

"That's three counts, I believe," she agreed. "Next lamentable mistake,—failure to see that democracy must be economic."

"Meaning socialism?"

"No, not exactly. Meaning what Socialism means, or ought to mean. You could not have a monarchy where the king was in no way different from his subjects. A monarchy must be expressed not only in the immediate symbols of robe and crown, throne and sceptre, but in the palace and the court, the list of lords and gentlemen-in-waiting. It's all part of monarchy.

"So you cannot have a democracy while there are people markedly differentiated from the others, with symbolism of dress and decoration, with courts and palaces and crowds of servitors."

"You can't except all the people to be just alike, can you?"

"No, nor even to be 'equal.' Some people will always be more valuable than others, and some more useful than others; but a poet, a blacksmith, and a dancing master might all be friends and fellow-citizens in a true democratic sense. Your millionaires vote and your day-laborers vote, but it does not bring them together as fellow citizens. That's why your little old New England towns and your fresh young western ones, have more of 'America' in them than is possible—could ever be possible—in such a political menagerie as New York, for instance."

"Meaning the Tiger?" I inquired.

"Including the Tiger, with the Elephant, the Moose and the Donkey— specially the Donkey! No—I do not really mean those—totems. I mean the weird collection of political methods, interests, stages of growth.

"New York's an oligarchy; it's a plutocracy; it's a hierarchy; it reverts to the clan system with its Irishmen, and back of that, to the patriarchy, with its Jews. It's anything and everything you like—but it's not a democracy."

"If it was, what would it do to prove it? Just what do you expect of what you call democracy? Don't you idealize it?" I asked.

"No." She shook her head decidedly. "I do not idealize it. I'm familiar with it, you see—we have one at home, you know."

So they had. I had forgotten. In fact I had not very clearly noticed. We had been so much impressed by their all being women that we had not done justice to their political development.

"It's no miracle," she said. "Just people co-operating to govern themselves. We have universal suffrage, you know, and train our children in the use of it before they come to the real thing. That far-seeing Mr. Gill is trying to do that in your public schools, I notice, and Mr. George of the Junior Republics. It requires a common knowledge of the common need, local self-management, recognizing the will of the majority, and a big ceaseless loving effort to make the majority wiser. It's surely nothing so wonderful, Van, for a lot of intelligent people to get together and manage their common interests."

It certainly had worked well in Herland. So well, so easily, so smoothly, that it was hardly visible.

"But the people who get together have got to be within reach of one another," she went on. "They've got to have common interests. What united action can you expect between Fifth Avenue and—Avenue A?"

"I've had all I can stand for one dose, my lady," I now protested. "From what you have said I should think your 'Splendid Child' would have died in infancy—a hundred years ago. But we *haven't* you see. We're alive and kicking—especially kicking. I have faith in my country yet."

"It is still able to lead the world—if it will," she agreed. "It has still all the natural advantages it began with, and it has added new ones. I'm not despairing, nor blaming, Van—I'm diagnosing, and pretty soon I'll prescribe. But just now I suggest that we change politics for tennis."

We did. I can still beat her at tennis—having played fifteen years to her one—but not so often as formerly.

7

In Our Homes

IF THERE WAS ONE THING more than another I had wanted to show Ellador it was our homes,—my home, of course, and others that I knew.

In all the peace and beauty of Herland there was nowhere the small lit circle of intimate love and mutually considered comfort which means so much to us. The love, the comfort, were everywhere, to be sure, but that was different. It was like reflected lighting instead of a lamp on the center table; it was like an evenly steam-heated house, instead of one with an open fire in each room. We had missed those fires, so warm to the front, so inadequate on the back, so inclusive of those who can sit near it, so exclusive of everyone else.

Now, as we visited far and wide, and as Ellador, in her new capacity as speaker to clubs and churches went farther and wider, she was becoming well acquainted with our American homes, it seemed to me.

But it did not satisfy her. She had become more and more the sociologist, the investigator.

"They are all alike," she said. "The people vary, of course, but the setting is practically the same. Why, Van—in all my visits, in so many states, in so many kind families, I've found the most amusing similarity in homes. I can find the bathroom in the dark; I know just what they'll have for breakfast; there seem to be only some eight or ten dinners or luncheons known."

I was a little nettled,—just a little.

"There is a limit to edible animals, if that's what you mean," I protested. "Beef and veal, mutton and lamb, pig,—fresh, salted and smoked—poultry and game. Oh, and fish."

"That's ten, and can be stretched, of course. No, I don't mean the basis of supplies. I mean only the lack of—of specialization in it all. You see the women have talked with me-eagerly. It really is pathetic, Van, the effort—effort—effort, to do what ought to be so easy. And the expense!"

"We know it is laborious, but most women hold it is their duty, dear. Of course, I agree with you, but most of our people don't, you see. And the men, I'm afraid, consider their own comfort."

"I only wish they did," she remarked, surprisingly. "But I'm studying the home not merely on the economic side; I'm studying it as a world institution—it's new to me, you see. Europe—Africa—Asia—the Islands—America—see here, dear, we haven't seen South America. Let's learn Spanish and go!"

Ellador spoke of learning a new language as if it were a dance, a brief and entertaining process. We did it, too; at least she did. I knew some Spanish already and polished it up with her new enthusiasm to help. It was not until observing her intellectual processes in our journeyings together that I had realized the potential energy of the Herland mind. Its breadth and depth, its calm control, its rationality, its fertility of resource, were apparent while we were there, but accustomed as I was to the common limitations of our own minds, to the narrow specialization with accompanying atrophy of other powers, to the "brain-fag" and mental breakdown, with all the deadly lower grades of feeble-mindedness and last gulf of insanity—I had not realized that these disabilities were unknown in Herland. A healthy brain does not show, any more than a sick one, and the airy strength of a bounding acrobat can hardly be judged if you see him in a hammock.

For this last year or two I was observing a Herland brain at work, assimilating floods of new impressions, suffering keen and severe emotional shocks, hampered by an inevitable nostalgia, and yet picking up languages in passing as one picks flowers by the roadside.

We made our trip to South America, with Spanish history carefully laid in beforehand, and learned what everyone of us ignorant United Statesians ought to know,—that "America" is a world-spanning double continent, not merely a patch on one, and that, if we do our duty by our brother countries, we may some day fill out legitimately that large high-sounding name of ours and really be The United States of America.

"I certainly have enough data now to be fair in my deduction," Ellador said, on our home trip. "It has been awfully interesting, visiting your world. And coming back to your country now, with wider knowledge and a background of experience, I think I can be fairer to it. So if you're ready, we'll go back to where we left off that day I jumped to South America."

She turned over her book of notes on the United States and looked at me cheerfully.

"Homes," she said, "The Home, The American Home—and the homes of all the rest of the world, past and present——"

I tucked the Kenwood rug closer about her feet, settled my own, and prepared to listen.

"Yes, ma'am. Here you and I, at great expense, have circled the habitable globe, been most everywhere except to Australasia and South Africa—spent a good year canvassing the U.S.—and if you're not ready to give us your diagnosis—*and* prescriptions—why, I shall lose faith in Herland!"

"Want it for the world—or just your country?" she asked serenely.

"Oh, well, give us both; you're capable of it. But not quite all at once—I couldn't take it in. America first, please."

"It's not so long," she began slowly. "Not if you generalize, safely. One could, of course, say that because the Jones children were let alone they spilled the ink, teased the dog, hurt the kitten, let the canary out, ate too much jam, soiled their clothes, pulled up the tulip bulbs, smeared the wall-paper, broke the china, tore the curtains—and so forth, and so forth, and so forth. And you could tell just how it happened in each case—that would take some time. Especially if you added a similar account of the Smith children and the Brown children and so on. But if you say: 'Neglected children are liable to become mischievous,' you've said it all."

"Don't be as short as that," I begged. "It would not be illuminating."

We spent many hours on the endless subject,—rich, fruitful hours, full of insight, simplification, and hope.

"I'm not so shocked as I was at first," she told me. "I've seen that Europe goes on being Europe even if each nation loses a million men—two million men. They'll grow again. * * * I see that all this horror is no new thing to the world—poor world—poor, wretched, blind baby! But it's a sturdy baby for all that. It's *Here*—it has not died. * * *

"What seems to be the matter, speaking very generally, is this: People have not understood their own works—their social nature, that is. They have not understood—that's all."

"Stupid? Hopelessly stupid?" I asked.

"Not at all—not in the least—but here's the trouble: their minds were always filled up beforehand with what they used to believe. Talk about putting new wine in old bottles—it's putting old wine in new bottles that has kept the world back.

"You can see it all the way long," she pursued. "New life, continually arising, new condition, but always the old, older, oldest ideas, theories, beliefs. Every nation, every race, hampered and hag-ridden by what it used to think, used to believe, used to know. And all the nice, fresh, eager, struggling children forcibly filled up with the same old stuff. It is pretty terrible, Van. But it's so—funny—that I can stand it. In one way human misery is a joke—because you don't have to have it!

"Then you people came over to a New Continent and started a New Country, with a lot of New Ideas—yet you kept enough old ones to drown any country. No wonder you've splashed so much—just to keep above water."

I didn't say much. I wanted her to work it out, gradually. She was letting me see her do it. Of course, in this record I'm piecing together a great many talks, a great many ideas, and I'm afraid leaving out some. It was no light matter she had undertaken, even for a Herlander.

"This family and home idea is responsible for a great part of it," she said. "Not, as I find you quite generally believe, as a type and pattern of all that is good and lovely, but as a persistent primitive social group, interfering with the development of later groups. If you look at what you ought to have evolved by this time, it becomes fairly easy to see what is the matter.

"Take your own case—with its wonderful new start—a clean slate of a country, and a very good installation of people to begin with. A good religion, too, in essence, and a prompt appreciation of the need of being generally educated. Then your splendid political opening—the great wave of democracy pouring out into expression. Room for all, wealth for all. What should have been the result—easily? Why, Van—the proudest Yankee, Southerner, Westerner, that ever lived doesn't begin to estimate what your people might have done!

"What they have done is a good deal—but, Oh—what they might have done! You see, they didn't *understand* democracy. They began to play, but they didn't know the game. It was like a small child, running a big auto. Democracy calls for the conscious intelligent co-ordinate action of all the people. Without it, it is like a partly paralyzed king.

"First you left out half the people—an awful mistake. You only gradually took in the other half. You saw dimly the need of education, but you didn't know what education was— 'reading, writing, and arithmetic,' are needed, even in monarchies. You needed special education in the new social process.

"Democracy calls for the understanding, recognition, and universal practice of social laws,—laws which are 'natural,' like those of physics and chemistry; but your religion—and your education, too—taught Authority—not real law. You couldn't make a good electrician on mere authority, could you? He has to understand, not merely obey. Neither can you so make the citizens of a democracy. Reverence for and submission to authority are right in monarchies—wrong in democracies. When Demos is King he must learn to act for himself, not to do as he is told.

"And back of your Christian religion is the Hebrew; back of that—The Family. It all comes down to that absurd root error of the proprietary family."

We were easily at one in this view, but I had never related it to America's political shortcomings before.

"That old Boss Father is behind God," she went on calmly. "The personal concept of God as a father, with his special children, his benign patronage, his quick rage, long anger, and eternal vengeance——" she shivered, "it is an ugly picture.

"The things men have thought about God," she said slowly, "are a ghastly proof of the way they have previously behaved. As they have improved, their ideas of God have improved slowly.

"When Kings were established, they crystallized the whole thing, in plain sight, and you had Kings a very long time, you see—have them yet. Kings and Fathers, Bosses, Rulers, Masters, Overlords—it is all such a poor preparation for democracy. Fathers and Kings and the Hebrew Deity are behind you and above you. Democracy is before you, around you; it is a thing to do. * * *

"You have to learn it by trying—there is no tradition, and no authority. It calls for brave, careful, continuous, scientific experiment, with record of progress, and prompt relinquishment of failures and mistakes. It is open in front, and in motion—democracy is a going concern." (How a foreigner does love an idiom or a bit of slang! Even this Herland angel was not above it.)

"Now, you in young America had left off the King idea, for the most part. But you had the King's ancestor—the Father, the Absolute Boss, and you had a religion heavily weighted with that same basic concept. Moreover, as Protestants, book-worshippers, in default of a King, you must needs make a written ruler for yourselves, and that poor, blind, blessed baby, Democracy, promptly made itself a Cast-Iron Constitution —— and crawled under it."

That was something to chew on. It was so. It was undeniably so. We had done just that. We had been so anxious for "stability"—as if a young living thing could remain "stable"—the quality of stones.

"You grew, in spite of it. You had to. The big wild land helped, the remoteness and necessity for individual action and continual experiment. The migration of the children helped."

"Migration of the children! What on earth do you mean, Ellador?"

"Why, haven't you noticed? Hardly any of your children stay at home any more than they can help, any longer than they can help. And as soon as they are able they get off—as far as they can. They may love the old homestead—but they don't stay in it."

This was so, too.

"You see that steadily lightens up this old mistake about Authority. It is the change to the laboratory system of living—finding out how by doing it."

"It does not seem to me that there is much 'authority' left in the American home," I urged. "All the immigrants complain of just that."

"Of course they do. Your immigrants, naturally, understand democracy even less than you do. You have all of you set the word 'Freedom' over the most intricately co-ordinated kind of political relation. You see the Authority method is so simple. 'It is an order!'—and you merely do it—no thought, no effort—no responsibility. God says so—the King or the captain says so—the Book says so—and back of it all, the Family, the Father-Boss. What's that nice story: 'Papa says so—and if he says so, it is so, if it ain't so!' "

"But, Ellador—really—there is almost none of that in the American family; surely you must have seen the difference?"

"I have. In the oldest countries the most absolute Father-Boss—and family worship—the dead father being even more potent than the live ones. Van, dear—the thing I cannot fully understand is this reverence people have for dead people. Why is it? How is it? Why is a man who wasn't much when he was alive anything more when he is dead? You do not really believe that people are dwindling and deteriorating from age to age, do you?"

"That is precisely what we used to believe," I told her, "for the greater part of our history—for all of it really—the evolution idea is still less than a century old—in popular thought."

"But you Americans who *are* free, who *are* progressive, who *are* willing to change in most things—why do you still talk about what 'your fathers' said and did—as if it was so important?"

"It's because of our recent birth as a nation, I suppose," I answered, "and the prodigious struggle those fathers of ours made—the Pilgrim Fathers,

the Church fathers, the Revolutionary fathers—and now our own immediate fathers in the Civil War."

"But why is it that you only reverence them politically—and perhaps,
religiously! Nobody quotes them in business methods, in art, or science, or
medicine, or mechanics. Why do you assume that they were so permanently
wise in knowing how to govern a huge machine-run, electrically-con-
nected, city-dominated nation, which they were unable even to imagine?
It's so foolish, Van."

It is foolish. I admitted it. But I told her, perhaps a little testily, that I
didn't see what our homes had to do with it.

Then that wise lady said sweet, kind, discriminating things about us till
I felt better, and came back with smooth clarity to the subject.

"Please understand, dear, that I am *not* talking about marriage—the
beauty and joy and fruitful power of this dear union are a growing wonder
to me. You know that—!"

I knew that. She made me realize it, with a praising heart, every day.

"No, this monogamous marriage of yours is distinctly right—when it is
a real one. It is the making a business of it that I object to."

"You mean the women kept at housework?"

"That's part of it—about a third of it. I mean the whole thing: the men
saddling themselves for life with the task of feeding the greedy thing, and
the poor children heavily stamped with it before they can escape. That's
the worst—"

She stopped at that for a little. So far she had not entered on the
condition of women, or of children, in any thorough way. She had notes
enough—volumes.

"What I'm trying to establish is this," she said slowly, "the connection
between what seem to me errors in your social fabric, and the natural result
of these in your political action. The family relation is the oldest—the
democratic relation is the newest. The family relation demands close,
interconnected love, authority and service. The democratic relation demands universal justice and good will, the capacity for the widest co-ordinate action in the common interest, together with a high individual
responsibility. People have to be educated for this—it is not easy. Your
homes require the heaviest drain on personal energy, on personal loyalty,
and leave a small percentage either of feeling or action for the State."

"You don't expect everyone to be a statesman, do you?"

"Why not? Everyone must be—in a democracy."

"But we should not make better citizens if we neglected our homes,
should we?"

"Does it make a man a better soldier if he stays at home—to protect his family? Oh, Van, dear, don't you see? These poor foolish fighting men are at least united, coordinated, making a common effort for a common cause. They are—or think they are—protecting their homes together."

"I suppose you mean socialism again," I rather sulkily suggested, but she took it very sweetly.

"We isolated Herlanders never heard of Socialism," she answered. "We had no German-Jewish economist to explain to us in interminable, and, to most people, uncomprehensible, prolixity, the reasons why it was better to work together for common good. Perhaps 'the feminine mind' did not need so much explanation of so obvious a fact. We co-mothers, in our isolation, with a small visible group of blood relations (without any Father-Boss) just *saw* that our interests were in common. We couldn't help seeing it."

"Stop a bit, Sister," said I. "Are you insinuating that Mr. Father is at the bottom of the whole trouble? Are you going to be as mean as Adam and lay all the blame on him?"

She laughed gleefully. "Not quite. I won't curse him. I won't suggest ages of hideous injustice to all men because of the alleged transgression of one man. No, it is not Mr. Father I am blaming, nor his fatherhood—for that is evidently the high crown of physiological transmission." (Always these Herland women bowed their heads at what they called the holy mystery of fatherhood, and always we men were—well—not completely pleased.)

"But it does seem clear," she went on briskly, "that much mischief has followed from too much father. He did put himself forward so! He thought he was the whole thing, and motherhood—Motherhood!—was quite a subordinate process."

I always squirmed a little, in the back of my mind, at this attitude. All their tender reverence for fatherhood didn't seem in the least to make up for their absolutely unconscious pride in motherhood. Perhaps they were right——

"The dominance of him!" she went on. "The egoism of him! 'My name!'—and not letting her have any. 'My house—my line—my family'— if she had to be mentioned it was on 'the spindle side,' and when he is annoyed with her—what's that man in Cymbeline, Mr. Posthumous, wishing there was some way to have children without these women! It is funny, now, *isn't* it, Van?"

"It certainly is. Man or not, I can face facts when I see them. It is only too plain that 'Mr. Father' has grossly overestimated his importance in the part."

"Don't you think the American husband and father is a slight improve-ment on the earlier kind?" I modestly inquired. At which she turned upon me with swift caresses, and delighted agreement.

"That's the beauty and the wonder of your county, Van! You are growing swiftly and splendidly in spite of yourselves. This great thing you started so valiantly is sweeping you along with it, educating and developing as it goes. Your men are better, your women are freer, your children have more chance to grow than anywhere on earth."

"That's good to hear, my dear," I said with a sigh of relief. "Then why so gloomy about us?"

"Suppose everybody was entitled to a yearly income of five thousand dollars. Suppose most people averaged about five cents. Suppose a specially able, vigorous and well placed group had worked it up to $50.   *   *   * Why, Van—your superiority to less fortunate peoples is not worth men-tioning compared to your inferiority to what you ought to be."

"Now we are coming to it," I sighed resignedly. "Pitch in, dear—give it to us—only be sure and show the way to help it."

She nodded grimly. "I will do both as well as I can. Let us take physical conditions first: With your numbers, your intelligence and mechanical ingenuity, your limitless materials, the United States should by now have the best roads on earth. This would be an immediate and progressive economic advantage, and would incidentally go far to solve other 'prob-lems,' as you call your neglected work, such as 'unemployment,' 'the negro question,' 'criminality,' 'social discontent.' That there are not good roads in Central Africa does not surprise nor annoy me. That they are lacking in the United States is—discreditable!"

"Granted!" said I hastily. "Granted absolutely—you needn't stop on *that* point."

"That's only one thing," she went on serenely, "Here you are, a democ-racy—free—the power in the hands of the people. You let that group of conservatives saddle you with a constitution which has so interfered with free action that you've forgotten you had it. In this ridiculous helpless-ness—like poor old Gulliver—bound by the Lilliputians—you have sat open-eyed, not moving a finger, and allowed individuals—mere private persons—to help themselves to the biggest, richest, best things in the country. You know what is thought of a housekeeper who lets dishonest servants run the house with waste and robbery, or of a King who is openly preyed upon by extortionate parasites—what can we think of a Democracy, a huge, strong, young Democracy, allowing itself to become infested with such parasites as these? Talk of blood-suckers! You have your oil-suckers and coal-suckers, water-suckers and wood-suckers, railroad-suckers and farm-suckers—this splendid young country is crawling with them—and has not the intelligence, the energy, to shake them off."

"But most of us do not believe in Socialism, you see," I protested.

"You believe in it altogether too much," she replied flatly. "You seem to think that every step toward decent economic health and development has been appropriated by Socialism, and that you cannot do one thing toward economic freedom and progress unless you become Socialists!"

There was something in this.

"I admit the Socialists are partly to blame for this," she went on, "with their insistent claims, but do you think it is any excuse for a great people to say: 'We have all believed this absurd thing because they told us so?' "

"Was it our—stupidity—that shocked you so at first?" I ventured.

She flashed a bright look at me. "How brilliant of you, Van! That was exactly it, and I hated to say so to you. How can you, for instance, let that little bunch of men 'own' all your anthracite coal, and make you pay what they choose for it? You, who wouldn't pay England a little tax on tea! It puzzled me beyond words at first. Such intelligence! Such power! Such pride! Such freedom! Such good will! And yet such Abysmal Idiocy! That's what brought me around to the home, you see."

"We've wandered a long way from it, haven't we?"

"No—that's just the point. You should have, but you haven't. Don't you see? All these changes which are so glaringly necessary and so patently easy to make, require this one ability—*to think in terms of the community* * * * you only think in terms of the family. Here are men engaged in some absolutely social enterprise, like the railroad business, in huge groups, most intricately coordinated. And from the dividend-suckers to the road-builders, every man thinks only of his *Pay*,—of what he is to get out of it. 'What is a railroad?' you might ask them all. 'An investment,' says the dividend-sucker. 'A means of speculation,' says the Sucker-at-Large. 'A paying business,' says the Corporate-Owner. 'A thing that pays salaries,' says the officer. 'A thing that furnishes jobs,' says the digger and builder."

"But what has all this to do with the Home?"

"It has this to do with it," she answered, slowly and sadly. "Your children grow up in the charge of home-bound mothers who recognize no interest, ambition, or duty outside the home—except to get to heaven if they can. These home-bound women are man-suckers; all they get he must give them, and they want a good deal. So he says: 'The world is mine oyster,'— and sets his teeth in that. It is not only this relentless economic pressure, though. What underlies it and accounts for it all is the limitation of idea!

You think Home, you talk Home, you work Home, where you should from earliest childhood be seeing life in terms of the community. * * * You could not get much fleet action from a flotilla of canoes—with every man's first duty to paddle his own, could you * * *"

"What do you want *done?*" I asked, after awhile.

"Definite training in democratic thought, feeling and action, from infancy. An economic administration of common resources under which the home would cease to be a burden and become an *unconscious* source of happiness and comfort. And, of course, the socialization of home industry."

8

More Diagnosis

OUR STUDY OF AMERICAN PROBLEMS went on now with persistence. Ellador was as busy, as patient, as inexorably efficient as an eminent surgeon engaged in a first-class operation. We studied together, she wrote carefully, from time to time, and read me the results—or part of them. And we talked at all hours, not only between ourselves, but with many other persons, of all kinds and classes.

"I've seen the ruined lands that were once so rich," she said one day, "and the crowded lands now being drained by a too thick population. (Those blind mothers! Can't they once think of what is going to happen to their children?)

"But here I see land in plenty, carelessly skimmed and left, or not even skimmed, just lying open to the sun, while your squeezed millions smother in the cities.

"You are used to it, to you it is merely a fact—accepted without question. To an outsider, it seems as horribly strange as to see a people living in cellars thick and crawling, while great airy homes stand empty above.

"My study is mainly to get at your state of mind, to understand, if possible, what mysterious ideas and convictions keep you so poor, so dirty, so crowded, so starved, so ill-clothed, so unhealthy, so unhappy, when there is no need of it."

"Now look here, Ellador! That's rather strong, isn't it? You surely don't describe the American people that way."

Then she produced another of those little groups of assorted statistics she was so fond of. She gave the full wealth of the country—as at present administered, and showed that it ought to give nearly $2,000 to each of us. "That is per capita, you see, Van, not per family. For a family of five, that would be nine or ten thousand—not a bad nest egg, besides what they earn."

Then she showed me the estimate made by our latest scientific commission of inquiry, that "fully one-half of our wage earners do not receive incomes sufficient to maintain healthful conditions of living." A World Almanac was at hand, and she pointed out on page 228 the summary of manufactures.

"Here you have enough to show how people live in this splendid country, Van. See here—'Average number of wage earners 6,615,046. Wages, $3,427,038,000'—which, being divided, gives to each $518 plus—less than $520 a year, Van. Less than $10 a week—to keep a family—average family, five; $104 a year, $2 a week apiece for Americans to live on. And you know what food and rent costs. Of course they are not healthy—how could they be?"

I looked at the figures, uncomfortably. She gave me a few more.

"Salaried employees average $1,187 plus—that's a bit more than twice as much. About $4.40 a week, apiece, for Americans to live on."

"How much do you want them to have?" I asked a little irritably; but she was sweetly patient, inquiring, "How much would you be willing to live on—or how little, rather? I don't mean luxuries; I mean a decent, healthy life. Think you could do it on $4.40? Think you could do it on less than $6 say? Rent, board, clothing, car fares?"

Now I had spent a few months during my youth, living on a modest salary of $10 a week, and remembered it as a period of hardship and deprivation. There was $6 a week for board, 60 cents for carfare, 90 cents for my modest 15–cent lunches, 70 cents for tobacco—it left $1.80 for clothing and amusements, if any. I had thought it hard enough, at that time to endure life on $10 a week for one. It had never occurred to me that the working man had to keep five on it. And here were six million of them who did, it appeared, and a lot of clerks who were only twice as well off.

"Ten dollars a week, for each person is little enough for decent living in this country, isn't it, Van? That would call for $50 a week for a family of five—$2,600 a year."

"But, my dear girl, the business would not stand it! You ask impossibilities!" I protested. She turned to her figures again.

"Here is the 'value added by manufacture' " she said. "That must be what these workers produce, isn't it? $8,530,261,000. Now we'll take out these wages—it leaves $5,103,223,000. Then we'll take out the salaries, that leaves $4,031,649,000. Where does that go? Here is a four-billion dollar item—for services—whose?

"It must be those proprietors and firm members—only 273,265 of them—let's see, out of that four billion they get nearly $16,000 a year each. Don't you think it is a little-remarkable, Van? These services are valued at fourteen times as much as those of the salaries of employees and thirty times as much as the workers?"

"My dear girl," I said, "You have the most wonderful mind I ever lived with—ever met. And you know more than I do about ever so many things. But you haven't touched economics yet? There are laws here which you take no notice of."

And I told her of the iron law of wages, the law of supply and demand, and others. She listened, giving careful attention.

"You call them 'laws,' " she said, presently, "are they laws of nature?"

"Why, yes," I agreed slowly, "of human nature acting under economic conditions."

"Surely the economic conditions are those of soil, climate, materials available, the amount and quality of strength, intelligence, scientific and mechanical development."

"Why, of course; but also there are these I have mentioned."

"Do you mean to tell me that it is a 'law of nature' for men to arrange their working and paying so that half the people shall be unhealthy? Do you really believe for a minute that this has to be so?"

But I was not prepared to repudiate all my education in economics at once, and doggedly pointed out, "It is a law of human nature."

Then she smiled at me with cheerful derision. I am glad to say that Ellador had risen above the extreme horror and pain of her first year among us, and was able to smile at what used to bring distress.

"It must be male human nature," quoth she, "we have no such 'law' in Herland."

"But you are all sisters," I said rather lamely.

"Well, you are all sisters and brothers—aren't you? Of course, Van, I know the difference. You have had your long history of quarrels and hatred, of inimical strange races, of conquest and slavery. It looks to me as if the contempt of the rich for the poor was a lineal descendant of that of the conqueror for the vanquished. A helpless enemy, a slave, a serf, an employee, and the state of mind coming along unchanged. But the funny part of it is that in this blessed land, with more general good will and intelligence than I have found anywhere, you should have allowed this old foolishness to hang on so long.

"Now, Van, dear, don't you see how foolish it is? This is a democracy. To be efficient, that demands a competent electorate, doesn't it?"

"Why, we know that," I answered, with some heat. "Those forefathers of ours that you so scoff at knew that much. That's why we have our great system of free public education—from kindergarten to college."

"And in 1914," said Ellador, turning to that handy volume again, "you had a public school primary enrollment of 17,934,982. A drop in high school enrollment down to 1,218,804—only one out of seventeen to get that far; and another drop to a college enrollment of 87,820. That free public education does not seem to go far does it?"

"But most of these children have to go to work early—they cannot take the time for more education, even if they could afford it."

"Does going to work early make them better citizens?"

"I dare say it does—some of the college graduates aren't any too good."

She shook her head at this, and confronted me with more figures. The college graduates certainly made a pretty good showing, and the terrible dregs, as she called the criminals and paupers, were not as a rule well educated.

"Do look at it reasonably, Van. I'm not trying to be unpleasant and I know I am ignorant of this 'economics' you talk of. But I'm looking as a stranger, of average intelligence, and with the additional advantage of an entirely different background at your country. You have natural advantages as good as earth affords. You have plenty of room. You have good racial stocks in large variety. You have every element of wealth. You have a good many true principles to go on. And yet—in the time you have been at it—in a hundred and forty years, you have built up the most crowded cities on earth, robbed, neglected and wasted the soil, made politics a thing of shame, developed private wealth that is monstrous and general poverty that is—disgraceful."

There was some silence after this.

It was extremely unpleasant. It was quite true.

"I knew it is better here than in Europe," she went on, "I know that, with all your imperfections and errors you are better off than Germany—poor, mistaken Germany, so authoritatively perfect that she became proud; so proud that she became hateful, so hateful that it will take generations before the world can forgive her. You are not lost, Van—not a bit of it. But surely you can see that it is as I say?"

I could. Who couldn't?

"It is very easy for me to show what could be done, how easily and how soon. In ten years' time you could see an end of poverty, in twenty of crime, in thirty of disease. This whole great land could be as fair and clean and healthy and happy as my own—and vastly richer in products. Even richer in happiness—with this heaven of married love to crown all else!"

She took my hand at the end and was still for a little. "But for the most part—you don't have that," she continued evenly. "Van, I've been reading. I've been talking with doctors and many wise persons, and, it seems to me, dear, that you don't appreciate marriage."

I had to grin at that. This Herlander, who never saw a man till a few years ago, and had only married one of them. Moreover, I recalled, with a momentary touch of bitterness, that we were not "married people" at present—not in the usual sense. And then I was ashamed. I had accepted my bargain, such as it was, with open eyes; I had had all this time of unbroken, happy love, living so near a beautiful woman who gave me comfort and rest and calmness in some mysterious, super-sexual way, and keeping always the dear hope of a further fulfillment.

We had had no misunderstandings, no quarrels, and while I own that at first there had been periods of some unease for me, they were as nothing to our larger joy. It was as if, in clean vigor and activity, I was on an expedition with a well-loved sister—a sister dearer and sweeter than all the world, and with that background of a still happier future.

From this I looked at the world about me, seeing it as I had never seen it before, as it was. All the eager, fresh young boys and girls, all the happy, hopeful lovers, the marriages, and then, how painful a proportion of miserable failures. It was not only the divorces, not only the undivorced ill-doing; but the low order of happiness among so many.

That was what Ellador had in mind, with her fine sense of personal relationship. She did not know as much as I of the deeper gulf; what she meant was the dreary level.

"You make fun of it, you know," she went on. "It's a joke, a question for discussion—'Is Marriage a Failure?'—it is being discussed by many, ignored, made the subject of cheap talk."

"There are many who feel this," I answered her. "There is great effort to check the divorce evil, to preserve the sanctity of marriage."

Another thing my Ellador had learned, I think from being in America, was a spice of mischief. It became her well. With a mind as keen and powerful as hers, lack of humor would have been a serious loss.

"Have they tried benzoate—to preserve the sanctity of marriage?" she inquired. "Or is it enough to be hermetically sealed—under pressure—at the boiling point?"

I'm not much of a cook, nor is she for that matter, but I could smile at that, too.

"Without going into the marriage question at present, I wish you would go on with your Herland view of economics," I told her. "It looks to me as if you wanted to adopt socialism at once. And that's out of the question— most of us don't believe in it."

"Most of you don't seem to understand it, it seems to me," she answered.

"If you mean by socialism, the principles of socialism—yes, that is the way we manage in Herland. The land is ours, visibly. We never divided it up into little bits as you people have. What we raised on it and out of it was ours, too, visibly—when there was little, we had little—children first, of course—and now that there is a balanced plenty why, of course, every one has enough."

"Had you no selfish women? No ambitious women? No super-women trying to get ahead of the others?"

"Why of course we had; still have some few."

"Well—how did you manage them?"

"Why that is what government is for isn't it?" she replied. "To preserve justice, to prevent the selfish and ambitious from injuring the others, to see to it that production is increased and distribution fairly carried on."

"We say that government is the best that governs least," I told her.

"Yes, I've heard that. Do any of you really believe it? Why do you believe it? How can you?"

"But look at Germany!" I cried; "there you see what comes of too much government."

"I wish you would look at Germany—every other nation might study Germany with great improvement," she replied, a little hotly. "Just because Germany has gone criminally insane, that is no reason for underrating all the magnificent work she has done. The attitude of some people toward Germany is like that of your lynchers. Nations that do wrong are not to be put to death with torture, surely! Like individual criminals, they need study—help—better conditions. I think Germany is one of the most glorious, pathetic, awful examples of—of the way our world works," she concluded solemnly.

"They wouldn't thank you for calling them pathetic," I said.

"No; I know they wouldn't. Their weakest spot is their blind pride. I find all of your nations are proud—it's easy to see why."

"Well—if you see it easily, do tell us."

"Why, it's one of your laws of nature," she explained, with a twinkle in her eye.

"You know something of perspective? The farther a thing is away from you the smaller it is, the less well you can see it, the less you are able to understand it, and by the 'law of nature' you look down upon it! That was the reason when nations were really far apart and separate. Now that you are all so close together you should have long since come to see and know and understand and work together—that means love, you know. But to prevent that are two big, unnecessary, foolish things. One is ignorance—the common ignorance which takes the place of distance. The man next door is as strange as the man in the antipodes—if you don't know him.

"The nations of the earth don't try to understand each other, Van. Then as a positive evil you have each built up for yourselves an artificial wall of brag and boastfulness. Each nation ignores the other nations and deliberately teaches its helpless children that It alone is the greatest and best——"

"Why, Van——" The tears always came when she touched upon children, but this time they vanished in a flashing smile.

"Children!" she said. "Anything more like the behavior of a lot of poor, little, underbred children it would be hard to find. Quarrelsome, selfish, each bragging that he can 'lick' the others—oh, you poor dears! How you do need your mother! And she's coming at last."

"I suppose you think she will solve these economic problems forthwith."

"Why not, Van? Look here, dear—why can't you people see that——" (Here she spoke very slowly as if she were writing some A, B, C's very large on a blackboard.) "There is nothing to prevent human beings in this historic period from being healthy, beautiful, rich, intelligent, good—and happy."

"That's easy to say, my dear," I remarked, rather glumly. "I wish it was true."

"Why isn't it true?" she demanded. "Do you think Satan prevents you, or God, or what? Don't you see—can't you see? God's on the side of all the growing good of life. God's with you—what's against?"

"I suppose it is only ourselves," I agreed; "but that's something. Of course I know what you mean. We could, conceivably, do and be all that you say, but there's an 'if'—an 'if' as big as all the world. If we knew what to do, and IF we would act together."

"That is not half such an obstacle, as you think, Van. You know enough now easily to set everything going in the right direction. It doesn't have to be done by hand, you know. It does itself, give it a chance. You know what to do for one baby, to give it the best chance of health, full growth and happy usefulness, don't you?"

"Well, yes; we do know that much," I admitted.

"Very well then, do it for all of them, and you lift the whole stock; that's easy. You know how good roads, waterways and efficient transportation build up the wealth of a community. Very well. Have them everywhere."

She was splendid in her young enthusiasm—that keen, strong face, all lit and shining with love for the naughty world and wise suggestions for its betterment. But I could not catch the fire.

"I don't want to dash your hopes, my dear," I told her gently. "You are, in a sense, correct; even I could make a plan that would straighten things out quite a bit. The difficulty is to get that plan accepted by the majority. No king is going to do it, and in a democracy you have to convince more than half the people; that's slow work."

She sat silent, looking out of our high hotel window, and thinking of what I said.

"It isn't as if our minds were empty," said I, "we don't think we're ignorant. We think we know it all. Only the wise are eager to learn, I'm afraid, and for everything you tell the people as truth there are no end of other teachers to tell them something else. It's not so easy as it looks. There's more excuse for us than would appear at first sight."

* * *

We had made special studies as we traveled about, of different industries and social conditions. Now we plunged more deeply into economics, politics and the later researches of sociology and social psychology. Ellador became more and more interested. Again and again she wished for the presence and help of certain of her former teachers in Herland.

"How they would love it," she said. "They wouldn't be tired or discouraged. They'd just plunge in and find a way to help in no time. Even I can see something."

From time to time she gave me the benefit of the things she saw.

"The reason we had so little trouble is that we had no men, I'm sure of that. The reason you have made so much progress is because you have had men, I'm sure of that, too. Men are splendid, but——" here was a marked pause, "the reason you had so much trouble is not because of the men, but because of this strange dissociation of the men and women. Instead of the smooth, helpful interrelationship, you have so much misery. I never knew—of course not, how could I?—that there could be such misery. To have two kinds of people, evidently adapted for such perfect co-ordinate action—once in a while you see it, even now—and then to have them hurt and degrade one another so."

Another time she propounded this suggestion:

"Can't some of your big men, and women, of course, work out an experiment station in methods of living—an economic and social unit, you know—to have for reference, to establish facts, as you do in other things?"

"What do you mean?" I asked her. "Compulsory eugenics and a co-operative colony?"

"Don't tease me, Van. I'm not as foolish as that. No, what I mean is something like this. Take a given piece of ground, most anywhere, and have it surveyed by competent experts to see how much it could produce under the best methods known. Then see how many persons it would take to do the necessary work to insure that production. Then see by what arrangements of living those persons could be kept healthful and happy at the least expense. For that unit you'd have something to go on—some definite proof of what the country could do."

"You leave out the human side of the problem, my dear. We have so many different causes for living where and how and as we do. Our people are not pawns on a chessboard; they can't be managed to prove theories."

It was no wonder that Ellador, for all her wonderful clarity of vision, her exceptionable advantage of viewpoint, should become somewhat overwhelmed in our sociological morass. The very simplicity and ease of living to which she was accustomed made her see a delusive simplicity and ease in attempting to solve our problem.

"How about the diagnosis?" I suggested. "Suppose we merely consider symptoms awhile. What strikes you most forcibly in the way of symptoms?"

"Physically?"

"Yes, physically, first."

"As to the land—neglect, waste, awful, glaring waste," she answered promptly. "It makes me sick. It makes me want to cry. As a mere wilderness, of course, it would be interesting, but as a wilderness with a hundred million people in it, and such able people, I don't know whether it is more laughable or horrible. As to the water, neglect and waste again, and hideous, suicidal defilement.

"As to means of communication——" words failed her. "You know how I feel about your roads, and the city streets are worse. One would think to see the way you rip up and lay down in your cities that an organized group of human habitations had never been built before. Such childish experiments. Over and over and over. Why a city, Van, is no new thing. It can be foreseen and planned for. That was done in ancient Egypt, in Assyria, and today, with all you know, with the whole past to learn from——Van, as I come into your cities, by rail, and see the poor, miserable, dirty, unhealthy things it makes me feel almost as badly as those European battlefields. They are at least trying to kill one another; you are doing it unconsciously. A city should be the loveliest thing. Why you remember—oh, Van!"

For the moment homesickness overcame her. I did remember. From that first low flight of ours, soaring across that garden land, that fruitful park and pleasure ground, with its little villages, so clean, so bright in color, so lovely in arrangement, lying here and there among the green, all strung together by those smooth, shaded roads and winding paths. From that bird's-eye view to my later, more intimate knowledge, I recalled them with deep admiration and with a painful envy. They had no slums—not in all Herland; they had no neglected, dirty places; they had no crowded tenements; they lived in houses, and the houses were in gardens, and their manufacturing, storing and exchanging—all the larger business of life was carried on in buildings, if possible even more lovely than their dwelling houses. It could be done—I had seen it.

"I don't wonder you cry, my dear."

9

[Democracy and Economics]

"THIS IS THE MOST FASCINATING STUDY," Ellador announced one day. "At home we are so smoothly happy, so naturally growing, that it's almost unconscious. Here, if you have not happiness, you have a call on all your sympathy, all your energy, all your pride—you have such a magnificent Opportunity.

"I've gone deeper into my diagnosis, dear," she continued, "and have even some prescriptions. Be patient while I generalize a little more. You see this 'case' has so many diseases at once that one has to discriminate a bit.

"Here is the young new-made country, struggling out of the old ones to escape their worst diseases, breaking loose from monarchy, from aristocracy, and feudalism with its hereditary grip on land and money, on body and soul, and most of all, from that mind-crushing process of Enforced Belief which had kept the whole world back so long.

"Note——" she interpolated. "It is easy to see that as man progresses in social relation he needs more and more a free strong agile mind, with sympathetic perception and understanding and the full power of self-chosen action. The Enforced Belief in any religion claiming to be Final Truth cripples the mind along precisely those lines, tending to promote a foolish sense of superiority to other believers or disbelievers; running to extremes of persecution; preventing sympathy, perception, and understanding, and reducing action to mere obedience.

"There," she said cheerfully. "If America had done nothing but that—establish the freedom of thought and belief—she would have done world-service of the highest order."

"The Greeks allowed it, didn't they? And the Romans?" I offered.

"If they did it was 'a lost art' afterward," she replied. "Anyhow you did it later, and you have gone on doing it—splendidly.

"Then, in establishing the beginning of a democracy you performed another great service. This has not progressed as successfully, first because of its only partial application, second because you did not know it needed to be earnestly studied and taught—you thought you had it once and for all just by letting men vote, and third because it has been preyed upon by both parasites and diseases. In the matter of religion you threw off an evil restriction and let the mind grow free—a natural process. In the matter of government you established a social process, one requiring the utmost knowledge and skill. So it is no wonder the result has been so poor.

"Prescription as to government:

"A. Enfranchisement of all adult citizens. You have started on this.

"B. Special training—and practice—in the simpler methods and principles of democratic government as far as known, for all children, with higher courses and facilities for experiment and research for special students. You are beginning to do this already.

"C. Careful analysis and reports on the diseases of democracy, with applied remedies, and as careful study of the parasites affecting it—with sharp and thorough treatment. Even this you are beginning."

"A little severe on the parasites, aren't you?" I asked.

"It is time you were severe on them, Van. I'm no Buddhist—I'm a forester. When I see trees attacked by vermin, I exterminate the vermin if I can. My business is to raise wood, fruit, nuts—not insects."

"Except of course when the mulberry tree is sacrificed to the silk worms," I suggested, but she merely smiled at me.

"You need to transfer to your democracy the devotion you used to have for your kings," she went on. "To kill a common man was murder—to kill a king was regicide. You have got to see that for one man to rob another man is bad enough; for a man to rob the public is worse; but to rob the public *through the government* is a kind of high treason which—if you still punished by torture—would be deserving of the most excruciating kind. As it is you have allowed the practice to become so common that it is scarcely condemned at all—you do not even call it robbery; you call it 'graft'—or 'pork'—or a 'plum tree'—or some such polite term."

Of course I knew all this—but I never had felt it as anything particularly dreadful.

"Don't you see," she went on. "The government is the social motor system. By means of it society learns, as a baby learns, to check some actions and to make others. If your government is sick, you are paralyzed, weakened, confused, unable to act.

"In practical instance your city governments are frequently corrupt from the policemen up. Therefore when, with infinite labor, the public feeling has been aroused to want something done, you find that the machinery to do it with won't work. What you do not seem to realize at all is that the specific evil you seek to attack is not nearly so serious as the generic evil which makes your whole governmental system so———so———"

"Groggy," I suggested with a wry smile.

"Yes—that's about it. As weak and slow and wavering as a drunken man."

"Remedy," I demanded, "remedy?"

"Why that comes under 'C' in those I just gave," she said. "It needs full study and careful experiment to decide on the remedies. But here is what might be done at once: A report be made which should begin with a brief survey of the worst cases of governmental corruption in other countries, past and present. Not only in general, but with specific instances, people called by name with their crimes clearly shown. What such and such a person cost his country. How such decisive battles were lost because of such crippling disorders in the government. Parallel made between conspicuous traitors already recognized and this kind. Report now brought to our own country with both summary and instances. Our waterways described, what has been done, legitimately, to improve them, and what has been done, illegitimately, to hinder, pervert, and prevent right government action. History of our River and Harbor Bills given, and brought down to date, with this last huge 'steal' now accomplished—and not even rebuked! Names should be given—and names called! The congressmen and senators concerned, and the beneficiaries in the localities thus nefariously fattened.

"This kind of thing could be put simply and briefly so that the children could understand. They should be taught, early and steadily, how to judge the men who corrupt the very vitals of their country. Also how to judge the lazy shirks who do not even vote, much less study how to help the country."

"It needs—it needs a new kind of public opinion, doesn't it?" I ventured.

"Of course it does, but new public opinion has to be made. It takes no great genius to recognize a thief and a traitor, once he is shown up; but yours are *not* shown up."

"Why, Ellador—I'm sure there's a lot about this in the papers——"

She looked at me—just looked at me—and her expression was like that of an over-ripe volcano, firmly suppressed.

"For Heaven's sake! Let it out, Ellador. Say it quick and say it all—what's the matter with the papers!"

She laughed. Fortunately she could laugh, and I laughed with her.

"I couldn't say it all—under ten volumes," she admitted, "but I'll say some of it. This is a special department—I must begin again.

"This whole matter of societies, parasites and diseases is intensely interesting. We in Herland, being normal, have not realized our society much, any more than a healthy child realizes her body."

I noticed that Ellador and her sisters always said "she" and "her" as unconsciously as we say "he" and "his." Their reason, of course, is that all the people are shes. Our reason is not so justifiable.

"But the rest of the world seems to be painfully conscious of its social body—without being able to help it much. Now you know there are diseases and diseases, some much preferable to others. In their degree of danger they vary much, and in what they are dangerous to. One might better have a very sick leg than even partly sick heart or brain. Rheumatism for instance is painful and crippling, but when it reaches the heart it becomes fatal. Some creatures cannot have certain diseases for lack of material; one does not look for insanity in an angleworm, or neurasthenia in a clam.

"Society, as it has developed new functions, has developed new diseases. The daily press is one of the very newest social functions—one of the very highest—one of the most measureless importance. That is why the rheumatism of the press is worse than rheumatism of the farm, or the market."

"Rheumatism of the press?"

"Yes—that's a poor figure perhaps. I mean any serious disease is worse there than in some lower or less important function. Look at the whole thing again, Van. Society, in the stage of democracy, needs to be universally informed, mutually sympathetic, quick and strong to act. For this purpose it must introduce machinery to develop intelligence, to supply information, to arouse and impart feeling, to promote prompt action. The schools are supposed to train the intelligence, but your press is the great machine through which the democracy is informed, aroused, and urged to act. It is the social sensorium. Through it you see and hear and feel—collectively.

Through it you are incited to act—collectively. It is later and by that much higher than the school and the church. It is the necessary instrument of democracy."

"Admitted, all admitted. But isn't that our general belief, dear, though perhaps not so clearly put?"

"Yes, you seem to think a grant deal of your press—so much so that you can not see, much less cure, its diseases."

"Well—you are the doctor. Pitch in. I suppose you know there are many and fierce critics of 'our sensational press' and 'our venal press.' "

"Oh yes, I have read some of the criticisms. They don't touch it——"

"Go on, and touch it yourself, Sister—I'm listening."

She was too serious to be annoyed at my light manner.

"It's like this," she said slowly. "This great new function came into being in a time when people were struggling with what seemed more important issues,—were, perhaps. In Europe it has become, very largely, a tool of the old governments. Here, fearing that, it has been allowed to become the tool of individuals, and now of your plutocratic powers. You see you changed your form of government but failed to change your ideas and feelings to go with it. You allow it to go on over your heads as if it were a monarchy and none of your business. And you jealously refuse to give it certain necessary tools, as if it were a monarchy and would misuse them. What you have got to learn is to keep your government the conscious determined action of the majority of the people, and see that it has full power. A democracy is *self*-government, the united self of the people. Is that self control the best that self-controls the least?"

"Do you want a government-owned press?" I inquired. "We see that in Europe—and do not like it."

"You mean a monarchy-controlled press, do you not? No, I do not mean anything like that. You should have a press with democratic control, surely, and that means all the people, or at least the majority of them. What you have now is a press controlled by starkly mercenary motives of individuals, and the more powerful purposes of your big 'interests.' "

"What are you going to *do*—that's what I want to know. Lots of people criticize our press, but no one seems able to suggest the better method. Some propose endowment; we must have freedom of expression."

"You mustn't expect too much of me, Van. I can see the diseases easier than the cures, of course. It seems to me that you could combine perfect freedom of opinion, comment, idea, with the most authoritative presentation of the facts."

"Do you think a government-run paper could be trusted to give the facts correctly?"

"If it did not there would be heavier charges against it than could be survived over election. What you have not recognized yet is the social crime of misrepresenting the facts. Your papers lie as they please."

"We have our libel laws——"

"I didn't say libel—I said lie. They lie, on whichever side they belong, and there is no penalty for it."

I laughed, as an American would. "Penalty for lying! Who's going to throw the first stone?"

"Exactly. That's the awful part of it, Van. Your people are so used to public lying that you don't mind. You are paralyzed, benumbed, calloused, to certain evils you should be keenly alive to. There are plenty of much less dangerous things you make far more noise about. You see the press is suffering from a marked confusion of function. It makes all its proud claims for freedom and protection as an 'expression of public opinion,' as 'a medium of information,' and then makes its main business the cheapest kind of catering to prejudices, and to a market—the market of the widest lowest popular taste for literary amusement. Why does 'the palladium of your liberties' have to carry those mind-weakening, soul-degenerating 'comics'? They are neither information nor opinion—only bait."

"The people would not buy the papers if they were not amusing."

"What people would not? Wouldn't you?"

"Oh, I would, of course; I want to know the news; I mean the lower classes."

"And these 'lower classes,' so low that they take no interest in the news of the day and have to be given stuff suited to imbeciles, imbeciles with slightly criminal tastes—are they a large and permanent part of your democracy?"

"You mean that we ought to put out decent papers and see that the people are educated up to them?"

"Why not?"

I was trying to see why not, but she went on:

"If your papers were what they ought to be, they could be used in the schools, should be so used. Every boy and girl in the high school should take the Current Events course. Each day they should be required to read the brief clear summary of *real* news which would not be a long task, and required to state what seemed to them most important, and why.

"This array of 'crimes and casualties' you print is not *news*—it is as monotonous as the alphabet. All that needs is a mere list, a bulletin from the sick chamber of society, interesting only to the specialist. But the children should be taught to see the world move—every day; to be interested, to feel responsible. People educated like that wouldn't need to be baited with foul stuff to read the papers."

For the life of me I couldn't see anything the matter with this. If we can trust our government with the meteorological reports why not with the social ones?

"The best brains, the best backing, the whole country watching," she continued,—"papers that gave the news—and people who could read them. Then your comment and opinion could be as free as it pleased—on the side. Anybody could publish all of that she wanted to. But why should private opinion be saddled on the public facts, Van?"

"All right; diagnosis accepted with reservations; remedy proposed too suspiciously simple. But go ahead—what else ails us? With every adult enfranchised, the newspapers reliable, our natural resources properly protected, developed and improved—would that do for a starter?"

"Not while half the people do not earn enough to be healthy."

I groaned. "All right. Let's get down to it. Bring on your socialism. Do you want it by evolution, or revolution, or both?"

She was not deceived by my mock pathos. "What is your prejudice against socialism, Van? Why do you always speak as if it were—slightly ridiculous?"

I considered for a moment, thoughtfully.

"I suppose it is on account of my college education, and the kind of people I've lived with most," I answered.

"And what is your own sincere view of it?"

That had to be considered too.

"Why—I suppose the theory is right enough," I began, but she stopped me to ask:

"What is the theory—as you see it?"

Then I was obliged to exhibit my limitations, for all I could produce was what I had heard other people say about it, what I could remember of various articles and reviews, mostly adverse, a fruitless excursion into the dogmatic mazes of Marx, and a most unfavorable impression of certain socialist papers and pamphlets I had seen.

"That's about what I find everywhere," she was good enough to say. "That is your idea of it; now, very honestly, what is your feeling about it—say it right out, please."

So without waiting to be careful and to see if my feelings bore any relation to my facts, I produced a jumble of popular emotions, to the effect that Socialism was a lazy man's paradise; that it was an effort of the underdog to get on top, that it was an unfair "evening down" of the rewards of superior ability with those of the inferior; that it was a class movement full of hatred and injustice, that nobody would be willing "to do the dirty work," and that "such a world wouldn't be worth living in, anyhow."

Ellador laughed merrily, both at this nondescript mass of current misconception, and at my guilty yet belligerent air, as who should say: "It may be discreditable, but that's the way I feel."

She sobered soon enough, and looked far past me—through me. "It's not you, Van dear," she said. "It's America talking. And America ought to be ashamed of itself. To have so little vision! To be so gullible! To believe so easily what the least study would disprove! To be so afraid of the very principles on which this nation rests!"

"This nation rests on the principle of individual liberty—not on government ownership," I protested.

"What individual liberty has the working man?" she countered. "What choice of profession has his ill-born, ill-fed, ill-clothed, ill-taught child? The thing you call 'free competition' is long past—and you never saw it go. You see ideas stay fixed in people's minds long after the facts have changed. Your industrial world is in a state of what Ghent called 'feudalism'—and he was right. It is like Europe under the robber barons, and your struggling trade unions are like the efforts of the escaping serfs in that period. It only takes a little history and economics to see the facts. The perplexing part of the problem, to me, is the dullness of the popular mind. You Americans are an intelligent people, and a somewhat educated people, but you can't seem to see things."

"Are we any blinder than other people, my lady? Do they recognize these glaring facts any better than we do?"

Ellador sat still a moment, running over her fresh clear view of the world, past and present.

"No," she said. "No other people is any better—in all ways—except New Zealanders perhaps. Yet ever so many countries are wiser in some particulars, and you—with all your advantages—haven't sense enough to see it. Oh I know you'll say the others don't see it either, but you ought to. You are *free*—and you are able to act when you do see. No, Van—there's no excuse for you. You had supreme advantages, you made a brave start, you established a splendid beginning, and then you sat back and bragged about your ancestors and your resources—and your prospects—and let the vermin crawl all over you."

Her eyes were grave, her tone solemn, her words most offensive.

"Look here, Ellador, why will you use that term? It's very disagreeable."

"What else can you call these people who hang like clusters of leeches on the public treasury, who hop like fleas to escape the law, who spin webby masses of special legislation in which to breed more freely, who creep and crawl on every public work that is undertaken, and fatten undisturbed on all private business? What do you call your 'sidewalk speculators' in theater-tickets, for instance—but vermin? Just to steal a ticket and go to see the play would be a clean manly thing to do compared to this. They are small ones, openly disgusting, yet you do nothing but grumble a little.

"To turn from little to big I want to know what you call your sleeping-car extortionists? What is the size limit of vermin, anyhow? I suppose if a flea was a yard long he would be a beast of prey, wouldn't he?"

"You certainly are—drastic, my dear girl. But what have you got against the sleeping cars? I've always thought our service was pretty good."

She shook her head slowly, regarding me with that motherly patient expression.

"The resignation of the American public to its devourers is like that of—of a sick kitten. You remember that poor little lean thing we picked up, and had to drop, quick, and brush ourselves? Why Van Jennings—don't you even know you are being *robbed*, to the bone, by that sleeping-car company? Look here, please——"

Then she produced one of those neat little sheets of figures I had so learned to respect. Most damaging things, Ellador's figures.

"Twelve double berths to a car, beside the 'stateroom,' or rooms which I won't count; twenty-four passengers, who have already bought a ticket on which they are entitled to transportation with accommodations in the day-coach. Usual price $5.00 for twenty-four hours. For this $5.00 the passenger receives by day a whole seat instead of a half one—unless there is a day crowd and then extra seats are cheerfully sold to other victims—I have seen sleeping-cars crowded to standing! By night he has a place to lie down—three by three by six, with a curtain for privacy."

"Well, but he is being carried on his journey all the time," I urged.

"So he is in the day-coach or chair-car. This money is not for transpor-tation—that's paid for. It is for special accommodation. I am speaking of the kind of accommodation, and what is extorted for it. The night arrange-ments are what you know. Look at the price."

"Two dollars and a half isn't so much," I urged, but she pursued relent-lessly. "Wouldn't you think it was much, here, in this hotel, for a space of that size?"

I looked about me at the comfortable room in the first-class hotel where we were then lodged, and thought of the preceding night, when we had had our two berths on the car. Here was a room twelve by fourteen by ten. There were two windows. There was a closet and a bathroom. There was every modern convenience in furniture. There was a wide, comfortable bed. My room adjoined it, equally large and comfortable.

"This is $2.00 for twenty-four hours," she remarked. "That was $5.00."

"Sleeping cars are expensive to build," I remarked feebly.

"More expensive than hotels?" she asked. "The hotel must pay ground rent, and taxes."

"The sleeping cars are not always full," I urged.

"Neither are the hotels—are they?"

"But the car has to be moved——"

"Yes, and the railroad company pays the sleeping car for being moved," she triumphed.

I wanted to say something about service; tried to, but she made merry over it.

"They have one conductor for their string of sleepers, and as to porters—we mostly pay them, you know."

I did know, of course.

"This is how I have figured it," said Ellador. "Of course I don't know the exact facts about their business, and they won't tell, but look at it this way: Suppose they average twenty passengers per car—staterooms and all—at $5.00 a day; that's $100.00 a day income, $36,500.00 a year per car. Now they pay the porter about $30.00 a month, I understand, or less, leaving the public to do the rest. Each car's fraction of the conductor's wages wouldn't be more than $20.00, I should think; there's $50.00 a month, $600 a year for service. Then there is laundry work and cleaning—forty sheets—pillow-cases—towels—flat-work rates of course; and renovating at the end of the journey. I don't believe it comes to over—say $800.00 a year. Then there is insurance, depreciation, repairs——"

"Look here, Ellador, where did you get up these technicalities? Talking with business men, I suppose—as usual?"

"Yes, of course," she agreed. "And I'm very proud of them. Well—I'll allow $1,600.00 a year for that. That is $3,000.00 for their running expenses. And remember they are paid something for running—I don't know how much. That leaves $33,500.00. I will magnanimously leave off that $3,500.00—for times when they carried fewer passengers—call it a clear income of $30,000.00 a year. Now that is 10 per cent. of $300,000.00.

You don't honestly suppose that one sleeping car costs three hundred thousand dollars—do you, Van?"

I did not. I knew better. Anybody knows better.

"If it costs $100,000 to build and fit a sleeping car," she went on calmly, "then they could charge about $1.75 for their berths, and still 'make money,' as you call it. If ten per cent. is a legitimate 'profit,' I call the extra twenty per cent. a grinding extortion. What do you call it?"

"Up to date I never called it anything. I never noticed it."

She nodded. "Exactly. You people keep quiet and pay three times what is necessary for the right to live. You are bled—sucked—night and day, in every direction. Now then, if these blood-suckers are beasts of prey—fight them, conquer them. If they are vermin—Oh, I know you don't like the word—but Van, what is your estimate of people who are willing to endure—vermin?"

10

[Race and Religion]

GOING ABOUT WITH ELLADOR among familiar conditions, and seeing things I never dreamed were there, was always interesting, though sometimes painful. It was like carrying a high-powered light into dark places. As she turned her mind upon this or that feature of American life it straightway stood out sharply from the surrounding gloom, as the moving searchlight of a river boat brings out the features of the shore.

I had known clever women, learned women, even brilliant women, a few. But the learned ones were apt to be a bit heavy, the clever ones twinkled and capered like spangled acrobats, and the brilliant ones shone, indeed, like planets among stars, but somehow did not illuminate much.

Ellador was simple enough, modest enough. She was always keeping in mind how little she knew of our civilization, but what she saw she saw clearly and was able to make her hearers see. As I watched her, I began to understand what a special strength it was not to have in one's mind all the associate ideas and emotions ours are so full of. She could take up the color question, for instance, and discuss it dispassionately, with no particular sentiment, one way or the other. I heard her once with a Southern sociologist, who was particularly strong on what he called "race conflict."

He had been reading a paper at some scientific meeting which we attended, a most earnest paper, full of deep feeling and some carefully selected facts. He spoke of the innate laziness of the negro race, their inborn objection to work, their ineducability—very strong on this—but his deepest horror was "miscegenation." This he alluded to in terms of the utmost loathing, hardly mitigated by the statement that it was impossible.

"There is," he averred, "an innate, insuperable, ineradicable, universal race antipathy, which forever separates the negro from the white."

Ellador had her chance at him afterward, with quite a group about, and he was too polite or insufficiently ingenious to escape. First she asked him what was the market price of a good, ablebodied negro before the war; if it was not, as she had read, about a thousand dollars. To this he agreed unsuspectingly. She inquired, further, if there had not been laws in the slave States forbidding the education of negroes, and if there were not laws still forbidding their intermarriage with whites. To this he agreed also; he had to. Then she asked whether the sudden emancipation of the negro had not ruined many rich men; if the major part of the wealth of the South had not been in slaves and the products of their labor. Here again could be no denial.

"But," she said, "I do not understand, yet. If negroes can not or will not work, why was one worth a thousand dollars? And how could the owners have accumulated wealth from their inefficiency? If they could not learn anything, why was it necessary to make laws forbidding their education; and if there is this insuperable antipathy separating the races, why are the laws against miscegenation needed?"

He was quite naturally incensed. There were a good many of his previous hearers about, some of them looking quite pleased, and he insisted rather stormily that there was this deep-seated antipathy, and that every Southerner, at least, knew it.

"At what age does it begin?" she asked him. He looked at her, not getting the drift of her question.

"This innate antipathy," she pursued gentry. "I have seen the Southern babies clinging to their black nurses most affectionately. At what age does the antipathy begin?" He talked a good bit then, with much heat, but did not seem to meet the points she raised, merely reiterating much of what he had said before. Then she went on quite calmly.

"And your millions of mulattos—they appear, not only against the law, but against this insuperable antipathy?"

This seemed to him so unwomanly of her, that he made some hasty excuse and got away, but his position was upheld by another man, for a moment. His little speech was mainly emotion, there are such hot depths of feeling on this subject in the children of slave owners that clear reasoning is naturally hard to find. This man made a fine little oration, with much about the noble women of the South, and how he, or any man, would lay down his life to protect them against the faintest danger of social contact with the colored race, against the abomination of a proposal of marriage from a black man.

"Do you mean," said Ellador slowly, her luminous eyes on his, "that if black men were free to propose to white women, the white women would accept them?"

At this he fairly foamed with horror. "A white woman of the South would no sooner marry a black man than she would a dog."

"Then why not leave it to the women?" she inquired.

Neither of these men were affected, save in the way of deep annoyance, by Ellador's gentle questions, but many of her hearers were, and she, turning that searchlight of hers on the subject, later announced to me that it seemed rather a long but by no means a difficult problem.

"About ten million negroes, counting all the mulattos, quadroons, octoroons and so on, to about ninety million whites," she said.

"As a mere matter of interbreeding, following the previous habits of the white men, it could be worked out mathematically—how long it would take to eliminate the negro, I mean."

"But suppose there remains a group of negroes, that have race pride and prefer to breed true to the stock," I suggested. "What then?"

"If they are decent, orderly and progressive, there is no problem, surely. It is the degraded negro that is so feared. The answer to that is easy. Compulsory and efficient education, suitable employment at fair wages, under good conditions—why, don't you see, dear," she interrupted herself to say, "the proof that it is not impossible is in what has been accomplished already. Here you white people wickedly brought over the ocean a great lot of reluctant black ones, and subjected them to several generations of slavery. Yet in those few generations these previously savage people have made noble progress."

She reeled off to me a list of achievements of the negro race, which I found surprising. Their development in wealth, in industry, in the professions, even the arts, was, considering the circumstances, astonishing.

"All you have to do is to improve the cultural conditions, to increase the rate of progress. It's no problem at all."

"You are a wonder," I told her. "You come out of that little far away heaven of yours, and dip into our tangle of horror and foolishness, and as soon as the first shock is over, you proceed to administer these little doses of wisdom, as if a mere pill or two would set the whole world straight."

"It would," said Ellador, "if you'd take it."

"Do you mean that seriously?" I demanded.

"I do. Why not? Why, Van—you've got all the necessary ingredients for peace and happiness. You don't have to wait a thousand years to grow. You're *here*. It's just a little matter of—behaving differently."

I laughed. "Exactly, my dear. And in Herland, so far as I make out, you behave accordingly to your perceptions and decisions. Here we don't."

"No," she admitted, grudgingly, "You don't, not yet. But you *could*" she persisted, triumphantly. "You could in a minute, if you wanted to."

I ducked this large proposition, and asked her if she had an answer to the Jewish race question as simple as that of the negro.

"What's the question?" she countered.

"I suppose there's more than one question involved," I answered slowly, "but mine would be: why don't people like Jews?"

"I won't be severe with your question, Van, though it's open to criticism. Not all people feel this race prejudice. And I'll tell you frankly that this is a bigger wide spread. It has deeper roots. I've one than the other. It's older. It's more looked into it—a little?"

I grinned. "Well, you young encyclopaedia, what did you discover?"

"I soon discovered that the very general dislike to this one people is not due to the religious difference between them and Christians; it was quite as general and strong, apparently, in very ancient times."

"Do you think it is a race feeling, then, an 'insuperable, ineradicable,' etc., antipathy."

"No," she said, "there are other Semitic and allied races to whom there is no general objection. I don't think it can be that. I have several explanations to suggest, of varying weight. Here's one of them. The Jews are the only surviving modern people that have ever tried to preserve the extremely primitive custom of endogenous marriage. Everywhere else, the exogenous habit proved itself best and was generally accepted. This people is the only one which has always assumed itself to be superior to every other people and tried to prevent intermarriage with them."

"That's twice you've said 'tried,' " I put in. "Do you mean that they have not succeeded?"

"Of course they haven't," she replied, cheerfully. "When people endeavor to live in defiance of natural law, they are not as a rule very successful."

"But, they boast the purity of their race——"

"Yes, I know they do, and other people accept it. But, Van, dear, surely you must have noticed the difference between, say, the Spanish and the

German Jews, for instance. Social contract will do much in spite of Ghettos, but it hardly alters the color of the eyes and hair."

"Well, my dear, if it is not religion, nor yet race, what is it?"

"I have two other suggestions, one sociologic, one psychic. The first is this: In the successive steps of social evolution, the Jewish people seem not to have passed the tribal stage. They never made a real nation. Apparently they can't. They live in other nations perforce."

"Why perforce?" I interrupted.

"Well, if they don't die, they have to live somewhere, Van. And unless they go and set up a new nation in a previously uninhabited country, or on the graves of the previous inhabitants, they have to live in other nations, don't they?"

"But they were a nation once," I urged.

"In a way,—yes. They had a piece of land to live on and they lived on it, as tribes, not as one people. According to their own account, ten out of twelve of these tribes got lost, somehow, and the others didn't seem to mind. No—they could not maintain the stage of social organization rightly called a nation. Their continuing entity is that of a race, as we see in far lesser instance in gypsies. And the more definitely organized peoples have, not a racial, but a sociological aversion to this alien form of life, which is in them, but not of them."

"But, Ellador, do not the modern Jews make good citizens in whatever country they are in?"

"They do, in large measure, wherever they are allowed," she agreed; "and both this difference and the old marriage difference would long ago have been outgrown but for the last one—the psychic one."

"Do you mean what that writer in *Blackwood's* said about Spain: 'There seems to be something Spanish in the minds of Spaniards which causes them to act in a Spanish manner?' "

She laughed. "All of that, Van, and a lot more." She stopped, looking away toward the far horizon. "I never tire of the marvel and interest of your mixed humanity," she resumed. "You see we were just *us*. For two thousand years we have been one stock and one sex. It's no wonder we can think, feel, act as one. And it's no wonder you poor things have had such a slow, tumultuous time of it. All kinds of races, all kinds of countries, all kinds of conditions, and the male sex to manage everything. Why, Van, the wonder is that before this last worldquake of war, you could travel about peaceably almost anywhere, I understand. Surely that ought to prove, once and for all how safe and quiet the world might be."

"But about the Jews?" I urged at last.

"Oh, yes. Well, dear, as I see it, people are moving on to a wide and full mutual understanding, with peace, of course, free trade and social intercourse and intermarriage, until everyone is what you call civilized. Against this process stood first total ignorance and separation. Then opposing interests. Then opposing ideas. To-day it is ideas that do the most damage. Look at poor Europe. Every interest calls them together but their different mental content holds them apart. Their egregiously false histories, their patriomanias, their long-nursed hatreds and vengeances—oh it is pathetic."

"Yes—and the Jews?"

"Oh dear me, Van, they're only one people. I get so interested in the world at large that I forget them. Well, what the Jews did was to make their patriomania into a religion."

I did not get that and said so.

"It was poorly put," she admitted. "They couldn't be patriomaniacs without a fatherland, could they? But it was the same feeling at a lower stage, applied only to the race. They thought they were 'the chosen people'—of God."

"Didn't other races think the same thing? Don't they yet?" I urged.

"Oh in a way, they do—some of them. Especially since the Jews made a Bible of it. You see, Van, the combination was peculiar. The special talent of this race is in literary expression. Other races had their sorrows but could not utter them. Carthage had no Jeremiah; nor has Armenia."

She saw that I was impressed by this point.

"You have Greece in its sculpture, its architecture and its objective literature. Even Greek history is a story told by an artist, a description. Rome lives in its roads, I have read, as well as its arts and its power of social organization. Rome, if it could have survived its besetting sins, was a super-nation, the beginning of a real world people. Egypt, India,—they all have something, but none of them concentrated on literature as the Jews did, having no other social expression."

"Why Ellador, don't you call their religion anything? Haven't they lifted the world with great religious concepts?"

She smiled at me, that gentle warm, steady smile of hers. "Forgive an outsider, please. I know that the Christian religion rests on the Jewish books, and that it is hard indeed to see around early teachings. But I have read your Bible carefully, and some little of the latest study and criticism upon it. I think the Christian races have helped the Jews to overestimate their religion."

"You've never said much about our various religions, my fair foreigner, What do you really think about them?"

This she pondered carefully.

"It's a large subject to try to comment on in a few words, but I can say this—they are certainly improving."

I had to laugh. This was such faint praise for our highest institution.

"How do you measure them, O casual observer?"

"By their effect upon the people, of course. Naturally, each set of believers holds its own to be the All True, and as naturally that is impossible. But there is enough truth and enough good will in your religions if you would only use them, instead of just believing them."

"And do you not think, especially considering the time of its development, that the Jewish concept of one God, the Jewish ethical ideal, was a long step upward?"

"It was a step, certainly, but, Van, they did not think their God was the only one. He was just Theirs. A private tribal God, openly described as being jealous of the others. And as to their ethics and the behavior of the people—you have only to read their own books to see how bad it was. Van, no religion can be truly good where the initial doctrines are false, or even partly false. That utterly derogatory concept of a God who could curse all humanity because of one man's doing what he knew he would, a God so petty as to pick out one small people for no better reason than that they gave him some recognition, and to set his face against all the rest of his equally descended 'children'—can't you see how unethical, how morally degrading, such a religion must be?"

"It was surely better than others at the time," I insisted.

"That may be, but the others of that period have mercifully perished. They weren't so literary. Don't you see, by means of their tremendous art this people have immortalized their race egotism and their whole record of religious aspirations, mistakes and failures, in literature. That is what has given them their lasting place in the world. But the effect of this primitive religion, immortalized by art, and thrust upon the world so long, has been far from good. It has well-nigh killed Christianity, from its cradle. It has been the foundation of most of those hideous old wars and persecutions. With quotations from that Hebrew 'voice of God' the most awful deeds have been committed and sanctioned. I consider it in many ways a most evil religion."

"But we have, as you say, accepted it; so it does not account for the general dislike for which you were offering explanations."

"The last explanation was the psychic one," she went on. "What impresses me here is this: The psychic attitude of this people presents to all the other inhabitants of the world a spirit of concentrated pride. It rests first on the tribal animus, with that old endogenous marriage custom; and then on this tremendous literary-religious structure. One might imagine generations of Egyptians making their chief education a study of the pyramids, sphynxes and so on, or generations of Greeks bringing up their children in the ceaseless contemplation of the Acropolis, or the works of their dramatists; but with the Jews, as a matter of fact, we do see, century after century of education in their ancient language, in their ancient books, and everlasting study and discussion of what remote dead men have written. This has given a peculiar intensity to the Jewish character—a sort of psychic inbreeding; they have a condensed spirit, more and more so as time passes, and it becomes increasingly inimical to the diffused spirit of modern races. Look at the pale recent imitation of such a spirit given in Germany. They have tried in a generation or two to build up and force upon their people an intense national spirit, with, of course, the indwelling egotism essential to such an undertaking. Now, suppose all German national glory rested on a few sacred books; their own early writings imposed upon the modern world; and suppose that German spirit, even now so offensive to other nations, had been concentrated and transmitted for thousands of years. Do you think people would like them?"

I was silent a bit. Her suggestions were certainly novel, and in no way resembled what I had heard before, either for or against this "peculiar people."

"What's the answer?" I said at last. "Is it hopeless?"

"Certainly not. Aren't they born babies, with dear little, clean, free minds? Just as soon as people recognize the evil of filling up new minds with old foolishness, they can make over any race on earth."

"That won't change 'race characteristics,' will it?"

"No, not the physical ones," she answered. "Intermarriage will do that."

"It looks to me as though your answer to the Jewish question was—leave off being Jews. Is that it?"

"In a measure it is," she said slowly. "They are world-people and can enrich the world with their splendid traits. They will keep, of course, their high race qualities, their special talents and virtues, by a chosen, not an enforced, selection. Some of the noblest people are Jews, some of the nicest. That can't be denied. But this long-nursed bunch of ancient mistakes—it is high time they dropped it. What is the use of artificially maintaining characteristics which the whole world dislikes, and then complaining of race prejudice? Of course, there is race prejudice, a cultural one; and all the rest of you will have to bring up your children without that. It is only the matter of a few generations at most."

This was a part of the spirit of Herland to which I was slow in becoming accustomed. Their homogeneous, well-ordered life extended its social consciousness freely, ahead as well as backwards; their past history was common knowledge, and their future development even more commonly discussed. They planned centuries ahead and accomplished what they planned. When I thought of their making over the entire language in the interests of childhood, of their vast field of cultural literature, of such material achievements as their replanting all their forests, I began to see that the greatness of a country is not to be measured by linear space, in extent of land, nor arithmetically by numbers of people, nor shallowly by the achievements of the present and a few leftovers, but by the scope of its predetermined social advance.

As this perception grew within me, it brought first a sense of shame for all the rest of the world, and even more intensely for my own country, which had such incomparable advantages. But after a little, instead of shame, which is utter waste, I began to see life as I never had before: as a great open field of work, in which we were quite free to do as we would. We have always looked at it as a hopeless tangle of individual lives, short, aimless threads, as blindly mixed as the grass stems in a haystack. But collectively, as nations, taking sufficient time, there was nothing we could not do. I told her of my new vision, and she was dumbly happy—just held my hand, her eyes shining.

"That's how to stand the misery and failure, isn't it?" I said. "That's how not to be discouraged at the awfulness of things; and the reason you take up these separate 'questions' so lightly is that none of them mean much alone. The important thing is to get people to think and act together."

"There's nothing on earth to hinder them, Van, dear, except what's in their heads. And they can stop putting it in, in the babies, I mean, and can put it out of their own, at least enough to get to work. They are beginning, you know."

She spoke most encouragingly, most approvingly, of the special efforts we were making in small groups or as individuals to socialize various industries and functions, but with far more fervor of the great "movements."

"The biggest of all, and closest related, are your women's movement and labor movement. Both seem to be swiftly growing stronger. The most inclusive forward-looking system is Socialism, of course. What a splendid vision of immediate possibilities that is. I can not accustom myself to your not seeing it at once. Of course, the reason is plain: your minds are full of your ancient mistakes, too; not so much racial and religious, as in beliefs of economic absurdities. It is so funny!"

It always nettled me a little to have her laugh at us. That she should be shocked and horrified at the world I had expected; that she should criticize and blame; but to have her act as though all our troubles were easily removable, and we were just a pack of silly fools not to set about it—this was irritating.

"Well, dear," she pursued pleasantly, "doesn't it look funny to you, like a man sleeping cold with good blankets at the foot of his bed; like Mr. Tantalus, quite able to get what he wanted, if he would only reach?"

"If what you said was so—" I began.

"And why isn't it, dear?"

"The trouble is, I think, in your psychology. You, as a free-minded Herlander, can not seem to see how helpless we are in our minds. All these ages of enforced belief have done something to us, I tell you. We can't change all in a minute."

"The worst thing that has been done to you is to fill your poor heads with this notion that you cannot help yourselves. Tell me, now, what is there to hinder you?"

"You had better be studying as to what does hinder us," I answered, "and explain it so that we can do something. We mean well. We are fairly well educated. We are, as you say, rich enough and all that. But we, up to date, seem unable to get together on any line of concerted action toward better living."

"I have been studying just that, Van, ever since I first came. Of course after I saw how things were, that was the only thing to do."

"Well?" I said, and again, "Well?"

She sat considering, turning over some books and papers that lay on the table beside her. A lovely picture she made, unique among the women of this land, she had the smooth rounded freedom of body we see in noble statues, and whatever her new friends tried to make her wear, she insisted upon a dress of such simplicity as did not contradict her natural lines and movements. Her face had changed, somewhat, in our two years of travel and study; there was a sadness in it, such as it never wore in Herland, such as I had never seen in anyone while there; and for all her quiet courtesy, her gentle patience, her scientific interest and loving kindness, there was a lonely look about her, as of some albatross in a poultry yard.

To me she was even more tender and delicately sympathetic than in our first young happiness. She seemed to be infinitely sorry for me, though carefully refraining from expressing it. Our common experiences, our studying and seeing so much together, had drawn us very close, and for my own part I had a curious sense of growing detachedness from the conditions about me and an overwhelming attachment to her which transcended every other tie. It seemed as if my love for her as a human being, such love as a brother, a sister, a friend might feel, was now so much greater than my love of her as a woman, my woman, that I could not miss that fulfillment much while so contented in the larger relation.

I thought of the many cases I had known where the situation was absolutely reversed, where a man loved a woman solely because of sex desire, without ever knowing her nature as a person, without even wanting to.

I was very happy with Ellador.

11

[Feminism and the Woman's Movement]

IT WAS INEVITABLE that my wife should take a large interest in Feminism. With that sweeping swiftness of hers she read a dozen or so of the leading—and misleading—books on the subject; spent some time in library work looking over files of papers and talked with all manner of people we met who had views on the matter. Furthermore, she thought about it.

As I grew more and more accustomed to seeing Ellador think, or at least to seeing the results of that process, I was sharply struck with the lack of thinking among people in general. She smiled sociably when I mentioned it.

"Why, yes, dear, that is largely what is the matter. You do not train your children to think—you train them not to. Your men think hard in narrow lines, just little pushing lines of their special work, or how to get richer, and your women——"

"Oh, come, let's have it!" I cried despairingly. "Whatever else you say or don't say you are always thinking about the women; I can fairly hear your brain click. And I'll tell you honestly, my dear, that I don't believe you can hurt me now, no matter how hard you hit them—or the men. It certainly has been a liberal education to live with you. Also I've had my time in Herland to show me the difference. I confess that as I now see this life of ours the women shock me, in some ways, more than the men. And I've been doing some reading as well as you, even some thinking. I suppose one thing that has made you so reticent about this is that you can't criticize the women without blaming the men. Perhaps it will encourage you if I begin to do the blaming."

She mildly said that perhaps it would seem more magnanimous, so I started in and found the case worse when stated at length than I had seen it in glimpses.

"Of course, there is no getting around Lester Ward," I began slowly. "No one can study biology and sociology much and not see that on the first physiological lines the female is the whole show, so to speak, or at least most of it. And all the way up she holds her own, even into early savagery, till Mr. Man gets into the saddle. How he came to do it is a mystery that I don't believe even you can explain."

"No," she agreed, "I can't. I call it 'The Great Divergence.' There is no other such catastrophic change in all nature—as far as I've been able to gather."

What Ellador had "gathered" in two years was perhaps not equal in detailed knowledge to the learning of great specialists, but she had a marvelous gift for selecting the really important facts and for arranging them. That was the trick—she did something with what she knew—not merely stored it.

"Well, he did take the reins, somehow," I resumed, "and we began our historic period, which is somewhat too large to be covered in an hour—by me. But in all this time, as far as I can make out, he has never been even fair to women, and has for the most part treated her with such an assortment of cruelty and injustice as makes me blush for my sex."

"What made you think so, Van? What first?"

"Why Herland first," I answered promptly. "Seeing women who were People and that they were People *because* they were women, not in spite of it. Seeing that what we had called "womanliness" was a mere excess of sex, not the essential part of it at all. When I came back here and compared our women with yours—well, it was a blow. Besides, if I'd had no other evidence *You* would have shown me—just living with you, my Wonder Darling."

She looked at me with shining eyes, that look that was more than wife, more than mother; the illimitable loving Human look.

"What I have learned from you, Dearest; from our companionship without the physical intimacy of sex, is this; that Persons, two Persons who love each other, have a bigger range of happiness than even two lovers. I mean than two lovers who are not such companions, of course. I do not deny that it has been hard, very hard, sometimes. I've been disagreeable to live with——" "Never!" she interpolated, "but somehow the more I loved you the less it troubled me. Now I feel that when we do reach that union, with all our love, with all the great mother purpose that is in your heart and the beginning of a sense of father purpose in mine, I'm sure that it will be only an incident in our love, our happiness, not the main thing."

She gave a long soft sigh of full content, still listening.

"All this makes me see the—limitations of our women," I continued, "and when I look for a reason there is only the conduct of men toward them. Cruelty? Why, my dear, it is not the physical cruelty to their tender bodies; it is not the shame and grief and denial that they have had to bear; those are like the 'atrocities' in warfare—it is the war itself which is wrong. The petted women, the contented women, the 'happy' women—these are perhaps the worst result."

"It's wonderful how clearly you see it," she said.

"Pretty plain to see," I went on. "We men, having all human power in our hands, have used it to warp and check the growth of women. We, by choice and selection, by law and religion, by enforced ignorance, by heavy overcultivation of sex, have made the kind of woman we so made by nature, that that is what it was to be a woman. Then we heaped our scornful abuse upon her, ages and ages of it, the majority of men in all nations still looking down on women. And then, as if that was not enough—really, my dear, I'm not joking, I'm ashamed, as if I'd done it myself—we, in our superior freedom, in our monopoly of education, with the law in our hands, both to make and execute, with every conceivable advantage—we have blamed women for the sins of the world!"

She interrupted here, eagerly—" Not *all* of you, Van dear! That was only a sort of legend with some people. It was only in the Jewish religion you think so much of that the contemptible lie was actually stated as a holy truth—and even God made to establish that unspeakable injustice."

"Yes, that's true, but nobody objected. We all accepted it gladly—and treated her accordingly. Well, sister—have I owned up enough? I guess you can't hurt my feelings any with anything you say about men. Of course, I'm not going into details, that would take forever, but just in general I can see what ails the women—and who's to blame for it."

"Don't be too hard on Mr. Man," she urged gently. "What you say is true enough, but so are other things. What puzzles me most is not at all that background of explanation, but what ails the women *now*. Here, even here in America, *now*. They have had some education for several generations, numbers of them have time to think, some few have money—I cannot be reconciled to the women, Van!"

She was so unusually fierce about it that I was quite surprised at her. I had supposed that her hardest feeling would be about men. She saw my astonishment and explained.

"Put yourself in my place for a moment, Van. Suppose in Herland we had a lot of—subject men. Blame us all you want to for doing it, but look at the men. Little creatures, undersized and generally feeble. Cowardly and not ashamed of it. Kept for sex purposes only or as servants; or both, usually both. I confess I'm asking something difficult of your imagination, but try to think of Herland women, each with a soft man she kept to cook for her, to wait upon her and to—'love' when she pleased. Ignorant men mostly. Poor men, almost all, having to ask their owners for money and tell what they wanted it for. Some of them utterly degraded creatures, kept in houses for common use—as women are kept here. Some of them quite gay and happy—pet men, with pet names and presents showered upon them. Most of them contented, piously accepting kitchen work as their duty, living by the religion and laws and customs the women made. Some of them left out and made fun of for being left—not owned at all—and envying those who were! Allow for a surprising percentage of mutual love and happiness, even under these conditions; but also for ghastly depths of misery and a general low level of mere submission to the inevitable. Then in this state of degradation fancy these men for the most part quite content to make monkeys of themselves by wearing the most ridiculous clothes. Fancy them, men, with men's bodies, though enfeebled, wearing open-work lace under-clothing, with little ribbons all strung through it; wearing dresses never twice alike and almost always foolish; wearing hats——" she fixed me with a steady eye in which a growing laughter twinkled—"wearing such hats as your women wear!"

At this I threw up my hands. "I can't!" I said. "It's all off. I followed you with increasing difficulty, even through the lace and baby ribbon, but I stop there. Men wear such hats! Men! I tell you it is unthinkable!"

"Unthinkable for such men?"

"Such men are unthinkable, really; contemptible, skulking, cowardly spaniels! They would deserve all they got."

"Why aren't you blaming the women of Herland for treating them so, Van?"

"Oh!" said I, and "Yes," said I, "I begin to see, my dear Herlander, why you're down on the women."

"Good," she agreed. "It's all true, what you say about the men, nothing could be blacker than that story. But the women, Van, the women! They are not dead! They are here, and in your country they have plenty of chance to grow. How can they bear their position, Van; how can they stand it another day? Don't they know they are *Women!*"

"No," said I slowly. "They think they are—women."

We both laughed rather sadly.

Presently she said, "We have to take the facts as we find them. Emotion does not help us any. It's no use being horrified at a—hermit crab—that's the way he is. This is the woman man made—how is she going to get over it?"

"You don't forget the ones who have gotten over it, do you? And all the splendid work they are doing?"

"I'm afraid I did for a moment," she admitted. "Besides—so much of their effort is along side lines, and some of it in precisely the wrong direction."

"What would you have them do?"

"What would you have those inconceivable men of Herland do?" she countered. "What would you say to them—to rouse them?"

"I'd try to make them realize that they were *men*," I said. "That's the first thing."

"Exactly. And if the smooth, plump, crazily dressed creatures answered 'A true man is always glad to be supported by the woman he loves' what would you say to that?"

"I should try to make him realize what the world really was," I answered slowly, "and to see what was a man's place in it."

"And if he answered you—a hundred million strong—'A man's place is in the home!'—what would you say then?"

"It would be pretty hard to say anything—if men were like that."

"Yes, and it is pretty hard to say anything when women are like that—it doesn't reach them."

"But there is the whole women's movement—surely they are changing, improving."

She shook off her mood of transient bitterness. "My ignorance makes me hard, I suppose. I'm not familiar enough with your past history, recent past history, I mean, to note the changes as clearly as you do. I come suddenly to see them as they are, not knowing how much worse it has been. For instance, I suppose women used to dress more foolishly than they do now. Can that be possible?"

I ran over in my mind some of the eccentricities of fashion in earlier periods and was about to say that it was possible when I chanced to look out of the window. It was a hot day, most oppressively hot, with a fiercely glaring sun. A woman stood just across the street talking to a man. I picked up my opera glass and studied her for a moment. I had read that "the small waist is coming in again." Hers had come. She stood awkwardly in extremely high-heeled slippers, in which the sole of the foot leaned on a steep slant from heel to ball, and her toes, poor things, were driven into the narrow-pointed toe of the slipper by the whole sliding weight of the body above. The thin silk hose showed the insteps puffing up like a pincushion from the binding grip of that short vamp.

Her skirts were short as a child's, most voluminous and varied in outline, hanging in bunches on the hips and in various fluctuating points and corners below. The bodice was a particolored composition, of indiscreet exposures, more suitable for a ballroom than for the street.

But what struck me most was that she wore about her neck a dead fox or the whole outside of one.

No, she was not a lunatic. No, that man was not her keeper. No, it was not a punishment, not an initiation penalty, not an election bet.

That woman, of her own free will and at considerable expense, wore heavy furs in the hottest summer weather.

I laid down the glass and turned to Ellador. "No, my dear," said I gloomily. "It is not possible that women ever could have been more idiotic in dress than that."

We were silent for a little, watching that pitiful object with her complacent smile as she stood there on those distorted feet, sweating under her load of fur, perfectly contented and pleased with herself.

"Some way," said Ellador slowly, "it makes me almost discouraged about the woman's movement. I'm not, of course, not really. I do know enough to see that they are far better off than a hundred years ago. And the laws of life are on their side, solid irresistible laws. They are women after all, and women are people—are *the* people, really, up to a certain point. I must make more allowances, must learn to see the gain in some ways even where there is none in others. Now that—that tottering little image may be earning her own living or doing something useful . . . . What's worst of all, perhaps, is the strange missing of purpose in those who are most actively engaged in 'advancing.' They seem like flies behind a window, they bump and buzz, pushing their heads against whatever is in front of them, and never seem really to plan a way out. . . . No, there's one thing worse than that—much worse. I wouldn't have believed it possible—I can hardly believe it now."

"What's this horror?" I asked. "Prostitution? White slavery?"

"Oh, no," she said, "those things are awful, but a sort of natural awfulness, if I may say so; what a scientific observer would expect of the evil conditions carried to excess. No—this thing is—*un-natural!* I mean—the Antis."

"Oh—the Anti-Suffragists?"

"Yes. Think of the men again—those poor degraded men I was imagining. And then think of some of them struggling for freedom, struggling long and hard, with pathetically slow progress, doing no harm in the meantime, just talking, arguing, pleading, petitioning, using what small money they could scrape together to promote their splendid cause, their cause that meant not only their own advantage, but more freedom and swifter progress for all the world. And then think of some other of those pet men, not only misunderstanding the whole thing, too dull or too perverse even to see such basic truth as that, but actually banding together to oppose it——!

"Van, if you want one all-sufficient and world-convincing proof of the degradation of women, you have it in the anti-suffragist!"

"The men are backing them, remember," I suggested.

"Of course they are. You expect the men to oppose the freeing of women, they naturally would. But the women, Van—the women themselves—it's unnatural."

With a sick shudder she buried her face in her hands for a moment, then straightened up bravely again, giving that patient little sigh of dismissal to the subject. I was silent and watched her as she sat, so strong, so graceful, so beautiful, with that balanced connection in line and movement we usually see only in savages. Her robe was simple in form, lovely in color, comfortable and becoming. I looked at her with unfailing pleasure always, never having to make excuses and reservations. All of her was beautiful and strong.

And I thought of her sisters, that fair land of full grown women, all of whom, with room for wide personal distinction, were beautiful and strong. There were differences enough. A group of thoroughbred race horses might vary widely in color, size, shape, marking and individual expression; yet all be fine horses. There would be no need of scrubs and cripples to make variety. And I looked again out of our window, at the city street, with its dim dirtiness, its brutal noise and the unsatisfied, unsatisfying people going so hurriedly about after their food, crowding, pushing, hurrying like hungry rats; the sordid eagerness of the men, the shallow folly of the women. And all at once there swept over me a great wave of homesickness for Herland.

Ellador was never satisfied merely to criticize; she must needs plan some way out, some improvement. So, laying aside her discouragement, she plunged into this woman question with new determination and before long came to me in loving triumph.

"I was wrong, Van, to be so harsh with them; it was just my Herland background. Now I have been deliberately putting myself in the woman's place and measuring the rate of progress—as of a glacier. And it's wonderful, really wonderful. There was the bottom limit—not so very far back—some savages still keeping to it—merely to live long enough to bear a daughter. Then there's the gain, this way in one land and that way in another, but always a gain. Then this great modern awakening which is now stirring them all over the world. By keeping my own previous knowledge of women entirely out of my mind and by measuring your really progressive ones today against their own grandmothers—that movement I was so scornful about now seems to me a sunburst of blazing improvement. Of course they 'bump and buzz' in every direction, that is mere resilience—haven't they been kept down in every direction? They'll get over that as they grow accustomed to real liberty.

"It would be inconceivable that they should have been so unutterably degraded for so long and not show the results of it, the limitations. Instead of blaming them I should have been rejoicing at the wonderful speed with which they have surged forward as fast as any door was opened, even a crack. I have been looking at what might be called the unconscious as apart from the conscious woman's movement, and it comforts me much."

"Just what do you mean?"

"I mean the women's clubs, here in this country especially; and largest of all the economic changes; the immense numbers who are at work."

"Didn't they always work? The poor ones, that is?"

"Oh, yes, at home. I mean human work."

"Wage earning?"

"That, incidentally, is a descriptive term; but it would be a different grade of work, even without that."

"So I've heard people say, some people. But what is there superior in doing some fractional monotonous little job like bookkeeping, for instance, as compared with the management and performance of all the intimate tasks in a household?"

I was so solemn about this that she took me seriously, at least for a moment.

"It isn't the difference between a bookkeeper and a housekeeper that must be considered; it is the difference between an organized business world that needs bookkeeping and an unorganized world of separate families with no higher work than to eat, sleep and keep alive."

Then she saw me grin and begged pardon, cheerfully. "I might have known you were wiser than that, Van. But, oh, the people I've been talking to! The questions they ask and the comments they make! Fortunately we do not have to wait for universal conviction before moving onward."

"If you could have your way with the women of this country and the others what would you make them do?" I asked.

She set her chin in her hand and meditated a little. "What they are doing, only more of it, for one thing," she answered presently, "but, oh, so much more! Of course they have to be taught differently, they need new standards, new hopes, new ideals, new purposes. That's the real field of work, you see, Van, in the mind. That is what was so confusing to me at first. You see the difference in looks between your women and our women is as one to a thousand compared to the differences between their mental content.

"Your conditions are so good, the real ones, I mean, the supplies, the materials, the abilities you have, that at first I underrated the difficulties. Inside you are not as advanced as outside, men or women. You have such antique minds! I never get used to it. You see we, ever so long ago, caught up with our conditions; and now we are always planning better ones. Our minds are ahead of our conditions—and yet we live pretty comfortably."

"And how are our women going to catch up?"

"They have to make a long jump, from the patriarchal status to the democratic, from the narrowest personal ties to the widest social relation, from first hand labor, mere private service of bodily needs, to the specialized, organized social service of the whole community. At present this is going on, in actual fact, without their realizing it, without their understanding and accepting it. It is the mind that needs changing."

"I suppose it seems a trifling matter to you to change the working machinery of twenty million homes—that's what it amounts to—doesn't it?"

"How long does it take to do up twenty million women's hair?" she inquired. "No longer than it does one—if they all do it at once. Numbers don't complicate a question like this. What could be done in one tiny village could be done all over the country in the same time. I suppose I do underestimate the practical difficulties here on account of our having settled all those little problems. The idea of your still not being properly fed!—I can't get used to it."

Then I remembered the uniform excellence of food in Herland; not only all that we ourselves had enjoyed, but that I never saw in any shop or market any wilted, withered, stale or in any way inferior supplies.

"How did you manage that?" I asked her. "Did you confiscate all the damaged things? Was there a penalty for selling them?"

"Does one of your housekeepers confiscate her damaged food? Is there any penalty for feeding her family with it?"

"Oh, I see. You only provided enough to keep fresh."

"Exactly. I tell you numbers don't make any difference. A million people do not eat any more—apiece—than a dozen at one table. We feed our people as carefully and as competently as you try to feed your families. You can't do as well because of the inferiority of materials."

This I found somewhat offensive, but I knew it was true.

"It's so simple!" she said wearily. "A child could see it. Food is to *eat*, and if it is not good to eat it is not food. Here you people use food as a thing to play with, to buy and sell, to store up, to throw away, with no more regard for its real purpose than——"

"Than the swine with pearls before him," I suggested. "But you know those economic laws come in——"

She laughed outright.

"Van, dear, there is nothing in all your pitiful tangled life more absurd than what you so solemnly call 'economics.' Good economics in regard to food is surely this: to produce the best quality, in sufficient quantity, with the least expenditure of labor, and to distribute it the most rapidly and freshly to the people who need it."

"The management of food in your world is perhaps the most inexplicably foolish of anything you do. I've been up and down the streets in your cities observing. I've been in the hotels and restaurants far and wide and in ever so many homes. And I confess, Van, with some mortification, that there is no one thing I'm more homesick for than food."

"I am getting discouraged, if you are not, Ellador. As compared with a rational country like yours, this is rather a mess. And it looks so hopeless. I suppose it will take a thousand years to catch up."

"You could do it in three generations," she calmly replied.

"Three generations! That's barely a century."

"I know it. The whole outside part of it you could do inside of twenty years; it is the people who will take three generations to remake. You could improve this stock, say, 5 per cent. in one, 15 in two and 80 per cent. in three. Perhaps faster."

"Are not you rather sanguine, my dear girl?"

"I don't think so," she answered gravely. "People are not *bad* now; they are only weighed down with all this falsehood and foolishness in their heads. There is always the big lifting force of life to push you on as fast as you will let it. There is the wide surrounding help of conditions, such conditions as you even now know how to arrange. And there is the power of education—which you have hardly tried. With these all together and with proper care in breeding you could fill the world with glorious people—soon. Oh, I wish you'd do it! I *wish* you'd do it!"

It was hard on her. Harder even than I had foreseen. Not only the war horrors, not only the miseries of more backward nations and of our painful past, but even in my America where I had fondly thought she would be happy, the common arrangements of our lives to which we are so patiently accustomed, were to her a constant annoyance and distress.

Through her eyes I saw it newly and instead of the breezy pride I used to feel in my young nation I now began to get an unceasing sense of what she had called "an idiot child."

It was so simply true, what she said about food. Food is to eat. All its transporting and preserving and storing and selling—if it interferes with the eating value of the food—is foolishness. I began to see the man who stores eggs until they are reduced to the grade called "rots and spots" as an idiot and a malicious idiot at that. Vivid and clear rose in my mind the garden-circled cities of Herland, where for each group of inhabitants all fresh fruits and vegetables were raised so near that they could be eaten the day they were picked. It did not cost any more. It cost *less*, saving transportation. Supplies that would keep they kept—enough from season to season, with some emergency reserves; but not one person, young or old, ever had to eat such things as we pay extortionately for in every city.

Nothing but women, only mothers, but they had worked out to smooth perfection what now began to seem to me to be the basic problem in human life.

How to make the best kind of people and how to keep them at their best and growing better—surely that is what we are here for.

12

[Conclusion]

AS I LOOK OVER MY MASS OF NOTES, of hastily jotted down or wholly re-con-structed conversations, and some of Ellador's voluminous papers, I am distressingly conscious of the shortcomings of this book. There is no time now to improve it, and I wish to publish it, as a little better than no report at all of the long visit of my wife from Herland to the world we know.

In time I hope, if I live, and if I come back again, to make a far more competent study than this. Yet why trouble myself to do that? She will do it, I am sure, with the help of her friends and sisters, far better than I could.

I had hoped that she could go blazing about our world, lecturing on the wonders and beauties of Herland, but that was all dropped when they decided not to betray their strange geographical secret—yet. I am allowed to print the previous account of our visit there—even that will set explorers on their track; but she did not wish to answer specific questions while here, nor to refuse to answer.

They were quite right. The more I see of our world, the surer I am that they are right to try to preserve their lovely country as it is, for a while at least.

Ellador begs that I explain how inchoate, how fragmentary, how dispro-portionate, her impressions necessarily were.

"The longer I stay," she said, "the more I learn of your past and understand of your present, the more hopeful I feel for you. Please make that very clear." This she urged strongly.

The war did not discourage her, after a while. "What is one more—among so many?" she asked, with a wry smile. "The very awfulness of this is its best hope; that, and the growing wisdom of the people. You'll have no more, I'm sure; that is, no more except those recognized as criminal outbreaks, and punitive ones; the receding waves of force as these turbulent cross-currents die down and disappear.

"But, Van, dear, whatever else you leave out, be sure to make it as strong as you can about the women and children."

"Perhaps you'd better say it yourself, my dear. Come, you put in a chapter," I urged. But she would not.

"I should be too abusive, I'm afraid," she objected; "and I've talked enough on the subject—you know that."

She had, by this time, gone over it pretty thoroughly. And it is not very difficult to give the drift of it—we all know the facts. Her position, as a Herlander, was naturally the maternal one.

"The business of people is, of course, to be well, happy, wise, beautiful, productive and progressive."

"Why don't you say 'good,' too," I suggested.

"Don't be absurd, Van. If people are well and happy, wise, beautiful, productive and progressive, they must incidentally be good; that's being good. What sort of goodness is it which does not produce those effects? Well, these 'good' people need a 'good' world to live in, and they have to make it; a clean, safe, comfortable world to grow in.

"Then, since they all begin as children, it seems so self-evident that the way to make better people and a better world is to teach the children how."

"You'll find general agreement so far," I admitted.

"But the people who train children are, with you, the mothers," she pursued, "and the mothers of your world have not yet seen this simple truth."

"They talk of nothing else," I suggested. "They are always talking of the wonderful power and beauty of motherhood, from the most ancient morality to Ellen Key."

"Yes, I know they talk about it. Their idea of motherhood, to what it ought to be, is like a birchbark canoe to an ocean steamship, Van. They haven't seen it as a whole—that's the trouble. What prevents them is their dwarfed condition, not being people, real, world-building people; and what keeps them dwarfed is this amazing relic of the remote past—their domestic position."

"Would you 'destroy the home,' as they call it, Ellador?"

"I think the home is the very loveliest thing you have on earth," she unexpectedly replied.

"What do you mean, then?" I asked, genuinely puzzled. "You can't have homes without women in them, can you? And children?"

"And men," she gravely added. "Why, Van—do not men have homes, and love them dearly? A man does not have to stay at home all day, in order to love it; why should a woman?"

Then she made clear to me, quite briefly, how the home should be to the woman just what it was to a man, and far more to both, in beauty and comfort, in privacy and peace, in all the pleasant rest and dear companionship we so prize; but that it should not be to him a grinding weight of care and expense, or an expression of pride; nor to her a workshop or her sole means of personal expression.

"It is so pathetic," she said, "and so unutterably absurd, to see great city-size and world-size women trying to content themselves and express themselves in one house; or worse, one flat. You know how it would be for a man, surely. It is just as ridiculous for a woman. And your city-size and world-size men are all tied up to these house-size women. It's so funny, Van, so painfully funny, like a horse harnessed with an eohippus."

"We haven't got to wait for Mrs. Eohippus to catch up to Mr. Horse, I hope?"

"You won't have to wait long," she assured me. "They are born equal, your boys and girls; they have to be. It is the tremendous difference in cultural conditions that divides them; not only in infancy and youth; not only in dress and training; but in this wide gulf of industrial distinction, this permanent division which leaves one sex free to rise, to develop every social power and quality, and forcibly restrains the other to a labor-level thousands of years behind. It is beginning to change, I can see that now, but it has to be complete, universal, before women can do their duty as mothers."

"But I thought—at least I've always heard—that it was their duty as mothers which kept them at home."

She waved this aside, with a touch of impatience. "Look at the children," she said; "that's enough. Look at these girls who do not even know enough about motherhood to demand a healthy father. Why, a—a—sheep would know better than to mate with such creatures as some of your women marry.

"They are only just beginning to learn that there are such diseases as they have been suffering and dying from for all these centuries. And they are so poor! They haven't any money, most of them; they are so disorganized—unorganized—apparently unconscious of any need of organization."

I mentioned the growth of trade unions, but she said that was but a tiny step—useful, but small; what she meant was Mother Union . . . .

"I suppose it is sex," she pursued, soberly. "With us, motherhood is so simple. I had supposed, at first, that your bi-sexual method would mean a better motherhood, a motherhood of two, so to speak. And I find that men have so enjoyed their little part of the work that they have grown to imagine it as quite a separate thing, and to talk about 'sex' as if it was wholly distinct from parentage. Why, see what I found the other day"—and she pulled out a copy of a little yellow medical magazine, published by a physician who specializes in sex diseases, and read me a note this doctor had written on "Sterilization," wherein he said that it had no injurious effect on sex.

"Just look at that!" she said. "The man is a doctor—and thinks the removal of parental power is no loss to 'sex'! What men—yes, and some women, too—seem to mean by sex is just their preliminary pleasure . . . . When your women are really awake and know what they are for, seeing men as the noblest kind of assistants, nature's latest and highest device for the improvement of parentage, then they will talk less of 'sex' and more of children."

I urged, as genuinely as I could, the collateral value and uses of sex indulgence; not the common theories of "necessity," which any well-trained athlete can deny, but the more esoteric claims of higher flights of love, and of far-reaching stimulus to all artistic faculty: the creative impulse in our work.

She listened patiently, but shook her head when I was done.

"Even if all those claims were true," she said, "they would not weigh as an ounce to a ton beside the degradation of women, the corruption of the body and mind through these wholly unnecessary diseases, and the miserable misborn children. Why, Van, what's 'creative impulse' and all its 'far-reaching stimulus' to set beside the stunted, meager starveling children, the millions of poor little sub-ordinary children, children who are mere accidents and by-products of this much-praised 'sex'? It's no use, dear, until all the children of the world are at *least* healthy; at *least* normal; until the average man and woman are free from taint of sex-disease and happy in their love—lastingly happy in their love—there is not much to boast of in this popular idea of sex and sex indulgence.

"It can not be changed in a day or a year," she said. "This is evidently a matter of long inheritance, and that's why I allow three generations to get over it. But nothing will help much till the women are free and see their duty as mothers."

"Some of the 'freest' women are urging more sex freedom," I reminded her. "They want to see the women doing as men have done, apparently."

"Yes, I know. They are almost as bad as the antis—but not quite. They are merely a consequence of wrong teaching and wrong habits; they were there before, those women, only not saying what they wanted. Surely, you never imagined that all men could be unchaste and all women chaste, did you?"

I shamefacedly admitted that that was exactly what we had imagined, and that we had most cruelly punished the women who were not.

"It's the most surprising thing I ever heard of," she said; "and you bred and trained plenty of animals, to say nothing of knowing the wild ones. Is there any case in nature of a species with such a totally opposite trait in the two sexes?"

There wasn't, that I knew of, outside of their special distinctions, of course.

All these side issues she continually swept aside, all the minor points and discussable questions, returning again and again to the duty of women.

"As soon as the women take the right ground, men will have to follow suit," she said, "as soon as women are free, independent and conscientious. They have the power in their own hands, by natural law."

"What is going to rouse them, to make them see it?" I asked.

"A number of things seems to be doing that," she said, meditatively. "From my point of view, I should think the sense of maternal duty would be the strongest thing, but there seem to be many forces at work here. The economic change is the most imperative, more so, even, than the political, and both are going on fast. There's the war, too, that is doing wonders for women. It is opening the eyes of men, millions of men, at once, as no arguments ever could have."

"Aren't you pleased to see the women working for peace?" I asked.

"Immensely, of course. All over Europe they are at it—that's what I mean."

"But I meant the Peace Movement."

"Oh, that? Talking for peace, you mean, and writing and telegraphing. Yes, that's useful, too. Anything that brings women out into social relation, into a sense of social responsibility, is good. But all that they say and write and urge will not count as much as what they *do*.

"Your women will surely have more sense than the men about economics," she suggested. "It does not seem to me possible for business women to mishandle food as men do, or to build such houses. It is all so—unreasonable: to make people eat what is not good, or live in dark, cramped little rooms."

"You don't think they show much sense in their own clothes?" I offered, mischievously.

"No, they don't. But that is women as they are, the kind of women you men have been so long manufacturing. I'm speaking of real ones, the kind that are there underneath, and sure to come out as soon as they have a chance. And what a glorious time they will have—cleaning up the world! I'd almost like to stay and help a little."

Gradually it had dawned upon me that Ellador did not mean to stay, even in America. I wanted to be sure.

"Like to stay? Do you mean that you want to go back—for good?"

"It is not absolutely clear to me yet," she answered. "But one thing I'm certain about. If I live here I will not have a child."

I thought for a moment that she meant the distress about her would have some deleterious effect and prevent it; but when I looked at her, saw the folded arms, the steady mouth, the fixed determination in her eyes, I knew that she meant "will not" when she said it.

"It would not be right," she added, simply. "There is no place in all your world, that I have seen or read of, where I should be willing to raise a child."

"We could go to some lovely place alone," I urged; "some island, clean and beautiful——"

"But we should be 'alone' there. That is no place for a child."

"You could teach it—as they do in Herland," I still urged.

"I teach it? I? What am I, to teach a child?"

"You would be its mother," I answered.

"And what is a mother to teach a solitary little outcast thing as you suggest? Children need the teaching of many women, and the society of many children, for right growth. Also, they need a social environment—not an island!"

"You see, dear," she went on, after a little, "in Herland everything teaches. The child sees love and order and peace and comfort and wisdom everywhere. No child, alone, could grow up so—so richly endowed. And as to these countries I have seen—these cities of abomination—I would die childless rather than to bear a child in this world of yours."

In Herland to say "I would die childless" is somewhat equivalent to our saying "I would suffer eternal damnation." It is the worst deprivation they can think of.

"You are going to leave me!" I cried. It burst upon me with sudden bitterness. She was not "mine," she was a woman of Herland, and her heavenly country, her still clear hope of motherhood, were more to her than life in our land with me. What had I to offer her that was comparable to that upland paradise?

She came to me, then, and took me in her arms—strong, tender, loving arms—and gave me one of her rare kisses.

"I'm going to stay with you, my husband, as long as I live—if you want me. Is there anything to prevent your coming back to Herland?"

As a matter of fact, there was really nothing to prevent it, nothing I might leave behind which would cost me the pain her exile was costing her; and especially nothing which could compensate for losing my wife.

We began to discuss it, with eager interest. "I don't mean to forsake this poor world," she assured me. "We can come back again—later, much later. My mind is full of great things that can be done here, and I want to get all the wisdom of Herland at work to help. But let us go back now, while we are young, and before this black, stupid confusion has—has hurt me any worse. Perhaps it is no harm, that I have suffered so. Perhaps our child will have a heart that aches for all the world—and will do more than any of us to help it. Especially if it is—a Boy."

"Do you want a boy, darling?"

"Oh, do I not! just think—none of us, ever, in these two thousand years, has had one. If we, in Herland, can begin a new kind of men!" . . .

"What do you want of them?" I said, teasingly. "Surely you women alone have accomplished all that the world needs, haven't you?"

"Indeed, no, Van. We haven't begun. Ours is only a—a sample: a little bit of a local exhibit. If what we have done is the right thing, then it becomes our clearest duty to spread it to all the world. Such a new life as you have opened to us, Van, you Splendid Man!"

"Splendid Man! Splendid! I thought you thought we were to blame for all the misery in the world? Just look at the harm we've done!"

"Just look at the good you've done, too! Why, my darling, the harm you have done is merely the result of your misunderstanding and misuse of Sex; and the good you have done is the result of the humanness of you, the big, noble humanness that has grown and grown, that has built and lifted and taught the world in spite of all the dragging evil. Why, dear, when I see the courage, the perseverance, the persistent growth you men have shown, cumbered as you have been from the beginning by the fruits of your mistakes, it seems as if you were almost *more* than human."

I was rather stunned by this. No man who had seen Herland and then come back to our tangled foolishness, waste and pain, could be proud of his man-made world. No man who had solidly grasped the biological facts as to the initial use of his sex, and his incredible misuse of it, could help the further shame for the anomalous position of the human male, completely mistaken, and producing a constant train of evils.

I could see it all plainly enough. And now, to have her talk like this!

"Remember, dear, that men never *meant* to do it, or any part of it," she tenderly explained. "The trouble evidently began when nobody knew much; it became an ironclad 'custom' even before religion took it up, and law. Remember, too, that the women haven't died—they are here yet, in equal numbers. Also, even the unjust restrictions have saved them from a great deal of suffering which the men met. And then nothing could rob them of their inheritance. Every step the men really made upward lifted the women, too. And don't forget Love, ever. That has lived and triumphed even through all the lust and slavery and shame."

I felt comforted, relieved.

"Besides," she went on, "you men ought to feel proud of the real world work you have done, even crippled as you were by your own excessive sex, and by those poor, dragging dead-weights of women you had manufactured. In spite of it all, you have invented and discovered and built and adorned the world. You have things as far along as we have, even some things better, and many sciences and crafts we know nothing about. And you've done it alone—just men! It's wonderful."

In spite of all the kindness and honest recognition she showed, I could not help a feeling of inner resentment at this tone. Of course, we three men had been constantly impressed with all that they had done in Herland—just women, alone—but that she thought it equally wonderful for men to do it was not wholly gratifying.

She went on serenely.

"We had such advantages, you see. Being women, we had all the constructive and organizing tendencies of motherhood to urge us on and, having no men, we missed all that greediness and quarreling your history is so sadly full of. Also, being isolated, we could just grow—like a sequoia in a sheltered mountain glade.

"But you men, in this mixed, big world of yours, in horrid confusion, of mind and long ignorance, with all those awful religions to mix you up and hold you back, and with so little real Happiness—still, you have built the world! Van, dear, it shows how much stronger humanity is than sex, even in men. All that I have had to learn, you see, for we make no distinction at home—women are people, and people are women.

"At first I thought of men just as males—a Herlander would, you know. Now I know that men are people, too, just as much as women are; and it is as one person to another that I feel this big love for you, Van. You are so nice to live with. You are such good company. I never get tired of you. I like to play with you, and to work with you. I admire and enjoy the way you do things. And when we sit down quietly, near together—it makes me so happy, Van!"

* * * * * * * *

There were still a few big rubies in that once fat little bag she so wisely brought with her. We made careful plans, which included my taking a set of thorough lessons in aviation and mechanics; there must be no accidents on this trip. By a previous steamer we sent the well-fitted motorboat that should carry us and our dissembled aeroplane up that long river.

Of baggage, little could be carried, and that little, on Ellador's part, consisted largely of her mass of notes, all most carefully compressed, and done on the finest and lightest paper. She also urged that we take with us the lightest and newest of encyclopaedias. "We can leave it in the boat, if necessary, and make a separate trip," she suggested. Also photographs she took, and a moving picture outfit with well-selected films. "We can make them, I'm sure," she said; "but this one will do to illustrate." It did.

After all, her requirements did not weigh more than the third passenger whom we might have carried.

The river trip was a growing joy; day after day of swift gliding through those dark, drooping forests and wide, reedy flats; and when at last we shot out upon the shining silver of that hidden lake, and she saw above her the heights of Herland—my calm goddess trembled and cried, stretching her arms to it like a child to its mother.

But we set swiftly to work on our aeroplane, putting it all soundly together and fastening in the baggage, and then sealed up the tight sheathed boat like a trim cocoon.

Then the purr of our propeller, the long, skating slide on the water, and up—and up—in a widening spiral, Ellador breathless, holding fast to the supports, till we topped the rocky rim, rose above the forest, her forest—and sailed out over the serene expanse of that fair land.

"O, let's look," she begged; "let's look at the whole of it first—it's the whole of it that I love!" So we swept in a great circle above, as one might sweep over Holland: the green fields, blossoming gardens, and dark woods, spread like a model of heaven below us, and the cities, the villages—how well I remembered them, in their scattered loveliness, rich in color, beautiful in design, everywhere fringed and shaded by clean trees, lit and cheered by bright water, radiant with flowers.

She leaned forward like a young mother over her sleeping child, tender, proud, gloating.

"No smoke!" she murmured; "no brutal noise, no wickedness, no disease. Almost no accidents or sickness—almost none." (This in a whisper, as if she were apologizing for some faint blemish on the child.)

"Beauty!" she breathed. "Beauty! Beauty!—everywhere. Oh, I had forgotten how beautiful it was!"

So had I. When I first saw it I was still too accustomed to our common ugliness to really appreciate this loveliness.

When we had swung back to the town where we had lived most, and made our smooth descent in a daisied meadow, there were many to meet us, with my well-remembered Somel, and, first and most eager, Jeff and Celis, with their baby.

Ellador seized upon it as eagerly as her gentle tenderness would allow, with reverent kisses for the little hands, the rosy feet. She caught Celis to her arms and held her close. She even kissed Jeff, which he apparently liked, and nobody else minded. And then—well, if you live in a country of about three million inhabitants, and love them all; if you have been an envoy extraordinary—very extraordinary, indeed—to a far-off, unknown world, and have come back unexpectedly—why, your hands are pretty full for a while.

* * * * * * * *

We settled back into the smooth-running Herland life without a ripple. No trouble about housing; they had always a certain percentage of vacancies, to allow for freedom of movement. No trouble about clothes; those perfect garments were to be had everywhere, always lovely and suitable. No trouble about food; that smooth, well-adjusted food supply was available wherever we went.

No appeals for deserving charity—no need of them. Nothing to annoy and depress, everything to give comfort and strength; and under all, more perceptible to me now than before, that vast, steady, onmoving current of definite purpose, planning and working to make good better and better best.

The "atmosphere" in the world behind us is that of a thousand mixed currents, pushing and pulling in every direction, controverting and opposing one another.

Here was peace—and power, with accomplishment.

Eagerly she returned to her people. With passionate enthusiasm she poured out, in wide tours of lecturing, and in print, her report of world conditions. She saw it taken up, studied, discussed by those great-minded over-mothers of the land. She saw the young women, earnest eyed, of boundless hope and high purpose, planning, as eager missionaries plan, what they could do to spread to all the world their proven gains. Reprints of that encyclopaedia were scattered to every corner of the land, and read swiftly, eagerly, to crowding groups of listeners. There began to stir in Herland a new spirit, pushing, seeking, a new sense of responsibility, a larger duty.

"It is not enough," they said, "that we should be so happy. Here is the whole round world—millions and hundreds of millions of people—and all their babies! Not in a thousand years will we rest, till the world is happy!"

And to this end they began to plan, slowly, wisely, calmly, making no haste; sure, above all, that they must preserve their own integrity and peace if they were to help others.

* * * * * * * *

When Ellador had done her utmost, given all that she had gathered and seen the great work growing, she turned to me with a long, happy sigh.

"Let's go to the forest," she said. And we went.

We went to the rock where I had first landed and she showed me where three laughing girls had been hidden. We went to the tree where they had slipped away like quicksilver. We went to a far-off, quiet place she knew, a place of huge trees, heavy with good fruit, of smooth, mossy banks, of quiet pools and tinkling fountains. Here, unexpected, was a little forester house, still and clean, with tall flowers looking in at the windows.

"I used to love this best of all," she said. "Look—you can see both ways."

It was on a high knoll and, through the great boughs, a long vista opened to a bright sunlight in the fields below.

The other side was a surprise. The land dropped suddenly, fell to a rocky brink and ended. Dark and mysterious, far beyond, in a horizon-sweeping gloom of crowding jungle, lay—the world.

"I always wanted to see—to know—to help," she said. "Dear—you have brought me so much! Not only love, but the great new spread of life—of work to do for all humanity.

"And then—the other new Hope, too,—perhaps—perhaps—a son!"

And in due time a son was born to us.

The End

Index

About the Author and Editors

CHARLOTTE PERKINS GILMAN (1860–1935) was an eminent feminist sociologist and novelist, perhaps best known professionally for *Women and Economics* (1898, repr. 1966) and, as a fiction writer, for her semiautobiographical novella, "The Yellow Wallpaper" (1892, repr. 1973).

MARY JO DEEGAN is Professor of Sociology at the University of Nebraska-Lincoln. Among her earlier publications are *Jane Addams and the Men of the Chicago School, 1892–1918* (1988); *American Ritual Dramas* (Greenwood, 1989); and *Women in Sociology: A Bio-Bibliographical Sourcebook* (Greenwood, 1991).

MICHAEL R. HILL is an interdisciplinary social scientist from the University of Nebraska-Lincoln and Iowa Western Community College. He is author of *Archival Strategies and Techniques* (1993); editor of Harriet Martineau's *How to Observe Morals and Manners* (1989); and coeditor, with Mary Jo Deegan, of *Women and Symbolic Interaction* (1987).